# LOOK LEFT, WALK GREEN

# Look Left, Walk Green

K. Rose Quayle

Cover Illustration Copyright © 2017 by K. Rose Quayle
Book design and production by K. Rose Quayle
www.lookleftwalkgreen.com

Published by K. Rose Quayle

Print ISBN 978-1-64008-848-1

Library of Congress Control Number: 2017908886

Typesetting services by BOOKOW.COM

*To*
*A. Quayle*
*For my curse is your burden.*

*V. Duncan*
*Remember that time when we were kids*
*and I thought you were my dog?*
*Yeah, me neither.*

*and Ah'sha*
*For remembering my baby-days.*

*For this thing I besought the LORD thrice, that it might depart from me.*
*And He said unto me, My grace is sufficient for thee:*
*for My strength is made perfect in weakness.*
*Most gladly will I rather glory in my infirmities,*
*that the power of Christ may rest upon me.*
*Therefore I take pleasure in infirmities,*
*in reproaches, in necessities, in persecutions, in distresses*
*for Christ's sake: for when I am weak, then am I strong.*

2 Corinthians 12:8-10

# Contents

Introduction 1

How to Use This Book 9

I Procedure 11

Tens and Twos Forever 13

If it Ain't Broke, Don't Fix it. If it *is* Broke, Break it Again. 34

So, You'd Like to Glow in the Dark 46

It Wasn't That Great of a Party if You Still Remember it 59

II Memory 73

Is, Was, and Will Be 75

Are You Doing the Taxes? 85

The Luxurious Curse of Not Knowing 96

Chronologic 114

III Effects 121

Every Silver Lining Has a Cloud 123

How Brilliant, the Dark 145

Singing Stories, Chasing Sound 163

I Only Come for the After-Party 184

IV   Support                                           197

Look Left, Walk Green                                  199

The Singular Burden of Remembering                     224


V    History                                           237

Before We Were Human                                   239

Holding on to One's Molars                             260

Washing One's Brain and Other Tales                    273

First Impressions are Everything                       288

Resources                                              299

Works Cited                                            301

About the Author                                       317

# Introduction

IF you stand at the edge of a cliff long enough, you'll either fall off or develop killer toe muscles. In the case of mental illness, it's often a case of having to do both over and over before you reach a semblance of balance.

I was standing on the cliff while writing this book; enmeshed in a struggle so entangled in my very sense of identity that my days were becoming filled with the same dread of waking that so plagues many across the country who deal with mental illness. I had had some spectacular episodes in the past but the routine, slow losing of my very self, invisible in plain sight, had stretched my well-trained toes to the point of snapping. I had been skating along with a projected sense of *ok*, a false persona of having gotten past everything that had happened to me with flying colors.

People now came to me for advice, and much like you're going to read in this book, I had a plausible answer because I thought and thought and *thought* about it. I thought about how I was going to go on without knowing what I was going on from.

Anyone who spends their life trying to outrun something that happened to them will know that they've got to stop at some point to breathe and that's when it comes up from behind, far closer than you ever thought it could get, and belts you in the head. You run until you stop or you run until you die.

Mental illness messes up your sense of self. It digs down into the brain and influences perspective, behavior, feelings and habits; the very things that make a person unique. Where does it end and a person begin? It's a question still unanswered thousands of years after mental illness first carved out a mention in mankind's history. And how far one will go to escape its oppression is a question that can never be answered; it's a question whose answer varies by person and by circumstance, sometimes changing a million times a day.

Because of the personal nature of mental illness, many patients feel they *are* their illness; that it is inseparable from who they were born as and this isn't seen as strongly in any other type of illness where the patient is trying their damnedest to get away from the disease, not identify with it. But I would argue that this view is one society impresses upon us and has for eons. We are not seen separately therefore we do not see ourselves as such. Others have realized this as well from time to time in recent history, from the "patient-first" language movement in healthcare (this person *has Bipolar Disorder* not, that person *is bipolar*) to the parity movement in healthcare coverage that seeks to make mental and physical illnesses equal by forcing insurance companies to cover them equally in the doctor's office.

It is not said to patients with mental illness, *let's all work together and get rid of this disease.* No end is projected as it is with other serious illnesses which have remissions such as cancer (which has come a long way from the days when even patients were shielded from the truth of their diagnosis and sent home to quietly live out their time). We all know someone with cancer or have experienced it ourselves these days in America. Cancer inspires awareness ribbons, bumper stickers, walks and marathons and positive speech. As well it should. It's been proven over and over what a positive attitude can do for healing and maintaining through treatments which make us wonder what devil thought this stuff up and why would anyone in their right mind choose chemo to begin with?

But an end point is always spoken of. There will be a day when chemo stops and labs come back good and remission will happen and *Science will find the cure.* Even when things are extremely dark, when we have to get very real and admit we all tried our best but the disease is taking its course, the attitude in healthcare is to keep looking up. Science is getting closer every minute; we're all in this together. We *fight* cancer.

With chronic illnesses such as Diabetes or Heart Disease we know that these things don't have remissions; they are ongoing problems that must be dealt with daily. We have to *maintain stability* with these diseases to keep them from getting worse. The focus is more about acceptance and doing what works. These are practical diseases. We are given a definite prescription of things to do to and if we follow these things we will be comfortable at best and have a pretty normal life and escape heart attack or amputation or be better equipped to survive it if it happens.

Chronic illnesses don't have the glory-of-battle aspect that cancer does but they're becoming more manageable and accepted as "actual illnesses". What I mean is that twenty years ago the assumption that *this illness is your fault* was much more prevalent. If you have type 2 Diabetes, usually diagnosed in adulthood, that surely has something to do with the donut you eat every morning. With heart disease and even stroke, immediately those around you started looking at your chubby midsection, all the butter you put on your bagel and how many months it's been since anyone saw you at the gym.

Public education has greatly helped us as a whole nation understand lifestyle factors, genetic risk and how illness itself works to be able to support those around with who struggle with them. We *battle* heart disease, stroke, Diabetes.

In the case of congenital and degenerative diseases we know these things will get worse, or, not get *better*. A person born without necessary genetic material is not going to grow it spontaneously. How they *are* is how they were *made* and I don't think I have to state that as people they are just fine as they are nor convince anyone else of the same. In times past though, a parent presented with a child with serious disability or sickness at birth would have been told to take them home, do the best they can and mourn an early death or to put them away in an institution and try to have another child.

Not so anymore. From Down Syndrome to Autism to Progeria, conditions one may have been born with are no longer a death sentence. The focus on such things is, happily, what the person *can do* rather than what they cannot, or helping them to do it *differently* in their own way. With degenerative diseases such as Multiple Sclerosis, Multiple Dystrophy and ALS for example, great strides have been made in educating patients about their treatment options; modifying workspaces in the business world and in school to accommodate maintaining a normal life as long as possible with the potential havoc these illnesses can wreak on the body and mind. *Let's work with what we have* is the motto here. Those who brave such disorders are courageous, beautiful, inspiring.

The evolution of public awareness has not, of course, taken away the punch of death. It hasn't lessened the despair of saying goodbye to dreams held hostage or the sorrow of a life arrested. Public awareness on its own does not win the war, however, it can lend the strength to conquer the battles.

But mental illness has cultivated over the centuries a culture of negativity and fear it refuses to be freed of. Let me preface that by saying there are a great many courageous and compassionate social workers, therapists, nurses, psychiatrists and lay workers in the world of psychiatric care; excellent examples of the best of humanity who have saved lives and livelihoods as surely as any surgeon. But they are also confined by the framework of medical science and its forced segregation of mental and physical illness in language, prognosis and of course, funding. Many of these workers are underpaid, underappreciated and overworked like everyone else in healthcare but they also face a lack of esteem from their peers, criticism of the validity of their work and difficult patients who battle their illnesses, the world, and the therapist themselves.

Illnesses which affect the mind are still poorly understood. Are they a problem with the brain itself? With behavior only? Combination of both? No-one is 100% sure yet of the mechanism or cause. In the past, the focus with mental illness was to keep the patient from being a danger to others, to keep the world safe from the mentally ill rather than the ill safe from the *illness*. Mentally ill persons have been feared, misunderstood, shunned and cast out, locked away and sent away, jailed when there was a lack of anywhere else to put them, experimented on, thrown out of institutions in social endeavors to lessen the burden of treating them on taxpayers and *overall*, told that the best they can hope for is to stay out of the hospital for a while; to maintain a semblance of a life out of jail and on medication.

There is little talk of bravery in facing the illness or even the cause of it. For most of my life it has been the assumption of society that mental illness is a character defect; a weakness, lack of self-control or deviance in self. Regardless of recent film depictions of exceptional persons, for the masses there are no beautiful souls waiting to be discovered, no courage to be envied and where we go, we go alone. We do not *wrestle* mental illness, we throw a torch at it and run as if it were a wolf stalking us.

Yet the psychosis, suicidality and despair of psychiatric diseases are elements of nothing less than the horrors of war. The daily maintenance of mental illness isn't for the patient to rejoin society and thrive, it's for the benefit of humankind to refrain from having to put up with and fear the mentally ill. Even as I write this I recall the recent shootings across the country which prompted our former president to call strongly for better mental health treatment. It's heartbreaking that it takes mass murder to inspire such change and bring an illness to public conversation rather than personal suffering and family devastation and the assumption that this act, this particular evil, can only be the work of a mentally ill person. How should we feel about this assumption? It would seem how we feel is of little consequence.

There are grassroots groups working across the land to promote understanding and awareness of mental illness every day. They now hold fundraisers and walks, wear green ribbons and claim a week and a month. There is no doubt the work of such groups has brought positive change to legislation and practice in mental health that past generations did not have the privilege of experiencing.

But it's the battles that count when you go to bed with mental illness and get right back up again with it. For example, I often find on social media that if I post something regarding mental illness I get a lot of private messages thanking me for doing so on behalf of 'awareness' but few people risk publicly agreeing in front of their friends save a few crusaders I know to champion many social and human rights causes. I *believe* this is because we still wrestle with two main things: lack of understanding that mental illness is indeed a disease and indeed can be life-threatening to the patient, and disbelief that it can and *should* be treated, and that treatment *should* lead to something more than survival.

And I *believe* that overall, the stereotype of the mentally ill as a threat to the safety of society is still winning the war.

And because we wrestle with these things, a whole host of problems prevents wellness and in some cases, jeopardizes survival. One complication is that patients themselves don't give thought to their illness as requiring treatment when that need isn't validated by those around them. Another is that family members, peers and medical doctors don't recognize the seriousness of the disease and therefore feel there is no need for support or insistence on treatment.

Yet another consequence is the stigma of treatment or admittance to the issue. At this point in history with the projection that 1 in 5 Americans (NAMI, 2017) will experience mental illness in their lifetime, the odds we know someone with it or are experiencing it ourselves are extremely high if not impossible to run from. No one questions going to the doctor for cancer. No one thinks controlling one's Diabetes to keep from going blind is a bad idea. And now that attitudes towards hundreds of diseases are changing from hopeless to hopeful to *of course we should do something*, it's mental health's long-awaited turn.

And in saying that I come to the point of this book. Here you will find a story of one of the most controversial and feared of mental health treatments: electroshock therapy, properly called ECT. Though many famous mentally ill persons have gone through shock therapy from Carrie Fisher to Kitty Dukakis and Ernest Hemingway to Yves Saint-Laurent, it continues to be the backbone of horror movies and the elephant in the corner of many homes across the world. Whether it helps or harms is almost irrelevant in the face of being made so shameful as to be rendered invisible.

I wrote *Look Left, Walk Green* about the experience of having shock treatment and the effects, good and bad. I flatly refused to speak of the experience for some time because frankly, I felt I had earned equal footing at work with my co-workers and in coming out as a shock therapy patient I could visualize echoes of the past disasters of allowing others to know of my illness. There was often a subtle but definite step backwards by the other person; a reddening of the face as they grasped that the day they were laughing in the lunchroom about the antics of 'crazy people' they didn't realize they were also talking about me.

It was bad enough admitting to being bipolar; resorting to shock therapy almost gave complete credence to all the fears of the disease. In my mind I could hear the voices of coworkers thinking I must really be a stark-raving lunatic to require such measures. I wasn't as youthfully hopeful or dimwittedly naïve enough to believe that nicer words used in business meant anyone felt the meanings behind them. I didn't need to be knocked down a few years socially if people actually *saw* me picking up my cross and walking.

But my husband raised the point repeatedly of the solitude of mental illness; that which placed the sufferers and their families on their own sort of archipelago cut off from the world but also from other patients. Perhaps there were others so far out into the water on their own islands they didn't know they were surrounded by millions exactly like them.

When I was diagnosed with mental illness at age 15 there wasn't anyone to tell me how this was all going to go and certainly nothing of the sort when I went in to have shock therapy almost twenty years later. There needed to be some sort of general reference about this type of treatment outside of the general pamphlet stacked up beside piles of magazines in waiting offices people generally avoided picking up lest it signal to everyone else there was a problem. There needed to be a manual of sorts on ECT that said here's *what* it is, *how* it's done, what it's *like* and what it can *do*, what you can *do about it*, and *why* we do it at all. *Look Left, Walk Green* aims to be that; a field guide for the curious soul, the patient awaiting treatment, the patient with nobody else to turn to afterward, and those just looking into the dark history of the mentally ill in America to get a better picture of where we are now.

So back to that cliff. I was standing there thinking to myself, *"I just can't do this."* I'd done so much research into my own story and that of others that it started to dawn on me what had actually happened. Before, it was facts on paper as impersonal as transit timetables by the roadside. I knew my own narrative by recorded instances like the names and dates of ancestors written on antique photographs. I knew they existed and *when* they did, but not *how* they did. My facts didn't live until I had to really dive into them and puzzle out why they had occurred to tell someone else.

That's when the cliff jumped up at me and I suddenly pitched backwards, wrenching my toes into a charley horse strong enough to snap them off.

Now, I value my toes; they keep me upright. I am vehemently *against* the snappage of toes.

And at some point I stared at my computer and thought, *"Don't let this be another one of your stupid projects you start and then drop because you're a coward or you lose interest."* To say it was that simple to get back on the horse would be a straight out lie but I did eventually push myself forward to flap my way across the canyon and back on track. It would have been poetic to say I soared forward into the future but if you know me, and you'll get to in these pages, you'll know the only soaring I've ever done was *up* stairs, *across t*armac and that one time straight down the stairs in a refrigerator box. But I do, in fact, flap.

# How to Use This Book

*L*ook Left, Walk Green is organized so the reader can read straight through or skip to the sections needed. It is intended for a variety of audiences without representing any one in particular. The information in this book is intended for your edification, not to be used in place of a doctor's advice. Unfortunately, when it comes to ECT there are a lot of unknowns, roadblocks and frustrations. It is my hope that no matter what your relationship to ECT you can find something helpful here.

**Part One:** *Procedure* goes over the mechanics of ECT and what makes it so daunting. *Procedure* answers such question as what is ECT and what is it used for? How much electricity is used during a treatment? How does this measure of electricity compare to those of other everyday applications? What does the patient go through in preparation for treatment?

**Part Two:** *Memory* examines the profound effect of ECT on memory. *Memory* investigates the brain's method of encoding and recalling memories, the personal experience of memory loss and the unforeseen effects on loved ones.

**Part Three:** *Effects* takes into account the controversy surrounding ECT. *Effects* looks at the many cognitive changes occurring during and after treatment, citing personal experience of what it's like to go through ECT.

*Part Four: Support* offers practical ways for patients to navigate life with the effects of ECT to be their best at any level. *Support* also gives suggestions for caregivers and families going through the process to take care of themselves while taking care of their loved one.

*Part Five: History* looks into the history of mental health treatment in America starting in the 18$^{\text{th}}$ century and following up into the early part of the 20$^{\text{th}}$ century. In the aim to understand why such a treatment was needed, *History* looks at the surrounding circumstances that catapulted ECT to the forefront of psychiatric care and dropped it into obscurity before making a comeback to the modern mental health care.

Lastly, *Resources* is a list of helpful sources for both patients and carers.

# Part I

# Procedure

# Tens and Twos Forever

"*It's not ten and two anymore. You remember that, right? Hands don't go there anymore. You're putting hand over hand, you want to pass the wheel from one hand to the other.*"

My husband was begrudgingly trying to teach me to drive in an empty mall parking lot in his slick, black, brand new-ish car. His baby.

"*Well where am I supposed to put them?*" I asked, exasperated and clearly not seeing what the sense was in changing from the old standard ten and two. Not that it mattered because I could barely read a clock face anyway.

"*Here,*" he placed my hands in the correct position and directed me to pull out, put my indicator on, look both ways and turn a left. It was too many directions at once. I pulled out, didn't look, got the left but swung much too wide and was very lucky the lot was indeed empty. I could see him twitching out of the corner of my eye, exerting the sort of control a man has to have in the face of his car being potentially creamed by something so inelegant as a concrete balustrade. It is the sort of control I can only admire with my innate fly-off-the-handle temperament.

"*Right over left,*" he admonished. "*Your hands. You don't pass across your hands!*" Here he did a sort of flailing motion I knew darned well was overexaggerating. But somehow it was warranted. I had no idea what he was talking about with the hands. "*Why?*" I asked, hoping it was some personal preference of his and not required on the road test. I think that's when the lightbulb turned on for my husband and he realized I actually didn't know what he was talking about. Problem was, neither of us knew which part was the mystery or how to communicate it.

*That's what memory loss is like.* You know something is wrong but not exactly what and there's no way can you tell someone else about it because the words are gone too. I think of it as having a second toddlerhood.

Ever have a toddler do a meltdown on you in public? It's distressing and embarrassing because you can't figure out what's wrong to help them or stop them. Toddlers don't have enough vocabulary to tell you and the words they do have aren't always delivered in context. It takes a lot of observation of just what made your 26-month-old start screaming murder right now to compare with what you already know provokes the caterwauling in rapid stride to calm them down successfully.

*This is what memory loss is like.* You either have nothing to compare anything with, a few out-of-order shreds or some impressions which are completely out of context. One thing is clear; that tantrum is for a reason. Something is clearly wrong. In the case of memory, you have that slight feeling that something is off but there are no words for it. My husband tried mightily to show me to hand the steering wheel from my right hand to my left hand. He described it, showed me with his own hands and then put his hands on my hands and guided me in the motion. I could clearly see what he was doing with his own hands. But when it came to hearing the direction and putting it together with my own motions opposite him, something was out of sync. Unconsciously, as I was made to keep on turning 'til I got it, my hands went right back to how I'd seen my grandfather turn the wheel when I was a young child riding with him in the car to the supermarket (and wondering how many times we had to go around the car park until we could actually park somewhere to get that Cherry Whitehouse ice cream...).

And though I couldn't really *visualize* ten and two anymore, I could recall my mother's hands at that position on the wheel when I was small. I had learned to drive when I was younger but never got a license. I had lived in several places as a teen when most get their licenses and so wasn't privy to a car and instructor at the same time long enough to get the hang of it and pass a test. As an adult, I lived alone and was either in school or working too much to really find someone with a car to teach me. Most of my adult life was either on foot or bus-bound. Even my husband, a Manx citizen, didn't have U.S. residency until we'd been married 4 years and then went out and got a license and bought a car. But this car I was trying not to demolish was the first *new* car, a thing which must be cared for like the first child and my right-and-left issues caused no end of anxiety on his part.

We gave up that day. He drove us home and on the way remarked that we needed something I could practice on before driving the actual car again. Something like...

*"Do we have any big plates? You could practice on a plate. It's wheel-shaped."* I thought about this a minute and said, *"Not any unbreakable ones."*

After a knowing chuckle he remarked, *"Put it on the shopping list"* I never did get back behind the wheel and I didn't buy a plate. When I tried to puzzle out this whole passing from right to left or left to right or whatever, my head hurt. My thoughts became foggy and I gave up. Months later, however, we took a bus trip to New York City and happened to pop into the M&Ms store in Times Square.

Dazzled by all the colorful candy, we made our way up to a small platform populated with candy merchandise; everything from aprons and hats to pillows and teacups. Amidst a gaggle of children milling around *ooh'ing* and *aah'ing*, I spied a stack of plates sorted by M&Ms character and snatched up a green charger. *"Plates!"* I exclaimed, showing my husband in glee. Unbreakable yes, but the melamine dinner plate was out of my price range just for practice.

He jumped in and stood behind me, placing the plate square in my hands and guiding me to "pass the wheel" properly. But still I didn't understand. My body still wasn't putting the spoken directions to the movement. I was clumsy and frustrated and aware of a growing audience of people wondering what the heck these two people were doing with a plate. It is lucky I have a sense of humor and was able to walk it off to laugh at the absurdity.

But during that exchange one thing was revealed: my husband told me over and over to pass the wheel from right to left and I flailed every time we got near the left. The frustration mounted until Mr. Quayle waved his left hand in the air to show me. *"To the left!"* he exclaimed. A light bulb (10-watt-frosted as my dad would say) flickered on and I said,

*"Oh, green!"*

My husband looked at me with his inborn sarcastic stare and muttered, *"Yeah ....sure."*

I nodded. *"You wanted me to go to the left."* He agreed, *"The other left, apparently."*

*"Left is green,"* I chirped matter-of-factly, glad we were finally on the same page. I set the plate down and moved out of the way for more shoppers to examine the shelves behind us. We were not on the same page.

A year passed by quietly and we still hadn't bought a plate.

Any type of cognitive dysfunction is a funny thing. You don't always know something's wrong until you send a thought out to test the waters and you expect it to come back with an olive branch but instead it's awkwardly lugging a refrigerator back with all the poise and grace of toting appliances. *"What is this?"* you ask and the thought answers rather saucily, *"You said you wanted an olive branch."* Then you immediately wonder if you did, in fact, ask for a refrigerator and somehow misplaced this notion between turning on the tap and putting the kettle to boil.

I have no idea why left is green. I have no idea what that even means, just that left, directionally, is *green*. I am quite certain of it, though at the same time

I know this isn't true. A color and a direction are not the same thing, nor are they related in the English language. But my brain has inextricably linked the two since having electroshock therapy in 2012.

When people ask what happened, my husband and I say it was an accident. You may wonder if this is truthful. When one says "accident" the general assumption is that it involved a vehicle or a fall or something else nobody intended to happen. Victims of abuse will often describe their injuries as being caused by an "accident" and not without reason; we live in a culture which assumes a victim always had *some* sort of hand in their situation. They chose the relationship, stayed with the abuser, denied the signs.

Truly, we *do* always have a choice in our own lives and it often is not a matter of a *right vs. wrong* or *good vs. bad* choice but perhaps two equally crap choices or two equally fantastic choices. Neither is preferable to human beings; we like things much more clear-cut. If there are two crap choices we grumble nothing will work out. But if the choice is put between two wonderful things and we have to limit ourselves to just one, the good doesn't look so attractive either.

Yet no-one can see the future. Most of our lives we spend a great deal of time playing defense over offense, no matter how wise our choices.

So, we choose to call it an accident when in reality my brain issues came after a medical treatment I *chose* to undergo in 2012. My husband and I don't use that word for sympathy or to confuse or deceive anyone. When I received a series of voluntary Electroconvulsive Therapy (ECT) treatments in hospital, no one knew what the effects to me personally would be afterwards. No one knew how much memory would be lost or how hard tasks such as addition and reading aloud would become. It wasn't possible for anyone to predict how my speech would change or how thinking itself would feel *different*.

And so, because it was no one's *intention* that any harm come to me, and it was not *possible* to predict that any would, the term accident perfectly fits the incident. Nothing more, nothing less. It was, as is more often the case then we want to admit, just something bad that happened; and life is full of such things. With our busy human brains always looking for cause and effect, that's a concept we all wrestle with naturally.

As Howard Dully, the youngest U.S. patient to receive a lobotomy at the age of 12 noted in an interview with *The Guardian* 47 years later, those he told about his experience later would "freak out," expecting him to be incapacitated (Day, 2008). As I read those words something in me sighed deeply with joy and sadness. Joy, because my soul knew exactly what that incongruity meant and sadness because it knew just the same for the place mental health occupies within society's eyes and what happens when we overstep public expectations.

New Zealand author Janet Frame wrote extensively in her autobiographies of the experience of being treated with ECT that echoed this same sentiment. Receiving over 200 treatments of unmodified ECT, she felt like a "non-person," inducted by her own diagnosis into a contained yet incoherent world by the very nature of mental illness, watching her mother enter the hospital fearful yet determined to keep up appearances even there that everything was fine (Frame, 1984).

Trying to deal with memory loss, persistent fears and nightmares of being taken for another treatment was only topped by her loss of rights to her life savings account and the fear and silence her family regarded her with on her return home. These are common experiences insofar as dealing with the attitudes of those who are not directly dealing with treatment. As for myself, I choose to believe that if there were a malicious intent or intentional leading astray, it's done with and over.

But for some of my family members it is much harder to process and move on because of the relationship they have to what happened and how it continues to affect them. The other reason we call it an accident is that the vast majority of people either of us comes in contact with outside of the psychiatric world either don't know what Electroconvulsive Therapy is or react with a variety of negative responses.

It's true that most of us have a cousin in therapy or work with someone whose sister takes antidepressants or perhaps someone even closer who goes to Alcoholics Anonymous meetings. But most of the population is not part of the closed and suffocating world of psychiatric hospitals; a kingdom unto itself with its own limitations and triumphs, laws and social structure. I am often frustrated by this and as a person with mental illness who is used to constantly having to hide portions of my life from others not acquainted with such things in order to protect myself *or them* from what can be a very harsh existence.

When I was younger, I felt the world owed me some understanding, as I think all teenagers do. What 15-year-old doesn't fancy themselves tragic and misunderstood at some point? But as I have grown older I am brought to the reality that most 15-year-olds are pleading their case to their parents to break curfew on a Friday night, not pleading their case to a mental health court judge to escape commitment to a state hospital. Likewise, most adults spend their mornings stuck in traffic waiting for the jerk in front of them to move, not in a recovery room waiting to remember who they are and how they got there.

Knowing that the majority of those I come in contact with have never seen 'behind the curtain" (to borrow a phrase from my husband), it was perhaps a misplaced sense of protectiveness that compelled me to keep the fact of ECT in my own life in the background unless directly asked. I took great solace in the writings of Janet Frame again as she clearly narrated that strange place of visible invisibility one enters after diagnosis, saying that suddenly the world around her felt divided even in those walking in the street between ordinary folk and "secret" people. These people were ridiculed and feared by the mainstream yet rarely even seen by them (Frame, An Angel at My Table, 1984).

The natural pathway of a life commandeered by mental illness constantly intersects with that of those around it, yet maintains a completely separate reality, with hospitalizations creating such lags in normal development that one can never catch up. The experience of the mental ward was, and indeed still is, widely different for each patient because it is based on so many factors:

*Socioeconomic background.* Do they have a place to return to afterwards or insurance for follow up appointments and medication? *Social status.* Will their family be ashamed to come visit or will their social circle suddenly and silently close so that they have no place in it anymore? *Employment status.* Do they have to return right away or have they been fired for being off too long? Will they be free to tell their coworkers where they have been or would this be "social suicide"? *Diagnosis.* Were they put in the correct treatment and ward for their diagnosis and will they be followed up with appropriately afterwards? *Personal demographics.* Mothers may feel they are not good mothers for having to leave their children for treatment, men may feel they can never admit to being hospitalized for a mental illness.

One thing is for certain: leaving the psychiatric hospital is as traumatic as going in and many patients find themselves caught in a tightly bound trap, unwilling to stay or leave. That may seem unthinkable to an outsider and is a mystery to the patient as well, but so often, stepping back out into a land where the general populace is fearful of you is sometimes the worst of what seems to be two bad places to end up. Because of this, there was much too much to explain; from the psychological effects (desired or not) to the technical aspects to the very big and omnipresent *why?*

Why would someone purposely want to be electrocuted to have seizures? Wasn't the whole focus of medicine on the subject of seizures to *prevent* and *stop* them? Yet controversial treatments have kept society busy debating for years now from stem cell treatments to the Marijuana legalization debates. There doesn't seem to be time or space to bring ECT to the forefront; if we cannot discuss it in the open it will remain forever chained by stigma and defined by outdated images perpetuated by media and the public's lack of resources or tolerance to other forms of evidence.

It is simply very hard for me to understand the silence all mentally ill persons run into when they reveal the details of those diversions from the routine path of humanity to their outside friends. It's probably not intentional and more to do with not knowing what to say out of a failure to relate to the situation. But that *silence-with-a-capital-S* which punctuates a statement such as "*I saw my psychiatrist...*" or "*My daughter has Schizophrenia*" or "*I have memory loss from shock treatment*" is *impenetrable*.

A line is crossed and though the other person has no idea what you're talking about, they instinctively swallow any attempts to learn more about it; creating a gulf impossible to cross which both parties are now responsible in some way for. Very frustrating, very defeating. I feel that every word I write is a brick I lay along a wall between myself and my family, my friends, my coworkers, my neighbors.

And yet, I feel compelled to go on.

I once asked my therapist why that silence reigned so strong still. Why did the very idea of mental illness make others so fearful in modern times? In ancient days, mental illness was thought to be a punishment from the gods, yet the ancestors were very practical about treating it with the means of the day and getting it done with so they could all get back to the daily business of proclaiming their Emperor's greatness. In modern America that is not the case, and we can make all sorts of arguments about the general decline of concern for the community, the increasing isolation of individuals in the age of social media and the rise of fear and crime across the country as strong contributors to an overall lack of empathy and identification towards those on the fringe of society for whatever reason.

We can also point out strong evidence of positive global solidarity through means of the internet, media bringing little known cultures and problems of poverty to light in wealthier parts of the world and the use of novelty to spread awareness of little known diseases like wildfire to bring in support and dollars for much-needed research. But fear of the mentally ill seems to survive social transition.

It was the therapist's belief that it was a general fear of illness that all of us have on some innate level as humans. Just the mention of a poorly understood illness such as Obsessive Compulsive Disorder or the Eating Disorders makes people feel as if they can catch it somehow (of course this is true of "medical" diseases, we are just much more likely to be educated in such or to ask about them to begin with). We fear that mental illness is communicable, like the flu or pneumonia when it is no catchier than gallstones.

While mental illness makes sense internally within the context of its own odd existence, the logic we apply to its handling often does not. It doesn't make any sense to avoid speaking about psychiatric disorders in the hopes they will cease to be. Not speaking about blood sugar levels did not magic away Diabetes. A diabetic patient is certainly more than the sum of their parts but their disease has a hand in who they are by the very act of influencing their behavior and routine every day.

The assumption that never speaking Diabetes' name will scrub it out of a loved one's pancreas is *ridiculous* and as adults we all are aware of this. Yet many people hold fast to a belief if they never mention mental illness, it will simply *not exist* or at the very least, *no one will have to know.* In doing this, a father or sister or coworker renders their loved one invisible. This does everything to foster the *Us versus Them* ideology so rampant still in the medical versus psychiatric community and the mentally ill versus neurotypical populations I have often subscribed to myself in resignation to the frustration of having a disease many think must be put out of sight, not cured.

Sight is so important to the stigma of the mentally ill. We *see* people talking to themselves in delusion. We *see* the dishevelment of the mentally ill homeless on the streets. We *see* the tears of spouses so brokenhearted that mental illness has brutally kidnapped their loved ones and their utter aloneness as the one who survives. We *see* gentle children becoming suddenly cruel, confident children being stricken by unimaginable terror or unreserved children disappearing deep inside themselves. We *see* teens and young adults, full of promise and dreams, suddenly ending their lives. This is the reality of mental illness. This is its toll and its price. What we don't see is how it happens.

We don't see it in concrete tests at the doctor's office, and though we know logically that it happens in the brain, we can't point to the side, the back, the top and say, "*There it is! This is where it all goes wrong!*" Science is getting closer and closer to that point, but human fear takes a far longer time to be assuaged of something that looks, for all intents and purposes, like a demon. It's no wonder the public at large has a very inaccurate and very negative view of mental health and mental health treatment (in Part Five of this book I will discuss some of the popular images we've been exposed to over the years in media that keep treatment shrouded in mystery and hope for recovery stamped down under the weight of stigma.).

I too came into treatment with these same images and misunderstandings over twenty years ago until I found myself to be one of those nutters being strapped down in an ambulance in the dead of night, peering out of a tiny glass window from the wrong side of the door. After I made the decision to write *Look Left, Walk Green*, my husband commented that I should have kept a journal because we'd determined the memory loss to encompass a period of approximately three years before ECT. "*It's no use now*," he said. "*You don't remember now*."

But one evening as I was cleaning our living room closet and going through old checque books and what, I found my original admission papers amid some other things: a mental health advanced directive; copies of treatment plans, a short diary written backwards in a composition book, and the very early outline of a book about ECT. So, it seems I had the same idea at one point and started out on that direction.

We went back and forth about it, me arguing more for the sake of defending my cognitive abilities more than anything, and I realized that actually, I didn't *want* to write a book on ECT. It was true I didn't remember a good 98% of any of the actual treatment and I quit several times before the final decision to get on with it.

One morning I was out with a friend getting coffee from a local chain and a family who came in regularly began talking to us. At one point I was asked if I had been working on any book illustrations lately, as this person was aware I had published a children's book titled *Little Quail* in 2005. I had been up quite late the night before writing and being tired and without my usual filter, found myself answering much too quickly.

I informed him I *was* working on another children's book actually (that was true insofar as the drawings were gathering dust on my dining room table) but also a *non-fiction* manuscript. This piqued his interest and I sat like a deer in headlights when he inevitably asked what the subject was going to be. I truly didn't know what to say and dearly wanted to stop telling obscured white lies because this was someone who did not know what had happened to me and was someone I would certainly see again on a regular basis.

I admit I took the coward's way out and told him a half- truth: "*It's about ...actually it's about the history of electroshock therapy and how media portrays that. And...*"

And I stopped because his face froze and the *Silence-with-a-capital-S* fell over the space between our chairs like a wet blanket. But I'd got myself into this hole and was going to have to deal with the people around me knowing at some point, so I started climbing back out by saying vaguely, "*I've been doing a lot of research.*"

A timid laugh echoed all round and some jokes were made about the types of caricatures I could do for the illustrations while admitting that wouldn't be politically correct and then I forcibly steered conversation towards the children's book, which predictably lightened the mood. Later I'd said to my friend, "*That just proved my point exactly. If I'd said, 'I'm writing a book on the history of chemotherapy and the portrayal of cancer in the media', someone would have shared that they have a relative who went through chemo or they themselves did or a friend is going to be going through it soon.*

*Cancer isn't something we all rush right into talking about, but we have a collective social knowledge about it as an illness."* Which makes sense with 1 in 3 Americans likely to get a type of cancer in their lifetime (American Cancer Society, 2016). Cancer touches *every* one of us in some way. Yet with 1 in 5 adults developing a mental illness in any given year (Mayo Clinic, 2015) , there is no argument we are all profoundly touched by these illnesses as well. With only a little over half of mentally ill adults receiving treatment in 2008 and around 100,000 of those adults receiving ECT every year (NIMH, 2008), it's nearly impossible to maintain any sort of belief that mental health is something still shut up in an asylum on the hill and not part of our everyday lives.

Let me clarify that the man who looked at me in the Silence is an educated, kind father of two teen boys who are nice, polite kids who will go on to better the world, no doubt. He and his wife are talented, faithful people you'd hope to move into your neighborhood. But it strikes me that our everyday lives are just worlds apart, as are the lives of most people with major mental illness from those around them while at the same time being incredibly similar.

Ultimately, these words become urgent when I see my fellow patients cowed into silent suffering because they are afraid to ask for help or admit what is happening to them. When I see them forsaken on their islands I want to *shake* someone. Mental illness is by no means the only illness or social problem put in the darkness; those affected by AIDS are *well acquainted* with that side-swipe of conversation as are victims of domestic violence and those with learning or developmental disorders, not to mention those cancer patients of the past when it was in *no way* acceptable to speak of the illness.

Countless others with a myriad of medical conditions not accepted by our world flounder to express that it's not *bad enough* to suffer an illness *and* try to protect their loved ones from stigma *and* garner up the courage to seek treatment and *then* actually go through it, so many times alone. Somehow their suffering is never enough to repay society's price for the invisible sin of being ill.

As time went on after my own ECT treatment, my family and friends opened up about how terribly stressful it had been and continues to be on them and as I spoke more and more to other patients having had ECT from the 1960s onward, I found that there were a few very common threads:

All experienced memory loss of some kind, and most experienced some permanent loss (for this book I define memory loss to have lasted over 2 years to be permanent or very unlikely to come back).

All were loath to admit to having the treatment because of stigma, even to other psychiatric patients.

All were told their memories would come back and many felt that they were somehow 'lied' to when these did no.

All felt the memory loss had either been downplayed (some felt purposely so) or not taken seriously by mental health personnel.

Many felt very much alone, experienced disappointment in their doctors and had periods of hopelessness that they would ever return to themselves.

Most had a somewhat poor understanding of ECT and its unintended effects or felt they should have been given more information.

Very few had been examined by a neurologist and as psychiatric patients, felt mistrustful of and looked down upon by that type of clinician.

Many thought well of their treating psychiatrist despite these concerns.

It was the day I discovered the very talented woman sitting next to me was having ECT but would not admit to it even a group of people who had gone through all sorts of treatments (as well as abuses and other very serious illnesses-there were no secrets there) that I decided Mr. Quayle had been right about the need to write such a book. This was not because there are no other books out there on the subject, but rather because the majority of available references are studies meant for reference by medical staff.

Other volumes referencing ECT were chronicles of the long and often dark social history of the treatment itself or personal memories of those with brain injuries caused by trauma such as a blow to the head, not the ECT experience itself. These have almost identical symptoms but still, were not accurate to what would have been helpful at the time I had needed it most. I found very passionate arguments both for and against ECT and I respected these but in a sense, I felt a bit suspicious at such polarity even where I agreed. I feel at that level of intensity the argument isn't totally truthful either way, whether or not it is *intentionally* so. There is too much in this life we can't ever know to make such strong claims; purity is an illusion. The only thing we can do is tell our own story as best we know it.

And while my sense of humor has gotten me through some very bad things, I wanted to steer clear of an open-mic competition because mental illness isn't funny. Screen writers seems to think it *is*, and therapists and patients know it *can* be, but what mental illness can *do* is downright devastating. And devastation commands its own respect.

To write this book I formed the following conjectures:

*ECT can cause brain damage* (can, not *does* or *does not*). This may be influenced by a myriad of factors such as physical background of the patient, duration of treatment, application of treatment, unknown existing neurological conditions, and abuse of treatment (which I assume is not common but can never be excluded as a potential factor).

*ECT patients report* the same cognitive and memory issues as do patients diagnosed with Mild Traumatic Brain Injury caused by a physical injury such as a blow to the head which were not present before the treatment. For the purposes of this book it is assumed that ECT can cause a type of mild brain injury.

*Because of this*, ECT patients would benefit from general knowledge of and treatments for mild traumatic brain injury.

K. Rose Quayle

*The ECT treatment I received* did cause such injury and the cognitive effects I have experienced are, in part, directly caused by this treatment. These are my own conclusions from research into brain injury, effects of ECT, my own medical records and observations from family and medical professionals.

*ECT is neither good or evil* but a means to an end of serious symptoms in certain clinical situations.

*Most patients* receiving ECT are woefully uneducated about the effects it may have on them post-treatment and this can affect the decision-making process to authorize treatment or continue with treatment.

*The majority* of doctors, nurses and staff in the medical and psychiatric disciplines act with the intent to help their patients with the information they have available to them, their past experiences, the observations they make in a clinical setting, and the current medical treatments available for their use.

So, without knowing very much about ECT and its effects, what brings people to this type of treatment? After so many people have walked away with cognitive and memory problems, what keeps ECT going even now? In the past those who were committed to asylums had little to no say in treatment options and ECT was used as the preferred treatment for Schizophrenia. In its most popular years the majority of hospitalized psychiatric patients received it automatically on admission.

Remember that psychiatric drugs only came into major use in the 1960s. It is very hard for us who grew up in the '70s and beyond to visualize when the reality of the psychiatric world was still very closed but publicly it was known that pills treated "those kinds" of problems; that a time before the pills even existed. Today there are multiple reasons for seeking out ECT as a treatment, multiple illnesses ECT is used to treat and across the world, and multiple demographics likely to use it.

By the time I was 33 years old and entering into treatment, I had been in the psychiatric system for almost twenty years. As a teenager, I had been treated in private practice, hospitalized in the public charity hospital, looked after by the state welfare system of social workers and EPSDT (Early and Periodic Screening, Diagnostic and Treatment) home visits, and had received good old-fashioned high school guidance counseling.

Unfortunately, these interventions did not prevent three overdoses and years of poor eating and deep depressions. Tough love didn't do the trick either, nor did switching schools, switching families, losing privileges, gaining weight back or a myriad of medications. I was started on Prozac at age 15 at a much higher dose than would be given today to someone under 18 and I soon found myself unable to distinguish reality from dreams.

What followed was a succession of different combinations of anti-depressants taken at night with the desired side-effect of drowsiness to also treat my persistent insomnia until I finally began having hypo-manias. My diagnosis of *Dysthymia* (chronic Depression) to *Major Depression* to *Bipolar II* came with a switch to Lithium and Depakote. I did all-right on the combination for a while in my late teens but my weight ballooned and by my early 20s I felt emotionally flat and dull. I asked for a switch.

Next, the antipsychotic class of medication seemed to do even better for me but I seemed to be prone to the rapid tongue and eye movements of their main side effect, *tardive dyskinesia (*also called *tardive dystonia)*, which can become permanent. Next, we tried anti-seizure medications, which have been in use to treat mood disorders for years "off-label," or unapproved by the FDA to treat mood disorders. However, doctors see success with them and so continue to prescribe.

You'll find a lot of that in Psychiatry: *"Looks like it works so let's try it, government –backing be damned!"* And this is either extremely foolhardy and stupid or really quite brave and innovative, depending on how you look at it. The first anti-seizure drugs I took caused skin rashes on my face and, barring how ugly that is, can be the beginning of a rare and deadly side effect called Stevens-Johnson Syndrome. Protocol for these (and others which cause the same rash) is to stop immediately.

My psychiatrist pressed forward, undaunted by my less than stellar track record of taking medication and my not-always-forthcoming method of reporting symptoms. My reputation for non-compliance even earned me the chance to star in a video for the local school of social work aimed at teaching seniors the multiple reasons patients chuck their meds.

Because Bipolar upswings are often pretty fun for a while it seems like crashing your own party to call the doctor and say, '*Yeah Doc, I'm having a fabulous time so maybe we ought to spoil it with some psychotropic drugs and don't hold the side effects!*' No. This is not what Bipolar patients think.

Bipolar patients, like many people with mental illness, think if it's not bothering them it's not worth bothering *about* and it doesn't bother them until it gets very out of hand.

After a combination of anti-depressant and anti-seizure drugs was settled on, I had a few years of hypo-manias and depressions but also more stability than I'd ever had in my short adult life. I earned my Associate Degree in Graphic Design, moved to New York City for additional schooling, kept a full-time job and attended therapy and had a few hospitalizations here and there but never missed a rent payment and stayed out of any legal trouble. It was a terrible shame then that the real end of my childhood was marked by a major overdose I was given little hope of surviving, only four months before my wedding.

But survive, somehow, I did, and ten years after the first go-round with psychiatric medications I was at a different place in development and I got very sick very quickly on retrying Lithium. Quickly I went back to the anti-seizure drugs, which have been a huge component in my wellness and have become a mainstay for me.

But though mental illness may take a nap here and there, it doesn't go away. Life and stress and grief and moving and jobs and marriages and births and happiness all bring it out in profound ways and by my 32$^{nd}$ year I was struggling heavily again with a deep depression and eating. The latter, I'd stopped almost altogether.

Nutrition has been found to have an immense impact on neurological health. Poor nutrition affects concentration, thought processing, reaction time, emotional stability and above that, metabolism of medication. So, take all the drugs you want, if you're not getting proper nutrition you're basically sweating and urinating that stuff back out. Depression can cause a person to under, or overeat and very poor nutrition can also cause Depression so it's difficult to say what caused what but I was in trouble and I knew it.

By then I had been married for eight years and life had thrown just about everything at us. My husband and I constantly took note that we were under stressors quite unlike those of our suburban neighbors and coworkers. So many times we ended up utterly alone with each other and against each other; others wanted to help but just couldn't relate and retreated from our lives. We weren't near family or friends and our early support system crumbled with the loss of my husband's job.

We nearly lost our apartment when my husband subsequently lost his U.S. visa. During the next twelve months he was not legal to work, I went through four jobs in the process to qualify as his U.S. sponsor and we found out first-hand the ignorance surrounding immigration in this country as we lost most of our friends. We pulled away further as a couple from the public eye, trying to encourage each other as we scrimped to pay for my court fees to file bankruptcy and then his court fees to file for residency. The tangle of shattered dreams that followed as we'd tried to start a family and then found ourselves with empty cupboards proved too much and the depression came back in full force.

I was hospitalized for tube feeding to gain weight, get back on medication and get on with what didn't promise to be a great life at the time.

But something had changed for me in those years on the inside; it wasn't just me on my own anymore fighting the usual fight. There was a dull but audible squeaking deep within that kept telling me I really didn't want to be the one to cause a funeral and I was surely on my way to my own. From my medical records and personal notes from the time, I know I felt extremely guilty for not caring; for not wanting to get better and I knew that it was Depression trying to squash my voice into nothing.

I was at my lowest weight and it was near impossible to cry from continual dehydration. My gums bled and the inside of my nostrils had tiny sores inside. It hurt to walk; my joints ached, my feet had started to lose their padding. And though the roar in my head screamed that it would be better for me to disappear and be off my family's hands; that voice I barely knew whispered off in the distance that I *had* to survive at any cost. I had to find a way to make myself care and I had no idea how to do it and neither did anyone else.

I often felt like I was walking against the wind in a dark tunnel, utterly alone, trying to make out the words of someone whispering at the other end. Because of this, I researched ECT and made my case to my therapist who tried to talk me out of it because of the effects on memory she'd seen before. My husband was extremely unsure that this was a good idea. But they did know I was strong-willed and didn't jump into anything; rather, I usually had to be coerced to stay on track.

I passed the pre-treatment evaluation and was cleared to start a therapy I had been afraid of most of my life and knew very little about other than reported success rate. At the time I used the information available to me, but ultimately a big leap of faith was involved. I'm not that great at faith, but it's clear from my writings during that time that I knew very well I was running out of time and I leapt, hoping something was going to catch me.

I'd had much practice with hospitalization in the past: there was a point when I learned that it would be much better for me if I signed myself in rather than resisting and ending up with a trip to mental health court and commitment. Signing myself in was like turning myself into jail for something I didn't do and was totally foreign to my sense of survival. But I found a place in myself to hide and disappear to when I knew I'd passed all my own safety checks and had to just have faith the worst thing possible wasn't going to happen when I signed those papers.

I knew that as a person with a mental illness, I was already judged guilty by the world of the crimes particular to the *crazy;* there was no way to redeem myself to it and I no longer cared to prove myself to it. But my loved ones, *well.* I either had to make the leap and risk death in trying, or certainly die.

ECT was my only ladder out of hell. I could only hope the rungs stayed steady enough for me to make it to the top.

# If it Ain't Broke, Don't Fix it.
# If it *is* Broke, Break it Again.

## You might just fix it.

You've probably heard of shock therapy at some point in your life, whispered at the far end of the dinner table in regard to a distant uncle or in confidence as you rode past that rundown place on the hill where some crazy widow lived and everybody knew the men in white coats came long ago and carted her away to be *shocked*.

While patients often still call it being "shocked" (the late actress, author and activist Carrie Fisher called it "riding the lightening"), in medical terminology shock therapy is properly called ECT, or electroconvulsive therapy. This is a much more accurate description of what happens during this form of treatment that's been around since the late 1930s in which an electric current is passed through the brain in order to create a seizure. The "shock" bit indicates that the body is shocked into a state of seizure with the prefix "electro" meaning the seizure is caused by administration of electric. Before ECT other types of "shock" therapies were also used to induce seizures.

And while in the '30s, the thought of using electric to cure disease might have been mysterious, novel and a vast improvement on the previous shock methods, in today's world it strikes us as dangerous, if not somewhat torturous.

Think for a moment of the popular modern picture of ECT: a patient is strapped down to a gurney against their will, straining at the restraints and alternately calling for help and protesting that they aren't crazy. A masked doctor and his nameless attendants hold the patient down, slip on what looks like a set of headphones and pull a huge lever on an ominous-looking machine. Electricity sparks and delivers a charge through the patient's skull that causes their back to arch upwards in spastic protest. The patient screams in what we assume is unbearable pain and then flop around aimlessly, in total loss of control. When the onslaught is over, the body falls lifelessly to the gurney and the attendants remove the machine from the room, leaving the unconscious patient alone.

Are they dead? Are they alive? Have they been tortured? *Brainwashed*?

To assume the patient in this popular vision is dead is natural given what we know to be the dangers of electricity and the assumed intent of those who deliver it. We assume someone who survives such a dangerous encounter must be "messed up" from now on rather than lucky or blessed. It's interesting that we also generally ascribe this to people who have been struck by lightning and survived as well. You just can't play with electricity and come out unscathed. Or can you?

Because we get hung up on the electric element in ECT, let's look at electricity for a moment and how it works. Electricity, we know, is a powerful form of energy made up of atoms. It flows as a *current* along a *conductor* or something that allows it to transfer its charge from one area to another. Conductors aren't mysterious items; everything physical is made up of atoms and some things allow electricity to flow through and some block that flow.

For example, a simple wire will allow electricity to flow quite nicely along it whereas a pillow will not because the pillow's atoms have more resistance to an electric current than the wire. There are three main parts to electricity:

The *current* (called an ampere) which is the measure of electric atoms (or charge) moving from one atom to another.

The *volt* is the measure of how much force or pressure it takes to transfer a current through a conductor.

And the *ohm*, which is the measure of *resistance, or* what blocks the current going through a conductor or *conductivity*, what allows it to go through.

A lot of different factors influence the movement of electricity, from magnetics to temperature so coating a wire (not too resistant) with a material like rubber (highly resistant) will slow down or stop altogether electricity's journey along it.

On the other hand, if you want to really get things moving, dissolve a relatively resistant item like a calcium crystal in salt-water, which has very high conductivity, and watch things get charged. So, while we can't control the natural molecular properties of conductivity and resistance in nature, we can use those properties to influence it for other purposes.

To move at all, electricity needs a conductor to move through. Since electricity is present in the atmosphere anyway (think of a humid summer's evening sky cut in half by the crack of lightning), to use it for our own purposes we must either harness what's already rolling around above us (extremely impractical as of yet) or generate it ourselves with some kind of generator to get things moving.

Very simply, to use electricity *efficiently* we have to manufacture some sort of circuit for it to move through and control that movement once it gets going so it's not just out running around causing havoc. The simplest sort of circuit goes like this: A light bulb is hooked up to a battery with 2 wires, one positive and one negative. In this scenario, the generator (the battery) generates electricity. Electricity travels through one conductor (the wire) to the *load* (the light bulb).

When either the light bulb is switched on or the battery is connected, the electric atoms come charging inside the bulb on one wire and back out to the battery on the other, making a continuous current until the generator is disconnected. In a very simple nutshell, that's electricity.

Now we use electricity in many ways and for some time now have been using it on the body to either help or harm. Thinking to what we just learned about electricity, there are a couple of things we have to remember when imagining electricity going through the body:

We are made up of almost three quarters of water in some form or another.

As our temperature rises, we sweat water quite high in salt content.

We do not all have the same resistance to electricity; men have lower resistance than women, larger versus smaller people differ in the amount of their resistant tissues, and we all have slightly different skin and fluid makeup.

What is touching the body is important. For example, wearing rubber soles will stop or "ground" the flow of electricity while wearing metal earrings (if electricity is moving from ear to ear) will keep it moving.

What path the current is taking is also important. Ear to ear, hand to hand, hand to foot or head to foot are the most dangerous paths as the current nears the vital organs.

If we use electricity in the body there are ways to make it safer or more dangerous by controlling these factors or using them in the evaluation of doing so.

It seems as long as wall outlets have been around, children have been running to stick their chubby little fingers in them and mothers have pole-vaulted over all manner of furniture obstacles to prevent the inevitable *very bad thing* from following. If your father told you not to go running around outside in a lightning storm holding a TV antenna, he wasn't just ruining all your fun. Alternately, your high school Science teacher wasn't going on about grounding just to fill in time before sending you off to PE. And even pet owners know to keep Sparky from chewing on wires unless they want him to start... sparking.

These are all practical and safe means of keeping electricity from running amok in our tissues because these examples are not deliberate, controlled applications of the force and we are not being mindful at those times of influencing factors of conductivity. But take this into consideration: each of us already have a controlled state of electricity within. In fact, we are generators in ourselves.

While extremely complex, our own brains are a veritable storm of electricity themselves within the circuit of the entire body. Their own microscopic neurons are constantly generating electrical impulses from one area to the other to "speak" commands, share information and check in with other parts of the body, with the granddaddy of all internal lightning storms being when the brain experiences a surge of electric activity resulting in a seizure.

You can think of the brain as the body's battery, with each neuron able to generate about 0.07 volts. Now that's kind of small potatoes compared to the AA's in your kids' nerve-shattering Christmas toys with each of their batteries at 1.5 volts, but considering that there are approximately 100 billion of those tiny neurons generating their little sparks (Herculano-Houzel, 2009), you can see how their voices combined in one mighty shout could produce an awesome power, particularly if we could master this by will alone. Of course, the brain's electricity is generated differently than that which lights up the skies in a summer storm or that which powers a lightbulb, but science and its handy equations are able to make accurate comparisons to what seems like an apples and oranges idea.

What has science found? That the electrical force produced when all 100 billion neurons get their singing voices together can generate up to 4 times the force used by the static present I the air to create lightening (lightening takes about 3 million volts). Now sit back a minute and allow yourself to be awed by that matter between your temples (Jones, Brain Battery, 2012).

And that's not to mention our never-tiring hearts. The human heart also generates its own electricity but its power is used to contract the heart's muscles and make it beat. Electricity in the heart follows a pattern or rhythm that must be maintained for the heart to do its job, just as electricity in the brain must be on an even keel for it to do its job. We are organisms naturally acquainted with electric energy.

We've established how electricity works and that the human body manufactures its own version within its own environment. We know that there are multiple factors that influence how electricity travels. And we know that harnessing these factors can influence our encounters with this force. Therefore, electricity doesn't need to be as harmful as we tend to assume it is. But without a doubt, it can be.

Let's take a quick look at the most lethal usage of this force against human life: capital punishment by electric chair.

America's preferred method of execution in the late 1800s was death by hanging until electricity was harnessed and applied to execute by the chair in 1890 by the dentist Alfred Southwick. Considered to be a most humane improvement upon hanging, if that seems a little contradictory it's because it is; death by the chair is pretty rough stuff. In this method of execution, electrodes are placed on the head and one leg and a first shock is given to knock the individual out at the rate of 2400 volts for 7 seconds using a current of approximately 12 amperes.

The second round of electricity is then given at 600 volts for 17 seconds to be repeated as needed. Because the current runs right through the heart from head to leg and is applied through salt-water soaked conductors, what seems like a lowly 600 volts becomes the magic number for death (deathpenaltyinfo. org, 1998). Though this sounds like an instant way to die considering the conductor is a sure-win and the path of electric current is through one of the most dangerous in the body, it's not, because conductivity isn't one size-fit-all when it comes to the body.

2400 volts sounds like a terribly large amount of volts and is certainly a measure of electricity you'd want to avoid to stay conscious to begin with. That is, unless you find yourself in the unlucky situation of cardiac arrest and your heart's electrical rhythm needs some help getting back on track, *stat*. If that's the case, those 2400 volts aren't going to be enough.

How can this be?

Well, remember that voltage is only one component of how electricity works so the number in itself isn't the be all-end all.

An automated external defibrillator (AED) delivers an electric current of anywhere from 120-200 joules (the measure of electricity used for AED) and up to 45 amps. Two-hundred joules is equal to approximately 3000 volts but instead of running through the head and leg, it's applied directly to the chest to enter the vital organ. The computer inside an AED assesses a person's heart rhythm before a current is run through its electrodes to the heart muscle because sometimes the heart balances itself out and so you wouldn't want to just shoot electricity through it pel-mel. With this technology the error of giving electricity when it's not needed is eliminated in the first place. Hence, delivered properly, in the right set of circumstances, a high voltage of electricity can save your life. (American Heart Association, 2017) (Resuscitation Central)

Then again, let's go back to what your mother knew all along- sticking your finger in a light socket will indeed hurt you (and under the right conditions can kill you) because of the path it takes through the body.

Most U.S. outlets in the home run about 120 volts with 20 amps of current and touching a live wire, while not as easy nowadays with current electrical safety practices and equipment, is one way to shoot a current right from the finger up through the arm and to the heart. So as before, serious injury can happen even with the modest living room light socket. Always do yourself a favor and don't put anything in it.

Then what actually *is* the most dangerous part of electricity? Is it the voltage? The method of conduction? These are important factors but in the end, it's the current that kisses or kills; specifically how strong the current is and how long it lasts.

Interestingly, it's not even necessarily a high current that kills outright, and this is due to how the body resists the shock. For example, you may have seen a television show in which someone grabs a wire and is shocked continuously, being unable to let go of the wire. This is true at lower currents. The contractions that happen in the muscles of the arm from a shock at as low as 10 milliamps (a milliamp being one thousandth of an ampere) prevent it from unclenching long enough to let go and stop the flow of electricity into the body.

The longer the current stays in the body, the higher the body's temperature rises, the more sweat is produced which makes tissue more conductive and the more damage can occur. As electrical current goes up in amps, the muscles react more and more strongly until around 200 milliamps. At this point the heart clenches and cannot move. But if the heart is paralyzed by current temporarily and is resuscitated, it can potentially be saved because the arresting of the muscle keeps it from going into the frazzled beat of ventricular fibrillation.

In essence, 200 milliamps in the heart can theoretically be something like putting someone into a medical coma. But of course, this is no guarantee for survival and a delivery of milliamps above 200 can cause what we generally associate with the "look" of either the electric chair or electroconvulsive therapy: convulsions and contortions, total loss of muscle control, death.

In short, we put together a mental image of the actual effects of the electric chair at 2400 volts and 12 amps of electricity at a steady rate with ECT which is administered at generally at 450 volts depending on the machine's manufacturer settings and .09 amps of electricity for approximately 6-8 seconds in pulses (ect .org, n.d.). Clearly using electric in and on the body isn't new and isn't limited to Psychiatry by a long shot; it's only been catapulted into our social awareness in a unique way by Psychiatry. (7)

Let's compare these applications of electricity in approximation:

We've established that in the case of current and time of application, ECT is one of the more benign exposures to the element a person can experience. We must allow at all times for variables which would cause a higher or lower application time or current; these being the make of the ECT machine being used, the seizure threshold of the patient receiving the shock (some people just don't seize without a longer application) and the physical makeup of a person in regard to how conducive their tissues are (Somatics, LLC, 1983-2015). But

| Application | Volts | Joules | Amps | Time |
|---|---|---|---|---|
| Capital Punishment | 2400 then 600 | | 12 amps | 7, then 17 seconds |
| AED | | 3000 | 45 milliamps (varies) | varies |
| Electrical Outlet | 120 | | | varies |
| ECT | Up to 450 | Up to 0.6075 | 0.09 amps | 8 milliseconds |

why bother with electric at all when so many pharmaceutical treatments exist? It's almost impossible to watch live television for an hour and not come across an advertisement for a drug of some sorts for just about anything that ails you.

In reference to the mental illnesses, the social isolation, stigma and multiple hospital rounds with the ever-present threat of suicidality (more for some illnesses, less for others, more for some life situations, less for others) is very real and very much a threat to quality of life. Quality of life in terms of mental illness is termed more in respect to functionality in life.

Is the patient able to work at all? Do they have the means to get and take their medication as directed? Are they able to maintain any relationships or social life while living with their Illness? Are they able to live on their own or without round the clock supervision? Do they feel safe, are they able to make goals or plans and are they able to see themselves having a future? Do they have days that are not continuously haunted by the persistent desire or compulsion to kill themselves? Are they productive members of society and if not, is the *illness* preventing this? Is it not medical science's mission and responsibility to remove this particular obstacle in any way it can?

And if these things are all a persistent problem, which doggedly refuse to be alleviated by first-line treatments such as therapy and medication, might we conclude that the brain *is* in peril and the person needs more serious help? Usually the first way of doing this, either through the patient's choice, a doctor's recommendation or what the insurance will cover, is to start with a psychiatric evaluation, therapy and then medication, usually in some semblance of that order. But barring the effectiveness of all that, ECT is currently considered a fallback for "hard to treat" cases in Psychiatry.

Primarily developed with the goal to treat Schizophrenia, Electroconvulsive Therapy was discovered second-hand to treat Depression quite effectively and later on, a myriad of other conditions as well, including:

Depression and suicidality

Severe manic states

Psychosis

Refusal to eat[1]

Agitation and aggression as an effect of Dementia

Catatonia

Parkinson's Disease

Neuroleptic Malignant Syndrome

Obsessive Compulsive Disorder

Depression as a result of Huntington's Disease, Multiple Sclerosis, Muscular Dystrophy and Central Nervous System Syphilis

Depression in the elderly population

Postpartum Depression (Gale Group, Inc., 2003)

And all this can be treated by causing the brain to have a seizure, with *reportedly* less overall side effects than years of medication and a rate of anywhere from 75-90% efficacy in treating Depression with about 25% of patients not receiving any effect either positive or negative (Hersh, 2013) (Somatics, 1983-2015) (Dukakis, 2007).

---

[1]Though not a treatment for Eating Disorders, ECT is sometimes successful in temporarily alleviating the depression and suicidal tendencies that can come with the malnutrition with these diseases.

Side effects from medications drive people off of them by the thousands every year, keep others from getting treatment and have spawned that generation of television commercials which always end up telling us the drug can kill us but *by all means*, go talk to your doctor for a prescription and keep your lawyer's number nearby.

A century ago, drug treatments would have been a dream come true for thousands but after decades of medications causing other conditions requiring more medications and thousands of deaths from accidental -and not so accidental- overdoses, it would seem we're back at the logical next step of searching out non-chemical treatments for just about everything.

Here I must caution: please don't take me the wrong way about medication. I've had many adverse reactions on medications, chucked more than my insurance ever wants to tabulate, and have proven conclusively to myself that I'm not so swift off of them for any amount of time. I would never dissuade someone from taking their psychiatric medication unless they really and truly feel with their physician's professional opinion that they have a good medical reason to.

Consider this: if the brain's electricity naturally gets off balance it goes into a seizure, a sort of lightning storm of activity one wants to avoid. But adding extra electricity to the mix to purposely knock the brain off-line works in theory much the way the AED does in the heart or your computer does during an electric surge by taking systems offline in order to allow them to reset, recalibrate and prevent further damage.

While it's still not known why ECT works or exactly how and theories have ranged widely since its discovery, there are currently two main theories at work. One is that the brain of the patient is already "broken" in a sense, that is, not working properly to begin with because it was either formed that way from birth or because it has become that way as a byproduct of illness. The second theory is that the seizure activity triggers the brain to release deadened and diseased cells so it can reset or reboot and begin to heal itself. *Mind exfoliation*: I can dig it.

But having *Epilepsy* where the brain naturally experiences seizure activity from a variety of factors doesn't guarantee an absence of mental illness as has been previously thought, in fact the suicide rate amongst epileptics is roughly 3.5 to 5.8 times higher than the rest of the population (Shafer, 2013). And receiving a seizure from applied electricity from the outside is not the same as the brain's own electrical system causing a seizure from within.

What we do know, for sure, is that ECT *can* work. It doesn't always, and we don't know exactly why, but it can. Next, we'll look at how ECT is applied to the brain, so let's imagine you have scheduled yourself for some electroconvulsive treatments.

How to get started?

# So, You'd Like to Glow
# in the Dark

JUST *what* in the physical sense is ECT?

To begin with, electroconvulsive therapy is not a single treatment or single seizure but usually a series of treatments somewhere around 8 to12 rounds with 2 to 3 days in-between.

Let's pretend then that you, yes you, have decided with your doctor to undergo ECT as a treatment for Depression. Incidentally, according to the National Institutes of Health, if you are having ECT in the U.S. you are most likely to be an elderly white woman but in the U.K. you could be as young as 16. In Turkey, you would most likely not be in your senior years yet, but on the African continent you would most likely be a young man. And in Saudi Arabia you would tend to be a married woman. (Leiknas, 2012)

You will find that though you may not know a single soul who ever had ECT to tell you of their experience, there are many famous people who have undergone ECT before you such as:

Sylvia Plath (writer)

Lou Reed (musician, *Velvet Underground*)

Kitty Dukakis (writer/ philanthropist)

Ernest Hemingway (writer)

Vivien Leigh (actress)

Judy Garland (singer/ actress)

Cole Porter (musician)

Harold Gimblett (cricketer)

Yves St. Laurent (fashion designer)

Connie Francis (writer)

Dick Cavett (talk show host)

Janet Frame (writer)

Carrie Fisher (actress, writer, activist)

Thelonious Monk (jazz pianist / composer)

Peter Green (musician, *Fleetwood Mac*)

Sherwin B. Nuland (surgeon / writer)

Spike Milligan (comedian / writer)

Francois Luong (gay rights activist)

David Helfgott (musician)

Dave Mustaine (musician, *Megadeth*) (Association for Natural Psychology, n.d.)

What makes you a candidate for ECT? You may not been helped sufficiently with medication, or are intolerant to the side effects. Maybe you're pregnant and unable to take medication, or have exhausted other therapy options. Maybe, like me, you've gone through nearly twenty years of medication therapy, multiple hospitalizations and suicide attempts and have developed a drug allergy list a mile long. ECT may be the only logical option between you and another suicide attempt. Though each hospital or clinic has varying treatment schedules, etc., the general procedure is the same for the actual treatment across the U.S.

You'll begin by having a medical evaluation with a physician who will review your medical and psychiatric history and current medications. A physical will be taken as well as blood tests, an ECG of the heart, an MRI of the brain and cognitive testing to establish how you, as you, work. You'll be given information on the procedure in person and you might watch a video on things as well. Because general anesthesia is given for a short period, an anesthesiologist will evaluate you to make certain you can safely tolerate it. Some people, like myself, are "slow to wake" from anesthesia and may need a little oxygen to get them going again or just permitted a much longer period to recover and allow their body to get back to normal functioning. That doesn't necessarily mean you'll be unable to have ECT, but it's something that everyone should be aware of in your care from start to finish.

Other pre-tests you may have include a CT of the brain, an EEG of brainwaves, x-rays and urine screening, and these will depend largely on whether or not you have other medical conditions present before treatment. Lastly, consent by you or your power of attorney must be signed before any testing occurs.[2]

Some medications must be discontinued temporarily during treatment such as Lithium, some antidepressants and anti-seizure or seizure threshold lowering drugs (because taking anti-seizure drugs while trying to create seizures would make for an extremely expensive visit to the doctor just to take a short nap). Your medications may be started again after treatment ends, or the dosage may be changed or discontinued altogether. Before ECT, I was taken off Lorazepam, Cymbalta and Tegratol and restarted on Lorazepam and Tegratol only after treatment ended.

Let's say you've passed all your evaluations with flying colors and are scheduled to start therapy in an outpatient clinic or possibly as an inpatient and then receive follow-up treatments as an outpatient. The night before a treatment you'll stop taking your medications as directed and stop eating or drinking eight hours prior to your appointment. For the most part you will have treatments in the early to mid-morning to allow recovery time and not less than two days apart, and you will begin a regimen of pain and anti-nausea medications something like this (from my personal notes in 2012):

---

[2]In the United States, by state law informed consent must be given unless you have pre-determined in a mental health living will that you elect ECT to be given automatically in certain situations in which you may be unable to give consent to treatment, or you have been involuntarily committed to a hospital by the state or are incarcerated with a mental health diagnosis and in these cases can be treated as ordered by a mental health court (Law, 2009).

*600 mg ibuprofen at bedtime prior to ECT and once after ECT*

*Naproxen 375mg 1 tab 2x daily on days off ECT*

*Motrin during the day on ECT days*

*Nausea meds (Zofran) night before ECT, morning of, and after treatment*

You will receive an IV line to administer anesthesia and in the U.S., also a muscle relaxant to prevent spasms which can occur normally during a seizure and can do serious harm. Using a muscle relaxant during ECT is referred to as the practice of "modified ECT" and is not always used in other parts of the world. In the actual treatment room a medical team will be waiting to monitor your vital signs and brain waves and you'll be given oxygen through a mask.

*Prep: dry hair. No meds past 7 pm. (they) use heart monitors. Blood pressure cuff on arm and foot. Socks are removed. Wheeled into a bay with other patients waiting for treatment.*

*A nurse goes over your name and birthdate and pins a yellow ID paper (*with allergy information*) to your blanket.*

*Head is prepped with EEG stuff.* (conduction gel for the electrodes.)

*Inside the treatment room anesthesiologist and psychiatrist introduce themselves and ask some medical questions...perform a "time out". They ask your name and (date of birth).*

*Anesthesiologist and psychiatrist say the weight of patient and what side of the head they will be doing treatment on and also the amount and then the nurse asks if all agree. They say yes and the nurse puts EEG leads on, gives anesthesia through the IV line and you are instructed to wiggle your toes if told to.*

*This lets them know your awareness during anesthesia.*

The purpose of using EEG recording during treatment is to show for sure if a seizure is going on because EEG records electrical activity in the brain. The blood pressure cuff prevents muscle relaxant from entering your foot so that the doctor can see your foot spasm when a seizure successfully begins. It seems a little low-tech to be watching feet but it's a reliable and non-invasive way to quickly tell if things are going the right way if something doesn't show on the EEG for some reason. Generally, you will receive a mouth guard as well to protect your teeth and tongue from any injury but this is fitted after you are asleep under anesthesia.

To create the seizure, a set of electrode pads is placed on your temples (one pad at both temples for *bilateral* ECT, one pad at the right temple and one at the crown of the head for *unilateral*) which have been prepared with conductive gel. Keep in mind this is a very controlled procedure and you must have dry hair to cut down on any extra moisture on the skin where the electrodes will go beyond that of the conductive gel because, as we've discovered, electric current follows along anything with good conductivity and the goal is to keep the current in one place. This also helps prevents burns on the skin occurring where the pads touch.

After getting gelled up, a medical professional activates the ECT machine which sends an electrical current through the electrodes and passes through your brain to induce a seizure. Now traditional ECT gives an electrical pulse at 8 milliseconds, considered a long pulse that stimulates a particular brainwave called the *sine-wave*. Advances in the treatment have taken that down to 0.5-1.5 milliseconds and stimulate another type of brainwave called the *square-wave*. Using these 'brief pulses' cuts down on side effects. This is now the standard of ECT in the U.S. though even shorter, "ultra-brief" pulses are being used in Europe and it's likely this will become standard here as well in future (Loo, 2012).

The seizure generated in ECT generally lasts 1-2 minutes and in the rare case it may last longer, Valium or Ativan may be given to you via IV to calm things down (Gale Group, Inc., 2003).

*Treatment takes about 10 minutes. Most of it prep.*

*EEG leads are removed before you wake in recovery bay. IV is removed, monitor tags taken off. Blood pressure monitored before release. Given another round of anti-nausea drugs and Motrin.*

*I'm not allowed to have breakfast because there's a tiny chance my stomach could aspirate anything still in there when the convulsions occur. These aren't huge convulsions– you can't even really tell they're going on from outside other than some twitches in the feet but it; enough internal motion that stomach contents can possibly be pushed into the lungs. Not good!*

The length of seizure, side of the head and toleration is recorded at each treatment. Afterwards you'll be taken to a recovery room and once you've awakened and are stable you'll be taken back to the hospital ward or released to go home with instructions not to drive during the course of treatment and likely some painkillers. You'll have two days off and then another treatment for a series of about 6-8 before some real progress is made in symptoms and a treatment team will determine if ECT needs to be continued, tapered off, or switched from unilateral to bilateral.

Bilateral ECT is called for with harder to treat illnesses or if a patient isn't responding quickly enough with unilateral treatment. You may need to come back every month for treatment after the initial block, or every 6 months or just every year or not at all. This is something a doctor must determine with you during treatment; it's a "see how it goes" sort of deal, monitored by weekly check-ins with the psychiatrist to go over a Depression scale (called the Hamm-D scale) (Hamilton Depression Rating Scale (HDRS), n.d.). Your progress is noted at every treatment so your physician can get a good idea on how to order those future treatments if needed:

*(Noted) There was an improvement in suicidal thoughts, easier to engage in conversation, showed some affect* (emotion).

And because we are all individuals who react in different ways to treatment, some people may need to scale back from all their activities during a course of ECT while some may even be able to work part-time and some may be able to resume some but not all duties.

But the million-dollar questions that so many wonder but don't quite know how to ask is, *how does it feel to be shocked*? Is ECT torturous? Does it paralyze and maim or fry the brain and curl the hair?

I'm not sure I want to know. The only memory I retain of actual treatment is that of looking up into a man's face and screaming as he put an oxygen mask on me and I'm pretty certain this was to do with the mask itself. But during the process I kept pretty detailed records for the first half of treatment as an inpatient from either my own observations or those of others telling me what they saw happening to me.

Luckily, most of us in modern times don't know what the actual shock feels like because they're out cold before it happens which was not the case in previous eras with unmodified ECT. But that doesn't mean there isn't still a physical "feel" to ECT; this just comes afterward and can be separated into two distinct parts, being the physical effects and the mental effects.

ECT used in the United States is modified with anesthesia and muscle relaxants which interrupt breathing, so oxygen is needed to deliver what your lungs can't as efficiently. In the past when these elements were not used at all, patients often passed out during the seizure and could also break or dislocate limbs (and often hips in bilateral shock), break and lose teeth, damage tendons and fracture the spine from the convulsions.

There is precious little recorded about the actual experience through these procedures in the patients' words except for the fear of what may happen ahead of time and the cognitive effects afterward. Writer Janet Frame, who received ECT before modification, said in her autobiography An Angel at My Table that it caused her permanent, grim memories of treatment and nightmares of being taken for another round, leading her to wake "in dread." (Frame, An Angel at My Table, 1984)

This was in a time when ECT was a very different procedure than it is today and properly commanded fear from those who underwent it. Keep in mind that

ECT causes a *grand mal*-type seizure, also called a *tonic-clonic* seizure. Tonic refers to the first 20 seconds or so of the seizure where, if you were conscious to begin with, you would be knocked unconscious. The clonic bit is the second, or convulsive part where muscles contract and limbs can flail so it's not a wonder pain is involved in some form.

And even with modification, a seizure is still a full-contact sport and the muscles still seize to *some* extent and again, this is where individuality comes into play. Unlike my fellow patients, I had been diagnosed previous to ECT with Fibromyalgia so was no stranger to muscle pain. As I noted in my journals, other patients had told me the amount of pain I experienced during treatment was pretty much par for the course. The duration may have had to do with my own makeup, but that's something we can't know in hindsight.

*When I turned my head at all I became very nauseous and dizzy. Excruciating pain in the right jaw and teeth. Jaw clenches when the (electric) current is run. It was very sore to talk, nearly impossible to swallow or chew without terrible pain for about 6 hours.*

*Took Tylenol every 4 hours for pain. Very sleepy.*

*Didn't remember getting to and from ECT. Faces in my memory from the day before were blanks. Woke up crying profusely – this is my usual wake up from anesthesia.*

*Legs extremely weak. Felt very shaky 16 hours after treatment.*

*Had to be carried and assisted to and from areas. Hands shook, spilled a lot of things. Grasp was very weak, had a hard time closing my hand to hold a spoon, pen, etc.*

*Constantly dizzy for 7 hours after treatment then this tapered down to just when my head was turned or tilted.*

*Other patients very concerned and scared, didn't know what was happening but very encouraging. Some friends curious outside of hospital but mostly frightened. Even met nursing staff who were frightened at the treatment.*

*Approx 8 hours after treatment recalled my entire name spontaneously.*

*Feel pretty much the same emotionally. Can't concentrate very much right now and pain/weakness has been acting up. I sort of don't want to do it again but next treatment is tomorrow. I am actually more upset/ scared about possibility of a PICC line.*

*Husband came to be with me, helped me dress and eat a little to keep Motrin down.*

*Throat and teeth and tongue very sore. Hurts to talk and swallow. Back of neck and upper back very sore, right hand. Dizzy on sitting. IVs difficult to get in- cried a lot. Had a lot of pain when anesthesia was given.*

*Pain extreme today. Leg weakness much worse to start but gradually got better. Slept 3 hours.*

*Pain is unbearable in mouth, back of head, hands, neck and spine. Hurts to talk, cough. Can't get over how much more painful it is today. Was advised of this by another patient but experiencing it is a whole new matter.*

*Must look down at the ground to keep upright when I walk. Turning is hard.*

*Feeling down because of pain. Cried a lot, feel miserable.*

*Unable to eat much because of swallowing pain; neck and left shoulder blade are very sore.*

Each person's choice of treatment to pursue is their own choice subject to the information they have, their past experience and their own personal biases. For many of us, ECT seems the ultimate act of desperation (as it did to me) and what causes us to become so desperate for relief that we would voluntarily submit ourselves to such a painful process nearly guaranteeing social misunderstanding and stigma afterwards?

To understand this we must understand that the conditions ECT offers hope for are still chronic and incurable at this time in medical history. Shock's greatest achievement is the temporary delivery from Depression (for some, a much longer relief) in a faster mode than the weeks of increasing medications can deliver. Nothing can come close to describing the seriousness of clinical Depression's consequences; how close to death it constantly forces its victims to walk.

Mental illness remains so tough to understand because it doesn't show up on blood tests or biopsies (though f MRI testing is beginning to shed some light on certain diagnoses). It comes out in the things we think and do; our inward and outward behavior. When someone has narrowing of the arteries as part of Coronary Heart Disease, this can cause a heart attack and end the person's life. Another person may have Depression on its own or develop it from the stress of living with chronic illness *such as* Coronary Heart Disease or the stress of abuse or work or a death which can alter thinking patterns and cause suicidal behavior and also *end that person's life.*

Kay Redfield Jamison notes in *Night Falls Fast* that in the context of Psychiatry, a suicide attempt which results in the death of the patient is considered a "successful suicide." (Jamison, 2000) This is for purposes of diagnosis of course but the wording is so fantastically ironic and unfortunate as many who are at the point that they feel they must end their lives do indeed consider the act the only *successful* and *right* thing they will ever do.

When we hear the almost cliché words, *the world would be better off without me*, it is many times this exact line of thinking that brings people to such desperate acts. A person in a deep depression often *cannot* reason with themselves that they only feel like a burden. They *cannot* think that their children wouldn't have a provider when they are gone or that their spouse would be *devastated* without them. They are *unable* to fathom that their own parents and siblings would have to go through the despair of burying them.

If we think of life-saving interventions, ECT becomes more logical as an emergency treatment to get people out of their depression long enough to save their lives and regulate their minds. Supporters of ECT as a front-line intervention and emergency treatment have a very logical argument that the cost of mental illness is extremely high in the U.S. in terms of failed medications, job loss, multiple hospitalizations and the emotional bankruptcy that affects not just the patient but their families and friends. What compels us to go through years of ineffective means to make it through the day when we could crank it up a notch and kick Depression to the curb if it means only having to do it a few times a year?

For one, most advocates of ECT aren't saying *let's chuck medication and therapy and go play with electricity*. Rather, they are for more education and access to the practice as well as respect from the community towards ECT being an option on par with the importance of using an AED on the heart. Right now in the 21st century the idea for pro-ECT advocates is not to force shock treatment on every patient who walks into a hospital but to make it available earlier on in the treatment cycle, to educate them on the positive effects it can have, and to make it available to doctors who deem their patient in need of mental health intervention.

They say, "*This is why*, ECT."

But something about the imagery and history of ECT makes us uncomfortable as a nation to allow such a treatment to come any closer past the asylum doors of old to our doctors' offices or hospital emergency rooms of today. It seems naturally related to those taboo subjects relegated to discussion in the *far* corner, not out in front by the water cooler. Such a stigma is not attached to the other medical therapies using electricity. Some of this has to do with public relations.

The National Heart Association has done a bang-up job of educating the masses about heart attack and what to do in the event of one. Their massive campaigns have educated us down to the grade-school level about the importance of CPR to save lives and the relevance of keeping AED machines in public places. The American Cancer Society has also done a wonderful job of taking the stigma away from cancer; advising us that cancer can't be given to someone else and when screened and caught early, has a good treatment success rate for many illnesses.

Who, facing a terminal illness, hasn't been put to the test of choosing whether or not to undergo life-saving surgery which may change the rest of their lives forever, or painful courses of treatments that have serious side effects? When someone is diagnosed with a terminal illness, there is no doubt about it, the big guns are called out immediately to fight a war for life. Choosing to undergo ECT is a serious decision, but one no less important or potentially life-saving.

When ECT came onto the world scene in 1938, it rode into the '40s and early '50s on a wave of PR through powerful and hopeful headlines in popular magazines of the era such as *Life* and *Time*, calling it a miracle improvement over the former treatments for Schizophrenia and Depression. So where are the sweeping campaigns today? We can look to the media's portrayal of ECT in the last half of the 20th century for contributing to our fear of the unknown factors of ECT but its history is much more complicated.

*My friends at home are afraid of ECT and as I talk to the staff I realize that many of them are too, it seems nobody knows too much about it. But the nurses say they've seen good results from it so that's promising.*

When we allow ourselves to "be real" as my therapist says, we will probably find that deep down, we ourselves are the roadblock to ECT. We forbid its mention in public, we shy away from the experiences of those going through it looking for support and we dare not ask. I don't believe that people develop such strong aversions for no reason, or that these aversions are for a bad reason. I do, however, believe that when the feeling is extremely strong, a little evaluation is in order.

We've looked at the mechanical workings of ECT and how it measures up to other experiences we have with its main component, electricity. We've looked at what it feels like in the body to go through a series of treatments. So let's get real and look deep down at what happens in the mind during and after treatment; the no-holds barred of what we naturally wonder when we hear the words "shock therapy."

# It Wasn't That Great of a Party if You Still Remember it

WE seek out novel treatments to cure what goes on inside our minds. People who do not experience mental illness engage in many activities to alter their thought states as well from eating (and maybe overeating) ice cream to alleviate the stress of a breakup to turning on upbeat music to feel happier to picking up a game of baseball to feel more like part of a group.

These are normal activities we all engage in, often without a whole lot of thought and many unique to our personal background (comfort food, anyone?). And even though we may not understand why someone on the other side of the world does something to feel joy that seems totally opposite to what we might do, as humans we recognize the *need* to.

Mental illness attacks emotions and thoughts in a way so personal it almost seems tailor-made to the sufferer. But just like we all long to feel happy and shy away from feeling sad, mental illness has hallmark effects on everyone who grapples with it. It takes someone from another race, another class, another gender, another socio-economic background, another country and equalizes them in a heartbeat. Depression on one side of the world is just as dangerous on the other side. Mania is just as destructive. Schizophrenia, just as isolating.

So when we look to unconventional treatments to assuage illness, we are looking for a lessening of what we already fight against. What we don't know is how it will feel as that lessening is taking place.

*Feels like: brain scramble.*

K. Rose Quayle

*I knew people but not their names, or names but not who they belonged to. I stuttered a lot-my mind had a lot of thoughts but it seemed like gathering them and forcing them out of my mouth was very tricky.*

For a procedure that seems to wipe out dreams, ECT appears to inhabit in an empyrean state itself, beyond the understanding of those going into it and those prescribing it. This completely leaves out the families of those undergoing the treatments themselves.

My husband explains, *"They told us, basically, that they didn't know how it worked. They said... that people with Epilepsy have seizures and not very much Depression so if they created a seizure...."* he waives his hand. *"That was pretty much it."*

*"I was amazed at how different people reacted. Some went in, did their treatment and came back out exactly the same. Then there was you. You came out and didn't know up from down, every time. They'd take you in early in the morning and by lunch they* [other patients] *would still have to help you walk to the dining room. They let me come in outside of visiting hours partly because of my work schedule and also because of how bad you were. I would just sit while you were conked out waiting for you to come round and then like I said, you had no clue. You would cry and cry suddenly, no one knew why or what to do."*

Years before I underwent ECT myself, I had been hospitalized on a floor where everyone except me was having ECT treatment. I'd only ended up on that floor because of a bed shortage and was very nervous around the patients who were plainly an almost even mix of those with Bipolar Disorder and Major Depression; people just like me whom I would ordinarily never be afraid of even in the most whacked-out of states.

The mystery surrounding ECT was very thick for me at that point, even while spending 24 hours a day with those undergoing it and even knowing that it helped a relative of mine whom I would later recall as proof that ECT and I had a shot together. My fellow patients would disappear for a few hours, come back in wheelchairs in various states of mild stupor and mainly sleep for a few hours until the next mealtime or straight through until the next day. Nothing terribly sinister seemed to be going on except that no one ever seemed to talk about it and no one wanted to answer my questions among the staff as to how this procedure actually worked. No one was willing to tell me what they thought, how they thought, if they *still thought at all* after being shocked. No one seemed to have courage enough to say, *We have no idea.*

My husband interrupts in frustration, "*That's it, isn't it? That's the thing. You can't remember. Anything could have happened to you but you wouldn't even know!* " I answer indignantly, "*You can't quantify my memory. You can't say this is what I've forgotten. It's not possible. I don't even know it's gone until someone else points it out. And how do they know what's gone from my mind?*"

"*Well. I guess it smacks of mind control and things like that,*" he concedes and the subject is dropped.

And I think that's ultimately what's so very bothersome about ECT. Beyond the idea of having an electric current purposely run through your brain and being shut up in a mental hospital with a bunch of loonies and keeping all that secret from everyone you know, what runs above and beyond with ECT are the unknown factors and the personal witness erased from the storyline that give it a sinister feel. Because if there was one thing more galling than anything else to my husband, friends and family, it was that the staff truly didn't know why.

Why *anything*, it seemed. Why it took so long, why I was so out of it, why ECT even worked. It's rather hard to put trust in a system no one knows the particulars of for certain. There's a reason people say *"the devil's in the details."* In rereading my notes, I could see immediately that my mind was changing from day one.

*(I have) lags in processing...don't understand humour... feeling flat emotionally by end of day, (I have a ) lot of crying without feeling during the day.*

*Unable to recognise people if their hair was worn differently.*

*Asked "who's that?" A lot.*

*Can't concentrate very much....head crammed with thoughts but there's a disconnect between thought and spoken word...stuttering, stammering, unable to find words. Hard to concentrate on reading or on one task- had a lot of walking from one thing to (another) thing but not really accomplishing anything.*

*Less interrupting thoughts (from bipolar).*

*Feel dull. Hard to sense any time has passed. Thoughts not readily accessible. Not frustrated, just impatient.*

*Sense of time is messed up .It's a very discombobulating feeling. It's like being able to say the alphabet as A to Z but nothing in-between. It's a little bit scary.*

The physical pain I experienced improved over the course of treatments, settling into a pattern of headaches and joint pain in my hands, toes and wrists. The "brain scramble" however, continued in strange and unexpected ways and any notable improvement wasn't observed until after my treatment was switched from unilateral to bilateral. Looking at my cognitive and depression scale scores it seems like a dramatic change and my treatment team noted particularly I was beginning to come out of my shell, having less *flat affect*. The term is sometimes interchanged with *blunt affect* which means basically "without emotion", though it is noted that some people develop a demeanor like this naturally in some cultures or situations at home when growing up and it is also present with certain neurological conditions.

For my husband and family, it was an improvement but there were deep concerns at what price. For one, during ECT my sleep pattern changed almost immediately. My mother has joked all my life that I never napped as an infant so she never got a break. I was one of those kids who had to be constantly moving and would sleep in a car, baby swing, rocking chair until it stopped and then *SCREAM*! But I was also used to my mother working 2nd shift when I was quite young and so late nights were a normal routine for me up until school began and I had to get on the rest of the world's schedule.

As I got into my school years I would sleep very deeply, thrashing out in nightmares and throwing myself onto the floor. This was remedied by metal rails installed on my bed but the pattern of nightmares mellowed in my early teens to rounds of nightly, lucid dreams in color, always playing out in four distinct parts. I was able to recall these in vivid detail, was often aware I was dreaming and could wake myself, and probably should have made it my business to write them down at the time and turn them into a book. Or at the very least some very trippy animation. Ah. *C'est la vie.*

Yet despite regular periods of dream-sleep and falling out of bed, I had trouble both getting to sleep and staying asleep and one night in elementary school I donned a pith helmet I'd found at a yard sale with my grandfather and took up my old army bugle to get some practice in during the wee hours. There weren't too many nights of that to follow. My mother then allowed me to listen to my little short-wave radio in the night as long as I stayed in my room and kept it on low for the benefit of other household members. No bugles at 2 am; Larry King and the BBC had to suffice.

By the time I'd become a young adult I was taking anti-depressants or anti-anxiety meds along with my usual anti-seizure drugs all in one cocktail at bedtime to combine side effects and knock me out for at least some of the night. It seemed after all those years of denouncing the Sandman and bawling *"I'm not sleepy!"* and meaning it, I'd managed to scare him off permanently.

Now only a fistful of drugs was bringing sleep anywhere near my bed. But ECT changed all that, at first with the normal exhaustion of going through the treatment itself and later with some unexpected and unexplained results.

On unilateral ECT: *Very sleepy. Asked if ECT would help with nightmares-general consensus was yes. However, 1st day (after treatment) every time I fell asleep I dreamed the same thing over and over on a continuous loop. I felt even more exhausted on waking.*

*Slept badly last night- dream loop again.*

*Woke up early- dreaming loop again. Felt restless and got up, wandered a little. Tried to nap a little but mind won't slow down enough to sleep.*

*Perhaps I'll ask the doc for something else to sleep tomorrow.*

*Didn't sleep for any(thing) last night. Still having these loops of dreams it's bizarre. I feel like I fought some sort of war last night. Got some melatonin from the doctor to start tonight. Still having constant cycles of repeating dreams though so not feeling too rested.*

On bilateral ECT: *Doctor talked me into trying some medicine for nightmares tonight. He said they don't know why it works, just that it's an old blood pressure medication and it seems to reduce nightmares in people with PTSD (*Post-Traumatic Stress Disorder*). I don't consider myself to have PTSD- this has just been tossed around during this admission. Whatever.*

After bilateral ECT was stopped, I experienced daytime sleepiness like never before and bouts of falling asleep anytime I sat still. My husband remarked that when I came home I was asleep much more than I was awake and probably making up for those years of insomnia. I was back on my old medications and sleeping badly as usual *at night* so what changed?

I'd stopped dreaming. Or at least, I'd stopped dreaming in full-color cinema quality and had either adjusted to not dreaming at all or such that I never remembered. The nightly show in my mind had gone the way of the drive-in and during my worst times after treatment I thought ECT had stolen my dreams away.

About three years after treatment I began to dream again, very rarely and in no way like I had prior. This was more like being aware something had just happened in between the time I laid down and the time my eyes opened again. My sleep got nominally better and then four years after, dramatically worse, with my dreams disappearing again. I began having extreme sleepiness in the daytime, falling asleep for a few seconds over and over again at work to the point I became disoriented, was unable to pay attention for even the small amount of time I'd become used to after treatment and my short-term memory began failing.

And when I say failing, I don't mean just didn't remember what I ate the night before, I mean leaving the back door wide open and letting the inside animals out and the outside animals in. It was a problem that broke me down enough to make an appointment with a neurologist. After scans and tests and a totally coincidental referral to a sleep surgeon from Otolaryngology, I was found to have Alpha-Delta Wave anomaly on a sleep lab study when everyone was betting the farm on sleep apnea.

In the simplest of terms, the brain is trying to stay awake while it moves into deep sleep so on an EEG readout the alpha brain wave intersects with the delta brain wave and the body isn't able to get the restorative healing sleep it needs every night to do repair work. It made sense that I was so tired and also getting sick over and over. Alpha-Delta Wave anomaly has been noted in psychiatric conditions as well as Fibromyalgia. I mentioned this to the doctor but that I had also noted in wonder that my pain had all but disappeared after ECT and I had thought I had been cured somehow as a byproduct.

The doctor was much more practical. He pointed out I'd been on anti-seizure medication and the dosages had changed at some point after ECT. Some of these medications are also used in treating neurological pain and sure enough, I was taking those. He felt they had been keeping the pain at bay and something had knocked this whole process off. Since poor sleep tends to make Fibromyalgia act up and had certainly started to do so in my legs and ribs, it was a safe bet the two were very closely linked and it wasn't really possible in hindsight to tell which began the whole process.

A plan was formed: I would change how I took my anti-seizure meds, drop a sleep medication and begin a short-acting anti-depressant to get to sleep. Slowly I began again to dream; a dim and distant memory always of *running*.

I'm not so sure ECT didn't play a part in this; possibly by setting me right to begin with in the short term before things got off again (breaking the already broken), but I'm not looking to sit in bitterness. I just like to understand the process to be able to fix things up. As it is, my sleep has improved slowly with anti-seizure medication and I have been sporadically dreaming in the classical sense. Mainly about my dog.

Sleep changes notwithstanding, the most immediate effect of ECT outside of pain was the requisite loss of memory which began with benign inconsistencies and ended with *great gaping holes* in my mind. For the first day or so minor things slipped away from me, getting to and from places mainly, or my own movement in the world.

*Some memories have holes in them or gaps...I know who I am, no ID (identification) issues. I can recognize everyone and name them. Don't remember waking up. Recall all names and faces this morning before treatment for the most part.*

Then this progressed to the things and people outside of me.

*Didn't remember getting to and from ECT. Faces in my memory from the day before were blanks.*

Next, the order of things began to twist around in my mind.

*Stared yesterday at dinner, couldn't recall what order I eat my food in, put condiments on, etc. Had a hard time recalling facts and moved everything on my plate to the opposite side for some reason and confused the hell out of myself.*

And then, my own sense of time itself.

*Holes in memory...can't recall facts I know... can't picture belongings or layout of (my) home. Sense of time is messed up. I can't remember the last time I was in my house (2 weeks ago, I've been keeping track) but I can't actually recall standing in the living room last or getting in the car. It seems like I haven't lived there in ages, maybe months! I hazily remember being at the (ER) but nothing before that and in fact nothing before I started ECT.*

*Woke up in the recovery room, or I guess I always did and didn't remember.*

*Was very upset when I woke up from treatment- don't remember getting there but I do remember coming back My husband was with me so he must have gone there with me. I was totally disoriented when I woke up- didn't know where I was, the date or my own name. Cried and cried and cried. I think I worried everyone.*

*I feel like I'm out of time. That's really all I can say. I feel like my thoughts and emotions are from when I was a kid, not the adult me I know. It's disturbing.. The worst about this is feeling like I don't have an age, I can't even describe that. It's just like I'm not an adult or a kid or a teen- I sort of mentally move through states. I feel lost in my own skin...*

*I'm not so keen on the feelings anymore. I'd like to stop feeling now, it's a bit too much for me . I wish I could shove it all back inside.*

Though I have seen my records pre-treatment and am confident from knowing my doctor for some time that I was warned about memory loss, I'm sure no-one could have told me exactly what it would be like without going through it themselves. There is a reason people who have witnessed the memory loss from Alzheimer's or stroke or Dementia and such know this effect is so devastating.

However, it seems no one was quite sure why suddenly *old* memories began cropping up for me at first during treatment and this remembering seemed to have been the most disturbing aspect to me; even more so than forgetting the present or losing my sense of age.

*Memories and impressions from when I was very small have been popping up today very strongly. They feel uncomfortable. They're very bittersweet.*

*Memories are bubbling up, they're uncomfortable because they are so vivid- it feels like the memory image blossoms softly like drops of food color in water but the center part of it is overwhelming. It's out of sync. I can smell it, feel it, taste it, etc. It's wonderful and horrible all at once.*

*Memories still seeping in- I told the doctor it wasn't necessarily a bad thing but it is bothersome.*

*Memories are still trying to 'sync' up- everything feels like it's a second off when it bounces through my head. It feels as if there was a filing cabinet of old memories*

*I'd long since filed away and it just got tipped over and everything's flying out of it around my mind. It's very hard to concentrate; it's hard to remember.*

*It's March. I can't remember Christmas just past.*

*I can recall my living room but not the feeling attached to it- there aren't any memories so it seems like I'm thinking of someone else's house. All I can say is it seems really silly but it's affecting my picture of who I am in my mind. I feel very unsteady and very unsure. Sort of like a balloon let go over the city.*

*I don't remember going to ECT or coming back, just waking up in recovery and not knowing who I was. I cried and cried. In fact I kept on going all day.*

*My memory is all messed up. I keep remembering things that happened so long ago- just random things but they're so intense it screws up my sense of where I am. I remember something like, earlier. A flash of picking up bottles (*as a teenager*), or setting on the porch swing in the middle of the night with my auntie in the summer (*as a toddler*) and I feel like I'm just a little girl with a little girl's feelings, all alone in a weird hospital and I'm scared!* (And I began to miss relatives I hadn't seen or thought about in years, people I had no correspondence at all with and had never wished for.)

*Still being bothered by memory snatches, even good memories disturb me, it's like looking into the sun. We all like the sun but in small amounts- too much hurts a person. I feel totally overwhelmed. Just looking at the intercom on the wall brought back an awful summer a few years ago and I burst out crying.*

*Bothered by some childhood memories-just of watching tv as a kid and being home alone but the feelings kick up like I'm there all over again. ...(because) I had been living in a memory as a child of walking in Niawanda park with (my grandfather), it hit me suddenly that I'd have no one to walk with- he was gone....it's like he's died all over again.*

*I think I am sad because all these things I am recalling as if they were now have come and gone...*

This was not the first round of memory loss for me. After taking Topiramate for seven years and doing well with my bipolar symptoms, I began to lose long-term memories from childhood. At the time, I was sent for cognitive testing that ended in the opinion that I had a delay of sorts in processing from the left side of the brain, and the medication was discontinued.

In my notes it's apparent that though I was disturbed at the sheer volume and speed of return, I wasn't going to lose them again and thus made additional detailed notes of what I was recalling. As it was, much later when I first read my own writing during this time, I was struck by my own preconception that ECT makes one "braindead" or "stupid" and so I was amazed that I'd written so clearly and succinctly in the midst of treatment.

But after I had been switched to bilateral ECT, it seemed as though my sudden upswing tapered to a steady hum and a sudden and all-consuming hole appeared in reality. This might possibly be owed to the fact that during my admission an event occurred in the hospital which left two dead and several others wounded, and we must be sensible and admit that the incidence of trauma in itself may have contributed to the wiping out of its memory.

What was later speculated to be a former hospital patient entered the building with a gun and shot a staff member before moving on up the floors bent on his own aims. The area around the hospital was shut down; the children's ward was evacuated immediately and the upper floors where I was admitted, were locked down. It was thought by law enforcement that the shooter was working with an accomplice so the SWAT team was sent in to route them out, though this was found to be untrue.

I have *no* memory of this event.

Per my family and friends, I called during the situation from the floor payphone and told my husband that I was ok and to turn on the news before hanging up. My therapist, who was supposed to be at the hospital around that time and would have been right in the middle of things had she not been running late, told me she visited me afterwards and we spoke of it.

K. Rose Quayle

I have read the news articles; I have seen the news clips. To me, in my own perceived *timeline*, it never happened. There are no shreds or shards or impressions left, nor associations that would lead me back to this experience or give me some sort of twilight awareness of it. There is simply void; *naught.* But clearly there is evidence that it did happen and then vanished, in my own handwriting:

*I think I'm a bit more emotional today because of the shooting that happened downstairs yesterday. It really bothered me to see the SWAT team having us all put our hands up so they could search the ward for the gunman. I think everyone had nightmares last night. We watched ourselves on the news. That was surreal.*

*Last night we had a special church service for the victims of the hospital shooting. It was nice, there were staff members there playing instruments and one of the patients sang His Eye is on the Sparrow.*

(On the day after) *Today I can't remember much of anything. I didn't know the year, month or season when I woke this time and I couldn't figure out half of the patients' names either. They told me this particular treatment was on both sides of my head.*

*My fellow patients were amazed I couldn't recall getting back at all, I went to church with the other girls but was pretty out of it- it was a Protestant service. They told me I usually go to it but I can't recall doing so. (husband) came to visit me this evening and I realized I couldn't recall what our house looked like (from the outside.) He said my dad had come to visit me in here (I barely recall this)… and apparently I stayed at (my best friend's) house recently. I also discovered a line in my arm. (husband) said I never remembered it and they always have to explain It to me that I had to get a PICC line in for IVS.*

*I always ask for my therapist when I wake from treatment.*

There are accounts of those receiving ECT who have lost memories of major life events, anything from their own weddings to world events to the births of their children and in the remarkable case of a 55-year old woman, an entire thirty years of her life (Grant, 2006). Of course, this is the more severe end of the spectrum of those who experience memory loss and it's heavily thought that in most cases memories do come back relatively quickly, though I've been told after six months, one year and even eighteen months.

Some patients forget a treatment entirely, some forget the whole experience completely, some forget it and then recall it after treatments have ended. According to the University of Michigan Health Department, memory loss of past events from two to six weeks before treatment can be affected (University of Michigan Department of Psychiatry, 2016). But what is very clear is that ECT causes *some* memory loss as a side effect in an estimated 85% of those who undergo it. And though the length of time this lasts and to what extent it continues remains hotly debated, the fact that it *does occur* is not contested and neither that bilateral ECT shows quicker positive treatment results but also results in more memory problems.

Why don't we hear about this? Some patients I've talked to had lived for years pretending to have memories they didn't so as not to hurt their families and remained silent about the gaps in their own personal stories. One estimation is that most patients who do experience lagging memory loss are told consistently it will go away. When they trust that this is sound advice from their doctor and it doesn't bear out, most will not return to that same physician later. It's estimated that because this majority will not come back, patient satisfaction surveys on treatment side effects therefore tend to swing to the positive (Boyles, 2003).

Of course they would; if no one actually experiencing the side effects aren't reporting them, how do doctors even know? I found myself in that same camp. At some point I stopped mentioning it; stopped asking the doctor when it would get better. My family and therapist could certainly see something was wrong. I was clearly missing a lot of information that was previously there in my mind and early on, I didn't seem to miss not knowing it, but it wasn't visible to anyone else outside of our little sphere.

I wasn't dragging a lame leg or missing an eye or spending enough time with anyone who clinically would have seen or noticed that a chunk of my life was gone to me. For one, you can't expect a doctor to treat a problem they're not aware of and you also can't expect a patient to know to keep trying once they've been told there's nothing to worry about. So on both sides there is a lot of misinformation and not quite accurate statistics.

*"I don't know what I don't know."* I said in anger to my husband one day but once tempers simmered down, it became a starting point to realize that we had to look at this side effect thing from a different angle. I had to name what was actually wrong before we could find a way around it.

Memory is an extremely important function of the brain. It's not just about what you ate for breakfast or where you left your keys. It functions to protect us from doing something dangerous, *again*:

*Note to self: fire is hot. Don't touch fire. Again.*

It bonds us with other people: *Remember that one time in high school when we snuck under the bleachers and ... I do too!*

It brings us pleasure: *When I think of blackberry ice cream I remember my father buying it for me down at the drug store on Sunday afternoons.*

It brings us home: *Down to the end of the lane, hang a ralph and over the broken fence. My house is the blue one on the left.*

And it reminds us of who we are: *After my mother died I began to lean a bit more toward the left in my views.* Would you rather lose your painful memories or your pleasurable ones? Seems like a no-brainer. Who wants to remember pain, embarrassment, shame, heartache, mistakes, the worst haircut to ever show up on a school picture? But I think most of us know just from being alive that we need even negative memories to make up the whole picture of our identity and the story of how we got to be where we are now. Then again, maybe not that school haircut unless you ended up in a blooming career in cosmetology.

Take away memory and you take away a vital piece of who you are.

# Part II

# Memory

# Is, Was, and Will Be

Iт's sort of like always having this nagging feeling that something is behind you, something is about to happen, someone is watching you, but you can't see it or feel it or catch it.

And then you look up and find your cat staring at you as if to say, "*Get up and get the damned can opener already so I can eat my dinner and get back to watching the neighbor's parakeet. We're on a schedule!*" Now where did that *cat* come from? Surely he wasn't here a minute ago. You've become all too aware of the existence of said schedule and it seems everyone else is on it but you're standing outside in your own timetable, unable to figure out when it's going to intersect with yours.

*This is what memory loss often feels like.* As I mentioned in chapter one, I could remember my grandfather turning the wheel a certain way and my mother placing her hands at the ten and two positions. My brain was becoming adept at "cobbling" together memories if it couldn't bring back the entire thing in technicolor. But my memories didn't always match up to those belonging to people around me, and sometimes I had no memory of an event altogether.

In 2004 when I got married my husband surprised me with a trip to New York City for our honeymoon. During that trip we stopped at Ground Zero, which was being leveled and cleared for what was still an incomplete plan of what would be eventually be built there. It might have seemed an odd choice of sightseeing on a honeymoon but my husband had done clean-up work at the site with some comrades from his country who came over from the U.K. in the weeks after the disaster. It was horrific but necessary work and closure was what we sought for him.

To me, September 11th was a close call. I had been out of Brooklyn almost a year when the disaster happened, having attended Pratt Institute. I came into Manhattan several times a week during school and often was near the World Trade Center. I recall standing at Ground Zero in 2004 was surreal but fitting and it didn't exactly bring what we sought, but then again we weren't totally sure of what that was to begin with.

Fast forward to a quick trip to the Google offices in New York to pick up a Google Glass in 2014. As my husband drove through crowded streets I looked up and saw a massive skyscraper like something out of a Dubai skyline and pointed, asking what this sleek new place was? My husband casually indicated it was the new World Trade Center.

*Back the truck up.*

When had this happened? How could they build something on the site of the towers? Who *let this happen*? I was aghast and I could see in regard to the subject matter he didn't want to break it to me that I had forgotten this was happening in the world. It was one more memory sucked down into that giant hole of things in my brain that didn't exist for me anymore including such public information as celebrities who'd died, laws passed through government and my home city's progress of rebuilding after Hurricane Katrina.

I went home and checked the World Trade Center website, staring at the photos of a massive plan of memorials and museums progressing along in construction. It was unbelievable and my feelings towards this event were extremely mixed between grief at the grounds being used for something else and amazement at the construction itself. At the time of the original talks of rebuilding I firmly believed the grounds as holy and as such should not be touched again so this was a particularly offensive re-discovery.

During a later trip the grounds were still under heavy construction but had just opened to the public and we went to take photos and stand reverently at the Memorial pools with hundreds of others. Both of us stood lost in our own thoughts and viewpoints coming from different countries and cultures, unsure if the scope could ever adequately express the many levels of grief present.

After spending some time in silence trying to forget the time lost, I felt reassured that the tribute had been constructed with such care and detail that a small sense of finality descended and whispered that yes, it was time to move on. But that sense spoke also to the shock of not having the progression of events to draw on, from having grief interrupted. September 11th didn't just happen and leave in the national sense, and it didn't leave our house either.

The nightmares that descended on my husband (like so many others present during those terrible weeks and months) prevailed for a long time after, and so when we came to the Memorial it was truly for as final a release as one could ask for us both. Just as it was time to accept we had, as a country, moved forward, somehow, having to live without memories freed me in a sense of having to hold back from life. There was nothing to go back to, hence, I could only go forward.

If I didn't remember the cat coming into the room, it was irrelevant. Here it was and it expected to be fed *now*.

We know from medical documentation and personal testimony that ECT effects memory in the vast majority of patients to some extent but the question is, why? For that matter, what actually *happens* to create and recall memories? Why is memory loss so damaging and painful rather than just a nuisance to wait out? I mean honestly, is it really so awful to forget your mother's disaster of a Thanksgiving turkey three years ago (*or was that mine?*)?

Let's start at the beginning: what types of memory are there?

Several, it turns out, that every human being experiences at some point in their life. Firstly, when we refer to *memory* we are actually using an umbrella term that encompasses what we experience as conscious recall as well as the process of storing information. The astounding brain performs a myriad of jobs in regard to memory processing so let's try and simplify things as much as possible so that we understand what memory is in order to see what happens when it goes wrong.

Overall, there are two main types of memory we think of when we're talking about the mechanism going on in our minds we are aware of daily. Memory can be a windy road but everything we're going to touch on flows from here: *short-term* and *long-term* memory.

**Short-term Memory:** Short-term memory can be thought of as being comprised of two parts beginning with *Immediate Memory*. Think of this as the first few seconds after you encounter new information. When I was a kid in school, the teacher would test us by having us stand in a line and repeat a string of numbers back backwards to what she'd told us. When we heard her telling us the numbers to remember, right in those very seconds our brain was processing these to immediate memory. It's very brief and if information doesn't pass on to the next stage of memory, you're not going to recall it (Johnson, 2010). Needless to say, I don't recall any of those numbers now and actually, I was pretty poor at it then.

**Working Memory:** Moving right along, the second part of short-term memory, also called *Working Memory*, occurs after immediate memory. It's sort of the deeper, more sophisticated version in which information does come and go but it stays longer, more like perhaps half an hour or so. If you like to watch comedies on television and can still remember the theme song by the end of the show, you're exercising your short-term memory. Short- term memory is often the most affected after a brain injury and it affects everyday life in surprisingly important ways.

**Long-Term Memory:** The other main type of memory we experience is *Long-Term Memory* and it is very individual, as are we. If you remember the theme song from that television show the next morning, it has passed into your long-term memory. Some people may recall it after a month; others may live to one hundred and still be able to whistle the same song. Long-term memory is often more or less intact with brain injuries but when it is not, huge impacts on a person's sense of self are felt. For how are we to know who we are if we can't *remember* who we are?

Long-term memory is then broken down further into the processes of the brain in which information stored there is recalled; namely, *Explicit* and *Implicit Memory*. You may have heard of these also referred to as *Declarative* and *Procedural Memory*, respectively.

**Explicit (Declarative) Memory**: This term refers to *conscious* memory. If you are awake and aware and you can recall that your name is Jim and you live at 555 Park Avenue and you are a piano salesman and last week you dropped a piano bench on a client's toe, you are using *explicit memory* to recall those facts (Kandel, 2007). Explicit memory itself is divided even further into *Episodic* and *Semantic Memory*.

**Episodic Memory** allows us to recall and reconstruct events in our own lives using emotion and context and has several subtypes of its own! For example, if you go to a play and tell your friend the next day at lunch how awful it was and spoil the entire storyline for her, you are using the process of episodic memory in constructing these personal events and the emotions that surround them. You swooned over the lead actor but were so appalled at how badly he delivered his parting lines you vowed to never watch anything with him in it again. "*The whole experience just spoiled him for me,*" you cried.

And this seems a real shame until you consider that episodic memory helps us recall highly charged situations in our own lives to protect us from doing the same things over again, badly. Maybe it's better you keep your money the next time Mr. Swoon comes to town and put it in the savings instead.

**A large subtype of episodic memory is Autobiographical Memory**. This refers to the process in which we recall distinct episodes from our *own* information; that is, the fixed events of our lives and past. This type of memory is more or less what we think of when we say, "I remember this one time when my Grandma and I made cookies."

The brain breaks information it contains about the self in autobiographical memory into three hierarchies of importance. From the top to the bottom:

Lifetime Periods: *I was a toddler when we made the cookies.*

General Events: *It was around Christmas when we made the cookies.*

Event-Specific times: *We made the cookies at night so they would be ready when Grandpa got off work at the factory.*

When we remember our own lives, as you can see, our brains pull from all three hierarchies to allow us to tell our own story. Without *all* memory types present, our lives would be very flat, dull, and without much emotion (Holland, 2010).

I.e.: *"One time we made cookies."*

*"That sounds nice. Can you tell me any more about them?"*

*"No."*

It's worth noting that every type of memory or memory function serves a purpose in our lives, no matter how insignificant it might seem at the time. When my husband, a volunteer fireman, was called out on a welfare check he had to crawl into the upstairs bathroom window from a ladder in his full firefighter gear. Unfortunately, the worst had occurred and the family had to be notified.

What my husband remembers to this day in the midst of that situation is the feeling of crunching under his boots and thinking *"oh, crap!"* at damaging the homeowner's property. When he'd entered the window he knocked some of the deceased's toiletries off of the window sill and when he stepped down, crushed several bottles. That moment became frozen in time for him, replaying in his mind for years after the fact.

He said to me that when he thought of it, he thought of the normalcy of it, the shampoo and toothpaste and shower gel we all use and thoughtlessly stash somewhere. He thought of this over and over while his brain knew full well what he discovered when he turned the corner. So in some cases, those tiny little details save us from darker truths that lurk within, because it is noted that emotion is very influential in how we record information into memory.

Autobiographical memory gives us the *context* in which we exist in the world. My best friend, one of the most generous people you will ever meet, once made it her mission to find a particular cream that promised to erase scars. It had been heavily advertised on television and I had thought about it in passing for the multiple chicken pox scars I have had since childhood and more so, the collection of deep scars I've acquired from skin infections, falls and whatever happened to my upper arm that I can't recall.

But by the time this wondrous new cream that promised to fade out scars had come to local stores, I found myself turning it down, saying very genuinely, "I don't want to lose my scars- they tell the story of my life." I had learned that, if my mind couldn't remember, my body would fill in the blanks. It comforted me somehow that after I died, someone would see part of my story unknown to anyone else, possibly even myself, and though it would only be a fraction of the truth, *someone* would know and be able to piece together a part of my story that would live on.

I would argue that autobiographical memory is perhaps the most important to our existence as human beings, because without it we cannot draw on our own experiences to create empathy towards others or realize our place within the brotherhood of man.

**Another subtype, Semantic Memory,** relates straight *facts* we recall that may be related to items in our episodic memory. You may recall that WWII ended for the United States on August 14, 1945 (V-J Day), which is a historical fact well documented that you may have read in a schoolbook. But what makes this fact important to you and to your *own* autobiographical memory, is that your grandfather was a U.S. soldier in that war and you know on that particular day he called your grandmother to tell her he was coming home and this was a treasured family story he recalled to you right up until the day he died.

So, as a child you may have been able to recall this date because you remembered this was the day Grandpa called Grandma but as an adult you recall it for the fact that it is, unchangeable in the fabric of history gone by. Once more, all types of memory work together to make us who we recall we are. The memory began as an emotional episodic memory but passed into semantic, factual memory (Matsin, 2010) where it became encoded in the brain for you to recall at a later date (Mastin, 2010).

**Still within explicit memory is another subtype; Spatial Memory.** That is, the process where the brain makes "maps" of incoming information. When you describe to your fiancé the ugly pink lamp your mother insists on keeping in her living room beside the left street-side window, you are using several memory processes along with spatial memory allowing you to recall where in space-time those objects are.

When I came home from the hospital from inpatient ECT treatment I discovered my husband had bought a new radio for the car and put a sunglass clip on his sun visor. Whenever we got into the car I asked when these things had appeared and he told me over and over again, but I had no spatial memory of these improvements existing in the car. During the next year I was off of work, the only times I got into the car was to go to the nearby hospital so I never really had enough time to encode these items in my spatial memory. I only knew there was something in those spaces that wasn't before.

**Implicit (Procedural or Physical) Memory** is the other type of long-term memory we observe and is what you recall *unconsciously*. For example, the saying that *"once you learn to ride a bicycle you never forget"* references this type of memory. You know those times when you have a brain fart so to speak and can't recall a phone number but you can somehow type in that same number on a phone or keypad accurately without looking? This is by the mechanism of implicit memory.

Luckily for us, the unconscious takes over and recalls that stored information for your lazy explicit memory so you can keep on keeping-on. Implicit memory is deeply important to everyday life in that it bridges the gap between action and thought. It would take us hours to purposely think of *every* step of *every* action we do *every* day. Implicit memory frees up the brain for explicit memory to record more immediate information (Kandel, In Search of Memory: The Emergence of a New Science of Mind, 2007).

Implicit memory is also the mechanism that recalls a lot of visual memory. It may take you a few times seeing a new type of flower to recall that you have seen it before but when you do, it is recalled by implicit memory. In a way you could think of explicit memory as a skill you practice daily and implicit memory as a reflex you develop that kicks in without thinking. While I never got a driver's license, before ECT, I did know how to drive at one time and had multiple permits.

Though I can't recall much about the steps of driving now or get the whole sequence together for anything past following an old country road, I still have a faint impression of the *feeling* of driving on actual roads from before treatment. The awareness of the wheels moving underneath me, the resistance of the pedals against my feet are so fleeting and at the edges of my mind that when I try to think of it with purpose, it flits away like a dream one tries to recall mid-morning. In fact, on rare occasions I dream I am driving and doing it like a champ!

What happened to my experience? Because my body still knows the feeling of doing it in some capacity, I assume somewhere in my brain some aspects of the skill itself is embedded but the process of recalling it enough to navigate a parking lot and heaven forbid, *parallel park*, has been interrupted or somehow lost.

Now, we don't *learn* without using healthy doses of both types of memory. For example, our conscious (explicit) memory records our environment while our unconscious (implicit) memory records the steps we are taking. For instance, we might be learning to build a fire and need to later recall on a camping trip how to do this. Implicit memory kicks in and directs our bodies to pick up tinder, pile it up, strike the match, etc., as our explicit memory recalls that we know the area is dry so we should have extra water on hand and the wind is blowing towards the north so we should build this fire in a south-facing direction to keep it from getting out of hand.

Both types of memory help us record new skills and learning to use them later and are constantly at work all throughout our lives because our brains are such very busy little bees.

Now that we know the basic types of memory, how exactly do these memory functions work? What's going on in our cells when we record information for later use?

# Are You Doing the Taxes?

*W**here* does memory happen, exactly?

Physically, the brain is divided into right and left hemispheres with right and left versions of its four lobes which sit at the top half of the brain if looking at someone head-on. Those all-important lobes are the:

*Frontal Lobe:* Right up in front just like it sounds.

*Occipital Lobe:* All the way to the back of the head.

*Parietal Lobe:* In the middle back near the crown.

*Temporal Lobe*: Directly in the middle and ends just at the temples.

All of these areas work together to help us perceive the world and ourselves in it and each is extremely unique in its work and role in who we are as individuals. Behavior, emotion and decision-making occur in the frontal lobe. The functions that allow us to work out mathematics, spell words and understand incoming information reside in the parietal lobe. How we process the information coming in through our eyes such as color, light, shapes and motion has to do with the work of the occipital lobe. And finally, memory, sound, smell and language processing are the main jobs of the temporal lobe.

Squished in-between the four lobes are the motor and somatosensory cortices who translate, respectively, movement of the body and sensory information. It was previously thought that the brain was designed to assign one structure to one purpose, so just as your feet are used for walking and your mouth is used for talking, so your temporal lobe was believed to be used specifically for memory. But obviously, your feet aid your legs to run, and your mouth aids your body to eat and digest. So it is also now known that several parts of the brain work together to manufacture what we would physically think of the process of memory, or the *cellular* part of memory (Kandel, In Search of Memory: The Emergence of a New Science of Mind, 2007).

If you recall, immediate memory has to "pass" through to short-term memory which also goes through a process to pass into long-term memory. To get down to the basics, information from the outside world comes into the brain via the senses of smell, touch, taste, hearing and sight (and probably that sixth sense most of us suspect we have, like when you aren't aware the dog is in the corner of the room but you can just fee his eyes attempting to teleport your dinner plate).

Once information has entered the body through these channels, it is inter-preted by the appropriate part of the brain. We've established that sight is the expertise of the occipital lobe, so when confronted with a beautiful sunset, the occipital lobe hollers to the rest of the brain, *"Hey, that's a sunset!"* The frontal lobe, ever the sentimentalist, echoes that *Sunsets make me cry* and the temporal lobe files that bit of information away to pull out later for a rainy day.

The lobes can't take total credit here; they get plenty of help disseminating this information to actually create memory. When information first comes in, the *thalamus*, a tiny little guy with the huge task of moving information from the brain to the spinal cord and out to the rest of the body, and the *hippocam-pus*, another small fry with big responsibilities in forming long-term memories, work together to move the unfathomable amount of stimuli coming in from the tops of our heads to the tips of our toes.

Once inside our heads and translated: *"Oh, this is a fire. It's very bright. It makes me nervous!"* information becomes encoded in immediate memory and then in short-term memory, depending on how long it has to bop around be-fore new stimuli come crowding in to take up brain power. Neuroscience has recently proven that memories do exist physically in cells; particularly spatial memory which creates a cellular map inside the brain it can later reference and be certain of where that ugly pink lamp is in your mother's house (Trafton, 2015).

One of the main physical differences in short term and long term memories is that long-term memory is manufactured in the brain by synthesizing particular proteins not present in short-term memory cells. In theory, this may be why some information doesn't pass into long term memory; the brain may not have had time or resources to manufacture the required protein to make long-term memory cells. Of course it's not quite as straightforward in the human brain, that organ we still know so little about, and much of what Neuroscience can tell us is based on what can be seen on a scan or observed in experiments with rats. And that's pretty good stuff but it can't tell us about all the invisible processes always going on behind our eyes.

Functional Magnetic Resonance Imaging (fMRI) scans at this writing are being used more and more to document problems in the brain's processing that aren't visible on current MRI, PET, CT and other scans. While neuropsychologic testing (cognitive testing) is used today to show the end result from damage not physically apparent such as problems in sequencing and short term memory, fMRI can show some problems in the brain in real-time as we think. Still inordinately expensive, fMRI has been receiving quite a lot of funding to test whether the function of lying can be detected to develop better crime conviction methods (UC San Diego School of Medicine, 2017). It is also being used to track subtle changes in the brain associated with neurological and psychiatric conditions.

Perhaps a better map of brain function will also result, which would be more accessible to physicians as a tool to diagnose that which lies beyond the physical. What *is* known is that different types of memories are encoded and stored in different places of the brain and if something happens to the process of encoding or storing or retrieving, both memory and learning are affected.

Explicit memories, dealing with people and places, events and facts are managed in the prefrontal cortex. Implicit memories dealing with tactile experiences are managed in the motor and somatosensory cortices. Those job descriptions remain as yet, unchanged. But the brain is more of a team-player than ever thought before, so while the lobes are extremely important in taking in information to be made into memories, the hippocampus, aided by the thalamus, motor cortex and somatosensory cortex, encodes and then pushes memories out to be stored in the lower parts of the brain such as the *cerebral, temporal,* and *visual cortices* as well as the *amygdala* and *striatum.*

That's *encoding* memory. When we *recall* memory, those stored parts are recalled through the hippocampus again and reassembled so you can remember making cookies with Grandma and all that information stored as Lifetime periods, General Events, and Event-Specific time is gathered up by the hippocampus and put back together into a sugar-scented, flour-coated, fuzzy feeling flashback. And the neat trick is, if you recall that memory enough times, the hippocampus steps back a bit to focus on new information and the elements of said memory become triggers or *cues* that can start your brain reassembling the past without bothering the busy hippocampus.

This is why you can be walking in the mall twenty years after Grandma has become late and as you pass by the cookie stall in the food court, you suddenly become surrounded in the memory of that night making cookies and the scent of Grandma's perfume though you haven't consciously thought about it since the funeral. The scent became a trigger and your mind grabbed those memory bits and put them right back together again.

What happens to memory when the brain itself is damaged?

It's not totally clear to what extent the brain can recover or if there is a magic formula to bring function back but recent studies have found that the marvelous human brain is more resilient and functional than we ever knew. In some instances when a pathway of the brain is damaged, other parts of the brain take over to compensate for some of that pathway's function. In people who lose their sight, for example, the brain takes in information from the other senses to compensate. While the person may not *see* someone else enter a room, the scent of cologne in the air, the vibrations of footsteps on the flooring and the jingle of keys are bits of information that come together to let the person know their favorite Uncle Lester has dropped by without using information obtained through the visual cortex.

Other systems in the body compensate in the same manner, with different parts of the intestinal tract taking on additional digestive responsibilities when a portion is removed (been there, bagged the t-shirt) to the kidneys adjusting output when one is compromised to make mention of a few. Because of this teamwork present in many of the body systems, including the brain, when a part cannot do its job anymore, other parts in the same neighborhood are already equipped to help out.

The brain's ability to do this has been demonstrated in studies of Epilepsy patients who experienced similar symptoms just before a seizure and mentally ill patients who experience hallucinations as part of their illness. Removing the brain tissue in the right frontal lobe of the epileptics resulted in verbal memory loss that resolved itself by twelve months after surgery; meanwhile other parts of the brain were still able to lend a hand in the usual duties of the frontal lobe (Gleissner, 2004).

But you can't expect the whole team to do each other's work all the time or nothing would ever get done! When damage occurs to areas of the temporal lobe or to the little hippocampus, turning short-term into long-term memories can indeed be affected permanently (as was found with the left frontal lobe in the Gleissner study with verbal memory). Remember that we said the hippocampus takes information from the lobes and sends it out to where it will be stored as long term memory and for long term memory to be made, certain proteins have to be manufactured. In sending information on down the chain, the hippocampus *consolidates* information from the lobes; the smell of cookies, the sight of Grandma's smile, the sound of the radio playing on the counter.

If something interrupts this process of consolidation such as an injury to the head or a seizure, the memory is never made into long-term. Let's imagine you and Grandma went to sit on the porch while the cookies baked and got to playing a card game. The time went by so fast no-one noticed the timer had gone off until you smelled something burning and it wasn't cookies. The oven had overheated and caught the kitchen on fire! Grandma called the fire department and you could only stand across the street and watch the house burn down.

But as the fire department came to the rescue, you fell to the ground seizing and were taken to the hospital. Two days later Grandma and Grandpa had moved in with your family and you sat around the table eating dinner. Your brother excused himself from the table and came back with a plate of cookies for dessert and everyone told him that wasn't funny at all but you didn't get what the fuss was about. Because while you completely remembered waking up in the hospital, choking down lime gelatin, getting an IV yanked out and thanking your cousin for the get-well teddy bear, you had no idea you helped burn down your grandparents' house with a sheet of cookies.

This is called *Retrograde Amnesia*. It's an all-time favorite plot device of television shows and movies and isn't always that total or that dramatic but it actually can be, and it neatly illustrates just what happens to memory when it is interrupted during consolidation. We know that when we learn, our brains build new information off of existing memories of what we already know. If you learn to ride a bike, the brain taps the *motor* memory you already have of walking and balancing to apply pushing the pedals with your legs and keeping the bike upright so you don't have to learn those skills again as well. It's a great shortcut built right into us.

But you can see where this is a problem if a person suffers frequent seizures, illnesses which affect the brain, malnutrition which interrupts brain function,

ECT which causes seizures repeatedly or frequent blows to the head such as in sports or an abusive situation. Not only is recollection of memories affected but learning new skills is as well for the time period affected.

According to a 2000 study by the Journal of the American Medical Association, retrograde amnesia is the most tenacious side-effect of ECT. After two month follow-ups with ECT patients the study concluded that both personal and impersonal memories are affected with memories around the time of treatment being most affected and impersonal memories being most affected long-term. Bilateral ECT seems to result in more and longer-term memory loss than Right Unilateral ECT but again, impersonal memories are more affected even then. Other studies found that memory loss could indeed be permanent (Sarah H. Lisanby, Jill J. Maddox, Joan Prudic, & al, 2000).

This is interesting when you take into consideration a 1981 study reported in Archives of General Psychiatry found that persistent memory loss occurred after bilateral ECT for events occurring just before treatment but that long-term memory loss was completely resolved by seven months after (L R Squire, 1983). But a follow-up study in a 1983 by the Royal College of Psychiatrists similar to the 1981 study reported that after three years had gone by post-ECT, 50% of patients receiving bilateral still reported memory loss and those receiving right unilateral having much less at that time. Recalling new information learned in the period of 1-2 years before ECT were also affected (Larry R. Squire, Slater, & Miller, 1981).

These studies used differing methods of testing patients to determine memory loss and therefore achieved slightly different results, which is common when comparing studies. Other factors that influence such research are other chronic conditions a person may have before having treatment which may influence memory, medications the person may be taking, stress and sleep disorders, etc. Conducting a perfect study is extremely hard and there are always variables one has to take into account when formulating results. For most of us, being aware that ECT causes memory loss in most people and may cause more serious issues has to be enough on the surface and anything more in depth we need to question on an individual basis.

I recall standing by the radiator in the living room of our new house, impatient to get to work as I'd just recently returned from medical leave. My husband stopped me just as I turned to open the door and asked, *"Are you doing the taxes this year?"*

I paused and then mumbled that he should do them but as I ducked out the door it hit me that I had no idea what he was talking about. *What were taxes and how did you do them?* Why was he asking me this? It seemed absurd and a silly distraction from what I needed to be doing at the time, which was getting to work on time.

As I sat at my desk later I found myself doing what I still find myself doing at times: asking Uncle Google rather than a Certified Human Being. At the time I couldn't form any type of mental picture of the actions involved in doing taxes or even what the words meant but at some point much later in the day I was able to recall a dim knowledge of paying tax on *candy* (one of my very favorite things and one I've plunked down a fair share of luxury tax money on over the years) but nothing further.

What had happened?

I had lost a portion of episodic memory while retaining the autobiographical portion. I didn't recall that my husband was asking me if I were going to do the taxes because previously I always had without discussion and probably didn't relish it, but I recalled the concept of sales tax because I knew I'd paid it throughout my life through various luxury taxes wherever I'd lived. Today I have a very dim awareness of having done taxes but no conscious memory of how; it's something I continue to ask myself every January when W-2's are issued.

While I was still fuzzy on current personal details and had a very hard time recalling new information about myself for months after treatment, the most embarrassing thing for me was not being able to recall what I had already learned and mastered. Anyone with memory loss quickly learns that not being able to recall is received in a very negative light in our culture. We see this as a death-knell of sorts; a hard and fast sign of getting old, of becoming senile, of developing Alzheimer's.

In the more benign set of responses we may encounter, accusations of not paying attention, of being stupid or lazy or *crazy* are the most common. Only very rarely outside my husband and very close friends do I ever hear someone offer to help or responses of good-natured humor. This lack of positive response only leads to a hopelessness that memory will ever return and a reluctance and outright refusal to ask for help.

I found myself often in this mindset because I felt like a little child, untrained and ignorant and I found myself soon inadvertently lying about what I did and didn't know. When I discovered that I indeed in times past did our income taxes myself online, even wading through the murky waters of claiming a home business, I was astonished. Who could figure this stuff out?

Yet I had for nearly seven years on my own before I married. Now my husband may as well have been speaking a foreign language to me. The next day at work I wondered all through the shift about how one went about doing taxes. When I had sufficiently researched the way to do it online I started bothering my husband to take them to someone professional to be done and *be quick about it* despite his assurances that he could certainly finish them himself and it would only take a day or so. After reading what I perceived as a Herculean feat, it seemed like utter lunacy to me not to go directly to a tax attorney. And not that I thought my husband was any less than heroic but come on now, let's be serious. We were talking *money*.

So we did the husband and wife dance where I nagged and he put it off and that year the taxes were done the day they were due, no penalties. This was just one example of me cowing to shame and not asking him to just show me what he was talking about. This was a big hindrance to me for quite some time. As I said, I found myself saying 'Yes!' immediately when someone asked me to do something, or if I knew how to do something, or if I recalled something. I quickly followed by then running to my smartphone to look up some instructions or a brief history of whatever I didn't know I knew.

At the time, Google, Instructables.com and eventually, Pinterest kept me running relatively smooth. Before ECT I wasn't too keen on the idea of smartphones and protested loudly when my husband insisted I get one so he could reach me when I went off on my usual adventures, being a natural wanderer. After treatment, however, I was constantly on my phone because two things kept coming up over and over in my practical day-to-day life:

I wasn't sure of what I didn't recall.

I wasn't sure of what I'd never learned to begin with.

Because memory is such a tangled mess of limbs rather than boxed into neat compartments, the usual building blocks of learning in which we draw from what we previously mastered were gone for me. When I went to climb onto the next block I met with a gaping hole of nothing. At first this simply confused me. I would hold my head cocked to the side, engaged in listening as if I could somehow hear the *voice* of memory. Though it's not logical to physically hear one's memory in the same sense as hearing voices from a television, nonetheless I found my body irresistibly attuned to trying. It seemed inexplicably determined to listen to its own past speak.

While writing, I wrestled with what to call this book because the subject is a serious one and I had what I thought was a serious, respectful moniker when I chose *Evanescent* to refer to the impermanent nature of memory. But one night coming home from the grocery store, my husband and I were sitting in traffic and he said to me, *"So did you figure out a title yet?"*

*"Yes I have!"* I chirped and then my mind came to that familiar halt and as I tried my best to stumble around in the dark of my brain without a torch looking

for something smaller than a paperclip. I found myself unable to control my giggles.

*"Well, what is it?"* he prompted.

*"I can't remember!"*

Having lived with me for several years after ECT, he knew this was entirely true so the both of us began to laugh unabashedly. *"Use it! Use that for the title: 'I had a title but I can't remember what it is!' You wanted the book to have humor, right? Oh, you have to!"* he insisted.

It was decided between us at the red light to name the book *The Incognizant Guide to ECT: I Had a Decent Title But I Can't Remember What It Is!* as a nod to the humor we've been forced to adopt and has saved us many times from total disarray.

Obviously, I didn't go with that. After much thought I decided on what I said in chapter one of this book, that despair commands its own respect. It would be a lie to gloss over the personal devastation that occurs with memory loss both in oneself and for others involved and I chose a title that reflected what was lost and how to move on, because life is about hope. And if we lose what is behind us, we have nowhere to go but forward.

# The Luxurious Curse
# of Not Knowing

"*Well aren't you lucky? You have the luxury of not knowing.*"

He spat the words out at me and at the time I felt so far away, so alone in the world. After an argument over something I'd done in the past but could no longer remember, my husband had found himself in his own particular solitude when it came to light I no longer recalled events from our history together.

*The Vow,* starring Rachel McAdams and Channing Tatum came out in 2012, the year I had ECT, and is based on the life and love story of Kim and Krickitt Carpenter (Okura, 2014). Krickitt suffered amnesia from brain trauma resulting after a near-fatal car accident, and while the film leaves out the more "real" aspects of healing from brain trauma and quite a lot of detail, it does bear striking resemblance to what being in a relationship in which a gaping hole in its timeline has been ripped is like.

When I had ECT I had been married for seven years and during those years we had gone through a tremendous amount on our own. Even immersed in our own reality, it was hard to recount the story of how we'd come to where we'd landed. It seemed impossible to pinpoint when exactly the world had stepped back and watched as we went on in the little country of two we'd become. And the thing about two is that it can so easily become one, that loneliest number.

When those words that would sear themselves into my mind were spoken in anger, it was anger at what had been lost to both of us. Some people in this world would feel angry and bereft if their loved one forgot *negative* experiences they'd gone through together. We are set up as human beings to recall negative experiences more strongly and this is perfectly logical; remembering the bad things teaches us not to repeat those experiences. Our conscious memories of bad experiences kept us alive from predators when mankind was young and now keep us functioning well mentally in a modern world where man is usually the top predator.

But the loss of positive memories can be just as damaging. In our lives we had gone through negative experiences so often and so back to back that they made the positive ones that much more powerful. This also is echoed in human behavior in the reward response, most strikingly with small children. Any parent or teacher of young children knows how powerful an influence a perceived reward can be and this works both ways. A child who thinks they will get to spend more time with daddy if they pick up their toys will be much more likely to do so when asked as opposed to a child who only sees he's being told to clean up his mess.

And parents work the same way. If they realize a correlation between giving in and buying the toy in the supermarket checkout lane and their child's bad behavior ceasing, they're going to be much more likely to buy it without much fuss on the child's part whether they should spend the money or not. It's a win-win: child is happy, parent is happy, who cares about an extra $5? So looking back, a parent will probably remember everybody was happy walking out of the store rather than that they spent their last $5 on something nobody needed to begin with.

When you are surrounded by loss and grief and upheaval and stress, those silly, carefree, everyday moments between members of your immediate circle take on a golden quality; they become in hindsight the stuff of dreams. I think of positive memories as what gets us through *right now*. People tend to divide into two separate groups: those who use sadness to get through today and those who use happiness. These groups also tend to view those respective experiences differently. I am a person who uses sadness to get myself through. It is through a past of sadness and the stories of others going through the same experiences that give me hope to go on. We've come this far, I tend to think, *therefore we can keep going on*!

My husband falls into the other group, and I wonder if being from a culture which tends to keep negative feelings more private has something to do with this. For him, positive experiences do the same thing. These show him there is a future and the injurious past can be overcome and somehow escaped. Negative experiences safeguard against a negative future and should not sully the present.

So for him, my memory loss wasn't as devastating over the bad things I'd forgotten as opposed to the good things. My husband found himself alone with not just the bad things we'd gone through, but the good things that had carried him through getting me through ECT and the effects afterwards. In his own experience, he was truly alone in that. We knew no-one who had experience with ECT and we could speak to very few about it without risking losing relationships. We found that when grief comes into our lives in any form, people will naturally move back away from us. Whether because of cultural conditioning or personal aversions or social alliances, people move away when you need them closest, leaving only those you can be sure are your true friends.

We were already so well-versed in losing what we had I wasn't willing to risk what we might in future gain. I had told him in no uncertain terms because of the stigma it carried that no one could ever know this had happened. And he, faithful to my honor, kept this secret safe. But at such price.

That day I had snapped back to him that *I didn't know what I didn't know*, he returned that I had that luxury, *of not knowing what was lost*. But how could it affect me if I didn't know? And how could we take comfort and hope in the good experiences we'd had if *we* no longer knew them? He was incensed and hurt that I wasn't incensed and hurt and I felt it wasn't fair of him to be because I didn't *know* what to be incensed and hurt about.

When you get married they say that two become one, joined together. Memory loss takes that two and makes it one half. What no-one anticipated with that isolation was the double-edged sword of regaining memory, because memories did in fact return in some form as time went on from seemingly insignificant details to full-blown episodes. But the return of these at first only reinforced that something had been lost, causing grief to begin anew for him and for the first time as a dull, persistent ache, for me.

I had become accustomed to asking people to tell me what had been, to fill me in on what I had lost and of course this was filtered through another person's perspective and what they could observe outside of me. My inner thoughts and feelings seemed lost to that ephemeral realm these things dwell in to begin with.

Is it better to dwell in happy ignorance or walk in troubled awareness? Of course awareness does not have to be troubled, but on the subject of the return of memory (or the awareness of the *absence* of it), there are few happy reunions. Memory can come back with the force of a freight-train; assaulting the senses as a clanging gong; blinding with the power of sun. The worse part? No one else knows what's going on or that something is going on at all.

In the business of war, sensory deprivation is used as a way to force enemy prisoners to forget their loyalties to their home country. In the business of memory, sensory assault is the way of recalling; confusion, the path to the past. When we listen to someone else tell an episode from our own narrative we listen with a propensity to match up what's being said with what we already know.

We say, "*I did not!*"

Or, "*It was certainly in the spring, because the crocuses were out that day.*"

We all naturally have an inner monologue chronicling our own story even as we live it. Growing up hearing my grandparents tell stories I had little trouble getting used to hearing about myself in this third party manner and indeed, hearing my own memories just sounded like another story about something someone did some time ago.

Listening, I was detached a bit, unsure of how things were going to come out. It was captivating in the same way as the promise of old photos from infancy are. We look at our own faces in a time before our awareness and try to mentally build a bridge between what we know and what we knew. During this time those around me were confused at first and stunned at the latitude of what I truly didn't know, but they too acclimated and became glad in the opposite way to share my own stories; to tell of themselves through me. So in that regard, I was hearing information for the first time. I was being told the story of me as I am in someone else's mind.

When memory started to return to me it was no smooth process. Like the childhood memories which bubbled up during treatment, the more recent lost memories had no hard and fast rules about how or when, how much or in what form they would appear. I was never able to think,
*Who is this person my husband keeps telling me I know?* to force anything about them to suddenly generate. When this did happen he would tell me to smile because I did in fact know them and that had to be enough.

I wasn't able to say *"Let's slow down tonight and try this again tomorrow"* when information populated where it hadn't been before and kept me awake at night. I found that while I couldn't *will* a memory to return, a sure-fire way of waking it up was to stumble onto something associated with it.

As we discovered previously, triggers such as the delicious smell of cinnamon buns at the mall food court can trigger memory recall of something related like making cookies with your Grandma and this happens to us all with regularity. After ECT I found that either the triggers which brought up old memories were either completely bizarre and unrelated or the information coming back was so incomplete I wasn't recognizing the relationship between it and the trigger. It became a sort of coffee-table sport in the house to figure out how A and B were related.

Though smell was never a real trigger for me before treatment, light and sound still seemed to have a powerful effect. It's almost impossible to describe, but I would come across a place under the trees or a hallway in a shopping center or even the space between windows in a church and the slant of light would suddenly transport me to the semblance of another place in my memory.

This was very unsettling to my husband who often worried I was having a seizure or nearing a point of passing out because I would stand transfixed to the spot, examining what I knew wasn't there in front of me but was so very strongly imprinted in the back of my mind. It was like seeing another place overlaid on what was right in front of me. The same could be said of music or sound.

Certain sounds or songs on the radio would call up places I'd been but these were always short snatches I could not catch for very long. After some time the memory information coming back fell into several distinct "categories" of memory or methods of recall for lack of better terms that I named in my mind to keep separate.

*Dim awareness.* So many things in my recent past were simply gone. There were no glimmers to hold onto or try to pull on to drag lost episodes into the light of day. Where there had been information there was nothing but a hole. These were episodes I referred to as *not existing* for me, because clearly they had happened in the past of the world, just no longer in my individual past. When tiny bits became to come back they came as a sort of dim or dull awareness that something was there that hadn't been previously. This was different than, say, learning about a historical fact one hadn't been aware of before because that is a flat fact. The awareness was just that; the full if darkish consciousness of something personal, like listening to the faint but audible crackling of electric lines after a deep snow.

*Impressions.* Though I had forgotten a lot of people I'd worked with or met casually during the few years before ECT, impressions of certain people's characters or auras remained as well as the semblance of places I had been. Like walking through mist, cognizant of the sounds and scents and character of a place but blind to its visage, the impressions of hospitals were especially strong to me having worked in one and visiting my mother and grandmother during their work shifts as I was growing up. The smell of antiseptic, the squeezing of my chest in apprehension at having to talk to yet another doctor or deal with yet another patient is just as tight as it was then. But then, so are the sweet memories of acceptance and inclusion at being a juvenile psychiatric patient on a juvenile psychiatric ward with others just like me for the first time.

*Disordered:* Sometimes I would recall something and be adamant that I was right when those around me were just as adamant what I was recalling was in the wrong time, that is, it happened in a different year or month than what I perceived. Other times, and much more confusing, were memories in which I *knew* elements were out of order. If you've ever seen of those "when you see it" photos on the internet that give you goosebumps when you see something sitting in the corner you weren't expecting to see, you've got the idea of what it feels like to recall something very clearly and strongly but out of order and not be able to discern which part is incorrect. The unfortunate part about these sorts of memories was that they usually were of things only I would have known to begin with so I had no one to corroborate my own thoughts. The most haunting part of these recollections was those which had no bridge at all; fond relationships that were suddenly no more and only I knew, or rather no longer knew, what had happened. These left me with an uneasy anxiety that I had done something terrifically wrong I had somehow forgotten and a compulsion to make things right.

*Echoes:* Imagine someone walks by you in the park wearing a light perfume. Ten minutes later you're on your own and detect the scent again, blown by in the breeze. Later you get off the bus and cut through the alley to go home on foot. Above you, somewhere in an apartment someone is blasting their music so loud you can feel it in the soles of your feet as they hit the bricks and the sound is so loud you can only hear the base but can still sing along in perfect pitch. Echoes of very sensory memories would come back to me at the strangest of times, dulled and filtered but recognizable. Though I often wouldn't know where the memory originated, I could always recognize that I'd experienced it more intensely before.

*Right-handed:* Curiously, visual memories of places I had been such as the hospital where I received treatment were decidedly right-handed. Though I had been on the same floor of that hospital in previous years and knew it very well, when I tried to think of it purposely the left-hand side of the halls, rooms and grounds had no left side. Rather, the left side of my mental picture faded and receded off like the waves from the shore. This extended to recalling things I had newly learned as well, but over time the left side returned, never totally but mostly from the first faint outlines to more fleshed out visages and details. In my memory those places remain washed away softly by the tide.

*Intense:* The popular image of 'flashbacks' is that of someone being knocked to the ground by an abrupt and intense assault on the senses so real it's impossible to discern one's bathroom from a battlefield and it's one used quite a lot in films portraying soldiers. While not frightening to recall, or violent in nature, these intense recovered memories were often so physically taxing because they involved every sense that I felt as if someone had full-body tackled me. Because of this, it was almost always observed by someone nearby that this was happening and after I assured them I was ok, I prayed nothing else came back. Again, these were not terrible memories that I would want to hide from, many times they were quite enjoyable later when I could actually recall them from a distance but up front they were so disruptive and forceful that I just wanted to escape the exhaustion of them. For this reason I hid when it happened, aware of and embarrassed by the smart mouth and awful temper I hid behind to do so.

*Suspended*: Someone asks me if I watch a particular television show and I answer no, I've never seen it or even heard of such a programme. Later I find out I have seen it and in fact loved all 157 episodes. I can't fathom it, why on earth would I have any interest in that type of show? But months later, something seemingly unrelated jogs my memory and the entire 157 episodes are instantly present in my memory as if they had never gone to begin with. It seems like a vision of Brigadoon; what was always there but not visible. At first, when there was a large, all-consuming hole "behind" me mentally, I had to ask about everything that may be lost in that hole.

This made me dependent on others and increasingly more unsure of what I could trust in myself. As little things began to come back I became distrustful of others, thinking perhaps I was being deceived but once facts were put to me, I could at least see that I may not know but I could at least suss things out. When I would sit and try to remember a certain look fell over me of listening intently, my eyes jammed down and all the way to the right. This also worried my husband into thinking something was terribly wrong and he would try to catch my attention to wake me out of it and as you can imagine, a spotty memory leads to all manner of misunderstandings.

*"What is this? Whose clothes are these?"* I demanded, holding up a pair of unders I'd found in my dresser that clearly were not mine. Firstly, I did not wear pink. Secondly, the shirts hanging in the closet were most certainly not ones I would choose. Ever.

My husband assured me these were my own clothes but I instantly accused him of having a girl up in the bedroom. We argued, I cried.

*How could he? And right in our own bedroom?* I was devastated. I had incontrovertible proof right in my hands and his denial made it all the worse. Did he think I was stupid? I felt stupid and now he was treating me like it as well.

*"Yes, Rose. I had a girl right up here while you were in the hospital. In fact she's the same size as you. And she keeps her clothes in your dresser,"* he said sarcastically.

It took me a bit to realize what he was saying. But when I did we had a good laugh that goes on still today. It highlighted how ridiculous memory loss can be, but also how frightening to not know your own likes and dislikes and be dead set on what you think is reality. The clothing I reacted to was that I had bought myself and had had well prior to ECT. But it was strikingly obvious to me that these couldn't be mine. I didn't even like the styles.

Another time the argument was hot and over a television show we used to watch.

*"Don't you want to watch with me?"* He asked.

*"Of course not. Why would I want to watch a show like that?"* I replied, completely confused and honestly repulsed. What did people see in those stupid shows?

*"Because we used to watch this. We used to have really great conversations about it,"* he pressed. I could feel my own blank stare. He tried again. *"We discussed stuff like alienation and how society views outsiders, and...?"*

*"No, we absolutely didn't. I'd never watch something like that and I won't watch it now."*

I had gotten a taste of what it feels like to dissociate from one's own self; a symptom of some mental illnesses and it was quite terrifying at times. Going forward I began to write my initials on the tags of my clothing with a permanent marker as one would do for a school-aged child. When you have a hole in your life you can only go forward with what you had from before that hole was ripped open; i.e. you judge your skills and body of knowledge by the period until then.

When those inevitable tales about you come out from the woodwork via family and friends who went through your life during that time, the first reaction is disbelief because all of the personal growth you had during that absent period is gone. I know for certain from the marked change in me and the notes that I kept during those years that profound things had happened in my thinking and decision-making that left me stranded as to how to backtrack to find the someone I knew inside my own head. The after effects of such changes may still be there but for the current incarnation of yourself, these things never happened;

the bridge between past and present has washed away, leaving you standing on an empty bank gazing across to the opposite shore.

And if you're not a very trusting person naturally (and I am not), this can cause a unique grief in so many ways. I didn't trust my husband right off the bat. My mind went back in time; not to before the treatment but to many years back when it wasn't smart or safe to trust men in general. When I had treatment, we had been married seven years but for me it was more like four and during those first years we had found ourselves often in the middle of embroiled cultural battles and battles of the sexes.

So, though I know my husband is a gentle and trustworthy person, there were times when I was irrationally afraid of this veritable stranger and times I thought he was an out and out liar because surely I would remember if I had *done that*, I'd know if I had *said that*. I would still *like* this or that or the other thing if he was telling me the truth because people don't just change on a dime! And as time went on I realized *no*, the essence of our real selves doesn't change regardless of outward behavior but truly, the essence of others doesn't either. If the people around me were trustworthy before, they were trustworthy now.

Now, it was time for me to be told my story. And though the words in my own voice had faded away, now the voices of others intertwined to sing a stronger future for me. It was time to pick up what I had and go with it, taking the gift of progress for what it was without reading into it. Personally that's a great challenge and one I work on every day because truly, that's what my husband spoke of when he said I had the luxury of not knowing. I didn't know what I was leaving behind. But only I knew to what extent I *did know* with the reverberations of the past.

It was sometimes dreadfully difficult to get through the minutiae of the day trying to reconcile past with present, express yet protect others from my own sorrow and deal with theirs at the same time. A favorite standby from the early days of our marriage that stayed strong even in the middle of treatment, humor came to rescue us and see us through in so many aspects of life and loss.

Directly after individual ECT treatments I didn't know my own name and when this came back to me I introduced myself as *Mrs. Quayle*, unsure of my first and middle name. This was odd as no-one ever called me this outside of my husband who did so mostly as an address over an endearment. Likewise, I did not recognize him at times but simply thought of him as a "very nice boy" who took care of me. I thought perhaps he was a nurse.

*"The standard of care must be quite high these days then,"* he mused later when he wasn't sure whether to be amused or insulted. *"The shots come with kisses now."*

Additionally, in the hospital it is apparent from my notes that the power of laughter cut through all damages.

*(the doctor) was interested about past memories coming up but said that's not unusual so I guess I'm just going to have to figure out how to get through it. This'll keep my therapist in paychecques for the next 40 years, haha.*

*Doctor has been leaving me notes so I know we've talked about stuff- I'm amassing a collection of post-its! It is helpful though. I'm going to make a fun Alzheimer's patient someday.*

*I read that magazine again and I know I have before but I can't ever recall it in my memory- that'll save some money on reading material!*

*Another both side of the head treatment today... woke up (I thought) they'd put someone else's socks on me, I couldn't recall owning the ones I woke up in!*

Interspersed with the tense, resentful responses my husband developed in response to the situation were his characteristic wisecracks reminiscent of Basil Fawlty which sometimes hurt my feelings until we established a rhythm to the routine:

*"No, you weren't dreaming,"* he said as we sat watching an advert for dishwashing liquid on TV. I looked quizzically at him and he repeated himself with a flourish of his hand.

Ah. He'd done the dishes that morning and was reminding me I'd somehow forgotten this minor miracle in the daily battle we often got into over this least-favored chore. I was chagrined. But we'd established that I needed frequent reminders, no matter how huge or how minute.

It seemed so did he and I pointed this out blithely. *"I do have memory loss, you realize. That's ECT humor for you."*

Sadly, it wasn't only episodes from my life or things that had happened that day that vanished for me. We hadn't lived very long in our apartment when I had my treatment and walking to the end of the street and back was an exercise in frustration when I couldn't recall how to get back, nor the left side of the street. Everything in the house seemed brand new. And riding a bike? I became famous for wrecking a ten speed every time I got on before I got ten feet along.

This is not to say that memory loss is a one-sided evil. As I have experienced, it is a multi-layered phenomenon that affects a multitude of things in one's experience. For those outside the situation the greatest joy is to be had in remembering what was lost, while those inside are alone in the grief of those same remembrances.

I found this to be searingly true with the death of my grandfathers who both passed a few months of each other around the time of my treatment. As I discovered while in hospital, the memory of their funerals had gone and I had to remind myself often that somewhere in that hole of vanishing things lied their passing and my goodbye. Without that memory I had to say goodbye over and over after the fact and I worried continually that I hadn't honored them *enough* because I couldn't remember doing so.

When my best friend's father, who had been a strong positive influence in my upper childhood years passed, I became haunted by a fixation to be present during the final hours of my loved ones, to somehow make up for something I felt I hadn't done. Being present had never been a strong point for me and coming from an estranged and long-distance family never taught me the finer skills of being the supportive daughter and granddaughter and sister and friend I wished I had been.

So it was no small struggle to do this but I felt compelled to sit alone with my grandmother as she died, insisting the other family take a break to go eat. It was not an act of guilt but rather from a deep sense that this was a vital act of growth for me and I would not have done it without that loss. If I hadn't lost my memory from shock treatment, I would have waited until I got the call that it was time to pull out the mourning dress and get in the car and arrange for work leave.

Now I was willing to fight myself to become who I needed to be. It was awkward, hard, it downright sucked and it took a good deal of blind faith to trust that I wasn't going to make a complete ass of myself even further than I already had in not remembering to begin with, as if I had somehow refused to recall on purpose.

Sitting with my grandmother brought me in a complete circle from detachment to full-throttle engagement at the most important moment of life; that second when we pass from it, co-equal with every other living being on earth in our mortality. Time hadn't been taken from me in punishment or maliciousness, it had been taken as a *part* of my timeline, an intrinsic stepping stone to where I was headed.

I didn't wake up one morning and declare myself discharged of all resentments that it had happened to begin with because memory doesn't disappear in neat, clean chunks for the most part because of how it's encoded and retrieved in the brain, and its loss doesn't neatly affect the present in clean fashion either. My best friend of nearly twenty-five years once told me afterward that she often didn't know what to say around me because she just didn't know what I knew or didn't anymore.

Commonality is what separates strangers from acquaintances and acquaintances from deeper relationships. If we have common past memories such as those of world events, school rituals or popular fads, we can find deep kinship with people who seem completely different to us or through the power of the written word, to those so far away from us we may never meet them face to face. Without those common memories, distance develops.

Part of accepting that there was a reality already gone by that I no longer knew and trusting others to guard that part of my past for me included an uneasy truce between my husband and I stating that we would assume I didn't know and he would just tell me rather than go through the song and dance of trying to sort out which bits I did and didn't.

After it became apparent I was completely unaware of a concert we'd attended and meeting the band afterward, my husband would sometimes say offhandedly, *"You wouldn't know anyway,"* which I took to mean, *"You're not bright enough to know anyway."*

Because I too was a person for whom memory loss incited fond pity or impatient belligerence most often in regard to the elderly in particular rather than respect for one who has lost a part of their life and its effects on their identity, I immediately felt I was being called stupid. And while there was great disappointment from him at my no longer knowing, there was also great disappointment in me at his all-too-human reaction over what I thought was the proper response; recognition that I did not choose to forget and frankly, not knowing me as well as I thought he did.

When memories first began to return to me I took a child-like glee in knowing, in catching up to everyone else. *"I know it! I know it!"* I'd howl, extremely pleased with myself. Once, standing in the shower at my grandmother's house, I turned around to grab a teacup to rinse the tub with and my mind burst open with the patchy memory of a show my husband and I once watched. In the car on the way home I accosted him with what I knew.

*"There was a funny little lady and she was always telling fat people how many cups of tea they were drinking and she put the food on a table. Why did she put the food on a table?"*

*"She measured how much they ate in a week and put it on a table so they could see,"* he explained.

"*Yes, and nobody liked her. And she was Scottish. And she was telling them what they ought to eat.*"

"*Yes.*"

"*And she looked at their poo!*" He smiled. "*Yeah, that was the poo lady.*"

"*Why did she do that?*"

"*To... measure what they ate,*" he shrugged. "*To tell them why they were un-healthy.*"

"*And she was ugly,*" I nodded with conviction.

It amazed him how I knew this and how suddenly it had come back. To me, it was exhausting to try and put together a story from the images I'd recalled because they seemed to be in real-time now, not from a time before.

"*How do you know that?*" He would ask again and again and I would tell him again and again, "*I just know it*". In my own mind it was if it had *always* been there, *always* missing some bits here and there. He insisted I'd always known why the food was on the table and why the poo was measured by the lady who was a *dietician*. I insisted I hadn't ever known those details.

Slowly I began to resent this blanket approach to saving time. I felt that, in this world so bound by shortcuts, headlines and saving every second only to cram it with as much productivity as humanly possible and more than so with the help of technology, I was *due* a little more patience than the immediate brush off. I began to hold my piece, to allow people to think I didn't know, believing it didn't matter. No one had time to listen anyway.

Certainly this ended in me losing my temper and becoming resentful every time, informing whomever I was with of what I *did know* in a terse, resentful tone or saving up my memories for one spectacular show-up that brought me no closer to the respect I wanted. It didn't help smooth things over with those outside of my story who were coming in at an angle and didn't know why this odd girl seemed so angry, so disjointed.

In the year after I came home from the hospital my husband and I purchased a house and he asked me one evening after we'd newly moved in if I wanted to sleep on his side of the bed, which was the side away from the door. I thought it was odd that he asked as we'd already picked our sides of a brand-new suite and I happened to be on the door side. I said no, where I *was* was fine but he asked me several other times, finally telling me that I was never able to sleep on the door side in the past and I ought to ask my therapist about it.

I did from curiosity and she confirmed that in the years she'd known me, I had some sort of fear about open doors from something that happened in my childhood and couldn't sleep on the door-side of a room. But now I no longer had the memory... so I had no fear of it. On the surface this seems like a fantastic side effect because who doesn't want to carve out the awful bits of their life and be unencumbered by their own phobias?

Like it or not, our own stories are part of a larger, finite world that must balance itself with us within its context and we are bound inside of that process. Fear, pain, sadness all serve their own good purpose and our brains are equipped to use these tools to help us survive. If we cannot remember these lessons we become like small children who run towards traffic, unaware of what it is about traffic that's frightening. Fear also often leads us to either avoid others to protect our own hearts or to lash out to protect our families or possessions. As humans we have enough foresight to be able to refrain from hurting those who have hurt us, from overcoming our own violent reactions to choose a different resolution. We are able to do this to prevent from becoming our own most feared predator, otherwise as a species we would die out.

We need to remember our fears to temper ourselves not just to survive, but to realize our potential. And who we are as humans builds throughout our lives based on what we've learned, what we've gone through, the strengths and weaknesses we see in others and how they've come through these. Everything we are is the culmination of what we remember.

Today when I run into something I don't remember I tend to be a bit impatient about it. I feel that I don't have time to mourn over these things anymore since time has disappeared from me. It wouldn't matter if it came back in bit or in full because I have outlived it and can never experience it the same way again.

So I say hurriedly, *tell me!* And this doesn't always take into account that the other person may be realizing for the first time along with me that I don't know. I have come to trust the idea that I may not remember or understand what is being told to me. I may have liked it, said it, or done it and no longer know the story but someday might meet that version of me in memories.

And perhaps we all should keep in mind that all of us at some point in our lives lose bits of our stories deep inside of ourselves through the distance of the past or the illness of the present. As humans beings we are always alone in our memories, in our uniqueness, in our thoughts.

We are, always alone, together.

# Chronologic

I was a happy, friendly baby.

Very imaginative at age 3.

With my grandpa.

My silly side started early.

K. Rose Quayle

Aged 15 when I was first diagnosed with Depression.

21 years old at Pratt Institute.

Mr. and Mrs. Quayle, 2004.

Photo booth fun.

Taken shortly before I began ECT.

Sleeping it off!

With a painting I did for a local NAMI fundraiser.

Mr. and Mrs. Quayle, 2017

# Part III

# Effects

# Every Silver Lining Has a Cloud

I T's an oddity.

ECT has been used for nearly a century as a treatment for mental illness and has secured itself a firm place in the popular consciousness as an instrument of torture and fear. The testimonies of how shock therapy has ruined minds and lives aren't rare. The testimonies of those for whom shock therapy has saved their lives are much less heard of.

Several things strike me as odd with this scenario. If ECT was as damaging to human beings as is postulated, why is it still being used at all? What would the therapeutic purpose be to cause irreparable harm to one's patient when millions are spent every year to research effective remedies for these illnesses? If so harmful, where are the mass lawsuits against doctors, hospitals and machine manufacturers splashed across the nightly news? Where are the mass recalls of shock machines, the FDA crackdowns? If ECT is so harmful, where are the millions lined up in protest?

Likewise, if this is such an extraordinary treatment why are those success stories so unheard of? Why aren't patients lining up to demand this miracle? For that matter, why aren't corporations lining up to make billions on it? And why aren't there protesters against monopoly in industry flooding the House with demands to allow competing machines to be manufactured, tweaked, *perfected*? Why isn't there *mass capital* being flooded into research on how many ways we can use shock therapy.

More importantly though, why do we have to dig so deep to find the answers? It seems no matter how you view it, something is being kept out of the story.

ECT has worked virtual miracles for some; I believe it and don't debate it. Compelling testimonies from its beneficiaries such as Julie Hersh (Hersh J. , 2016) who presented her story for the U.S. Food and Drug Administration Neurological Devices Panel, Risa Sugarman of the Jewish parenting blog Kveller.com (Sugarman, 2014), and Kitty Dukakis (Dukakis, Shock: The Healing Power of Electroconvulsive Therapy , 2007) amongst many others make the case that for those who have gotten to the end of their rope, ECT is the only way to escape certain suicide. Deafening our ears to their stories is harmful in that it silences knowledge of potential life-saving options to a population for whom medical science has so often been an utter failure in comprehension and results. It also smacks of the arguments of millions supporting the legalization of marijuana for pain treatment in those with chronic and terminal illnesses. Certainly, marijuana can be harmful if used improperly but for those who have no other hope, should it not be *considered* under controlled use?

For those individuals who have suffered for years through torturous side effects from medication or found no such relief in any other treatment or have had depressive episodes during pregnancy, some have chosen ECT as an alternative to medication when they'd had a long history of noncompliance for whatever reason.

One thing most readers will observe is that bad news travels faster than good news and sells exponentially more magazines and newspapers and garners many more likes and followers online. ECT has made its way into popular films and television shows in a negative light and when it is portrayed as a treatment rather than torture method, the outcome is still illustrated in little better than an obscure fashion.

Take, for instance, the film *Shine*, where a young David Helfgott is given shock treatment. We see the apparatus, the shaking of a limb conveying that

the seizure is happening and after a poignant glance at the young man's unconscious face we see him as a grown man seemingly cured of his younger bouts
of Depression. While film is a unique medium that opens our minds to new
facets of a story, keep in mind that film does takes some liberties to move along
a story and is influenced by popular culture and social norms, so how accurate
can this truly be? It is little wonder then that we do not hear more of the success stories and little wonder that those who have benefited wish to see this
treatment offered and easily accessible.

Which brings us to the bitter embroilment between beneficiaries and victims
over the classification of ECT devices under the FDA. To make a long story
short, an ECT machine is considered a neurological device and as such is under
jurisdiction of the U.S. Food and Drug Administration, which took over the
regulation of medical devices sold in this country in 1976.

Neurological devices are classed as I, II or III in regard to risk with Class
III being high-risk, of which the benefits of the device have not been shown to
outweigh the risks. If you take prescription medication you are already familiar
with this system with drugs being classed on schedules A, B or C, the most
referenced being Schedule C in which benefits do not outweigh the risks to
an unborn child when taken during pregnancy. These drugs are either held
altogether during pregnancy and breastfeeding or swapped out for a lower –
risk alternative.

The problem here is that the ECT device was classed as Class III in 1982,
and was not subjected to required safety testing because it had been on the
market prior to the 1976 takeover by the FDA. So go and test the thing, right?
Well not so simple. Where it gets tricky is this: those who have had radical
life-changes from the treatment want it knocked down to a Class II to be declared safer and made more accessible. Those who have had radical injuries
want it kept at Class III to be taken off the market altogether. In either case
however, the FDA's reluctance to enforce its own required human and animal

studies seems a little revealing, as is the American Psychiatric Association's ties with the two American manufacturers of these devices (International, 2017). In 2009 the FDA opened the matter to the public through what has been an ongoing Neurological Devices Panel to evaluate safety data from devices used for neurological purposes. Thousands of testimonials all around poured in to be collected and filed under FDA docket 82P-0316. There was enough opposition at that time to block the motion to reclassify and to follow up in 2015, the FDA drafted specifications for ECT Devices to be filed under Class II for the treatment of certain disorders (U.S. Department of Health and Human Services, 2016). This was supported by the APA in order to take the rating to what they called "low risk" on their website (Saul Levin M.D., 2016).

Regardless of the outcomes, for still others, ECT isn't effective at all but does no harm. And for still others, it's hard to tell if the treatment itself worked or the underlying disease went into a natural remission. As many have learned in the treatment of human diseases, earthly miracles can be finite. There will always be someone who benefits extremely well from a treatment, someone who is damaged profoundly by it and the vast majority who get a moderate benefit. What *is* generally the same in groups of people who have been helped or hindered in ECT treatment, however, are the general, or "milder" side effects.

It's been well documented for decades that ECT causes a myriad of side effects during the treatment period and shortly thereafter and these aren't debated. How long these effects last and *how* debilitating or permanent they actually are is debated hotly in the medical community and in patient groups all over the internet.

**On paper, side effects from and risks of ECT documented by various sources include:**

Anti-retrograde amnesia

Retrograde amnesia

Autobiographical amnesia

Verbal amnesia (bilateral ECT)

Weight gain

Menstrual changes

Brief elevations of hormones (Resuscitation Central)

Resetting of circadian rhythms

Jaw pain

Severe headaches

Acute mental confusion for 30-minutes to 1 hour after treatment

Burns at the electrode pad site

Breathing complications

Delayed onset seizures

Heart rate and blood pressure increases during treatment due to anesthesia

Nausea

Death (estimated currently as a 1 in 10,000 chance and this may be higher with patients who have concurrent or undiagnosed medical problems. Heart problems are the most common cause of ECT-related death. (Nancy A. Payne, 2009))

Prolonged seizures in patients taking medications that lower the threshold for seizures

Cognitive changes (nonverbal, visual, spatial relations, music and artistic ability, judgment and insight, intuition, personality, attention span)

Mania or hypomania in depressed or mixed-state patients

Brain damage (Dept of Psychiatry of University of Michigan Health Department , 2016) (Peter R. Breggin, 1997) (Mayo Clinic, 1998-2017) (Task Force on Electroconvulsive Therapy, n.d.) (U.S. Department of Health and Human Services, 2016) (Andrew C. Papanicolaou, 2005)

Again, the actual brain damage is generally what raises the hackles of many either for or against the idea with some individuals who believe that the treatment itself either made their symptoms worse or brought on disabling new symptoms, some who believe it doesn't happen at all and others supporting this as an "acceptable risk."

As a side note, the statistics on the rate of death caused by ECT have recently come under fire. In the 1990 APA Task Force report, reported deaths by ECT were defined as deaths occurring within twenty-four hours of treatment in the years between 1977 and 1983 in the state of California, which counted out to 1 in 10,000. Certainly the coincidence of death to the time of treatment is notable but has anyone actually studied these reports and patients post-mortem to find out if this is true? Shouldn't we be a little more concerned with proof? Journalist Sandra Boodman reveals the discrepancy in numbers when looking at ECT-related deaths reported in Texas, which became the first state required to report deaths occurring within fourteen days of ECT in 1993 and one of four states required to report at all. From the reports given in 1993, deaths in Texas "from ECT" were as high as 21 in 2,000. Within a three year report that number is closer to 1 in 95 (with suicides falling within the reporting period to be considered caused by ECT), yet most major literature on the subject still quote the 1990 figure from the APA (Boodman, 2016). Who's right? Until someone defines what criteria must be met to define a death as caused by ECT, no one can rightfully claim that title (Breeding, 2014).

While the specific biology and medical history of a patient will always influence how a treatment is received and how well it works, how the treatment is administered also has great consequence on its effectiveness and byproducts. The spacing and number of treatments, unilateral versus bilateral placement of electrodes, type of anesthesia, dosage of electrical stimulation and brain sine wave stimulation all make the difference in how intense and lasting cognitive effects of ECT are.

Studies have found that after ECT, the longer the time it takes to come around after anesthesia correlates to the amount of autobiographical memory loss in the long term. Which rather makes sense if you think of this in terms of computers: after an operating system update it usually bears out that the longer it takes your hard drive to boot up, the greater chance something from your desktop goes missing.

Three notable supporters of the idea that ECT damages the brain are Linda Andre, an activist for human rights and director of the Committee for Truth in Psychiatry as well as author of *Doctors of Deception*, Robert Whitaker, journalist and author of *Mad in America, Bad Science, Bad Medicine, and the Enduring Mistreatment of the Mentally Ill*, and Doctor Peter Breggin, former consultant for NIMH and author of multiple titles including *Talking Back to Prozac* and *Brain-Disabling Treatments in Psychiatry*.

These authors all believe that there is a distinct lack of quality modern studies on the effects of ECT on brain functions and that past post-mortem studies prior to the FDA takeover of medical device regulation in 1976 show definite changes and damage to the brains of animals as well as human studies showing cognitive changes and disability. Neuroscientist Peter Sterling, of the University of Pennsylvania, gave testimony in regards to the damage ECT is thought to inflict on the brain in a 2001 hearing before the New York Assembly Standing Committee on Mental Health, Mental Retardation and Developmental Disabilities. His testimony indicated that the rise in blood pressure noted in ECT-induced seizures can cause small hemorrhages in the brain, allowing irreplaceable nerve cells to die. He asserted that the blood-brain barrier, which protects the nerve cells from injury, is disrupted and neurons are compelled to release glutamate, a neurotransmitter (Leighton P. Mark, 2001).

The continual release of glutamate causes something called *excito-toxcity*. A cellular process relatively new to science, excito-toxicity refers to the concentration of glutamate in neurons in response to injury that kills neurons and raises glutamate in the neighborhood of surrounding cells, putting others as risk for death as well (Health C. o., 20002).

There is also the question of how safe are the actual machines being used to give shock, the reasons why the effects of ECT are not more closely investigated and how closely related the task forces set up to keep such things in check are to the industry that manufactures them. Add to this the question of whether or not ECT causes mental decline in the years post-treatment and what we know for certain is that we don't know a hell of a lot for certain.

On the other side of the fence, the National Institute of Mental Health, which is the largest funding organization of research on mental health in the world, *has* done numerous published studies of the effects of ECT on the brain and have come up with surprisingly little for what they have actually studied. The CORE research studies during the period spanning 1997-2011 found that cognitive impairment is gone by 4 weeks after a successful course of ECT and that overall the treatment is safe (Fink, 2014).

Likewise, a 1993 study referenced in *Biological Psychiatry* indicated ECT caused no permanent structural changes to the brain if used per safety guidelines (Bittar, 1999). Research in a 1994 study by the New York State Psychiatric Institute Department of Biological Psychiatry also found no credible evidence of damage to the brain's structures that could be attributed to ECT (Devanand DP, 1994).

And we can take this a few ways.

*One*, NIMH and its bedfellow the American Psychological Association have a less-than-stellar history in regards to the motivation for research at times and this is one of Dr. Breggin's chief points, having come from the position of supporting and administering shock treatment during the years it went from standard to modified. NIMH's background of using ECT as a means to build a better interrogation technique for the CIA during the years after WWII is one that has been admitted to by the government and documentation of this is available under the Freedom of Information Act. Its history of abuse is even admitted to in the 1985 National Institutes of Health Consensus Development Conference Statement on Electroconvulsive Therapy (US Department of Health and

Human Services National Institutes of Health, 1985). So we could take the position that NIMH is still up to the tricks of the past when it reports its studies say *"move on, nothing to see here, folks."*

*Two,* we could take the position that detractors of the belief that ECT does no actual damage are scorned in some way and are trying to take the system down. Dr. Breggin, for instance, previously consulted for NIMH. He believes that NIMH and the APA are very financially tied together and some psychiatrists were on the take to greenlight the usage of ECT for their financial benefit when it should have not been used in the interest of patient safety. The word controversial seems to follow him in media wherever he goes and often this term carries a hefty weight of evidence behind it. Ms. Andre is a former recipient of ECT. When a patient makes a very public stance against a treatment they have had in a negative light it is often assumed they wish for some sort of legal compensation.

Moreover, those who speak out against the established order of treatment standards are often regarded with a mixture of skepticism, fear and patronizing indulgence. It could be argued that Mr. Whitaker is a medical journalist, which can be construed as to convey a lack of legitimate medical degree to make such first-hand judgements on the effects of treatment. His heavy focus on pharmaceuticals in the psychiatric industry may also be seen as a single-minded focus.

*Three,* we can claim that those who give glowing testimonies to ECT's benefits are either receiving some sort of compensation for this or are being unduly influenced to paint ECT in a positive light.

*Four,* we could assume that NIMH and the APA are telling the truth. Or conversely, that ECT's opponents are.

*Five,* we can back the idea that there is a combination of sort of any of these factors to make up the truth.

*Six,* the theory that ECT isn't studied as much as it could be because it's an alternative to the much more heavily studied and trialed drug therapies may have a more significant weight in the puzzle than anyone's intentions on the positive or negative usage of ECT directly.

And lastly, we might put our faith in what's *lacking*. According to a study referenced in 1984 by Cambridge University Press (Weiner, 2010), a more middle of the road theory is put forward that ECT doesn't for the most part cause the devastating brain damage it's garnered a supposed reputation for but rather can be safely assumed to cause much more subtle changes in the brain, which would be much harder to predict based on individual biology and the outcomes of which may be wildly different depending on what area these changes occur in. Again, that much-cited 1985 Consensus found that ECT was known to be effective and beneficial to certain groups but was equally unknown to be safe in others; thereby making it foolish to assume this is a one-size-fit all treatment. In any study or trial of treatment the data is only as good as what's lacking: lack of control groups, lack of consistent results, lack of ability to reproduce the same results in another environment or situation.

One of the problems in proving whether or not it's true that ECT is harmful to the brain is the limits of what we can see on an actual brain scan. Structural changes of the brain are usually apparent on a CT scan, PET scan or MRI. In the case of MRI the brain can be divided into "slices" onscreen so that doctors can see deep into the brain's soft tissues to assess damage, tumors or lesions. But what cannot be seen at this time are the individual billions and trillions of neurons and synapses in the brain so that even in the case of having mild traumatic brain injury from something such as an accident, the damage is often not viewable. Of these, what can be seen is the activity of these structures on either a PET scan or the results of that activity in neuropsychiatric testing.

With even only 12% (Diane Roberts Stoler, 2013) of *concussion* sufferers kept overnight in hospital and the bulk of those patients showing no issues on a scan to begin with, we're left with one camp that argues no damage from ECT is *visible*, therefore it is not there at all and the other camp which argues the *effects* of the damage can be seen. *Psychology Today* reports that shock therapy has the positive effect of increasing brain-derived neurotrophic factor which stimulates brain cell growth (Hersh J. K., The Shocking Truth about ECT, 2015). I don't think there's a sure-fire way to tell if this *will* be the case beforehand with current knowledge and the elements of biological individuality.

What exactly is meant when referring to cognitive changes?

We can see how well the brain is functioning by measuring cognition, which is our conscious thought and thought processes. Learning is part of cognition, as is insight, discerning what we taste, feel, smell, see and hear and making judgements and assumptions about those things. When something goes wrong in the brain we can see the direct effects of that through changes in these processes.

It's interesting to compare the physical and cognitive symptoms experienced after a concussion (which is the cognitive *result* of a physical injury) with that of those experienced after a round of ECT. Immediate symptoms of concussion include:

Loss of consciousness up to one hour

Loss of memory from before or after the injury

Disorientation

Dizziness

Nausea

Headache

Fatigue

Delayed symptoms occurring 1-2 weeks after the injury include:

Headaches

Fatigue

Problems with attention and concentration

Problems with making decisions

Issues with sleep

Reading and communication problems

Behavioral problems

This collection of delayed symptoms is referred to as *Post-Concussive Syndrome*. Now, a concussion is generally thought of as temporary unconsciousness that has been caused by a blow to the head. Injuries to the brain in previous eras were termed as either closed- or open-headed injuries, with the World Health Organization using the identifier *acquired injury* to delineate that which is not already present at birth (Ed. David J. Thurman, 1995). Today such injuries to the head are referred to as mild, moderate or severe injury. These terms do not actually tell us about the *severity* of the injury but rather how long consciousness was lost from that injury.

Patients with concussion are often sent home from the ER and told to rest as there isn't much else to do because cognitive changes aren't bright and loud on a scan. Diagnosis is made on symptoms, like most illnesses are, but in this case, often only the symptoms are available to guide the way. If there are signs as described above *and* a catalyst event such as a fall, it's a safe bet to say this is a concussion. Likewise, ECT opponents argue, symptoms of cognitive dysfunction with a catalyst event of seizures caused by shock therapy should warrant a diagnosis of damage to the brain regardless of what shows up on a scan.

But when something such as Post-Concussive Syndrome sets in after a concussion, many patients feel invisible, depressed, frightened and isolated because their symptoms often aren't outwardly apparent or bothersome until they conflict with the person's job or relationships. This is a story all too-familiar to ECT patients experiencing the exact same symptoms post-treatment. It remains a perplexity to patients and doctors alike as to who should investigate and treat the ongoing problems after treatment and at what point it should be recognized as beyond the "it'll get better" stage.

It must be nearly as frustrating to doctors unarmed with more substantial knowledge on the subject when confronted with an upset patient or even worse, a patient who is either unaware of the extent of the problem or afraid to be forthcoming about it. The acute symptoms similar to those of concussion generally fade within a short time after treatment ends. However, there are lingering effects that continue down the road once the cycle of treatment is completed, staying in line with the cumulative effects of repeated seizures. These include measurable developments such as:

Development of seizures where there were none previous

Psychomotor epilepsy

Atrophy of brain visible on scans

Abnormal EEGs

Changes in the central nervous system Babayan, 1985

Nerve cell and vassal wall changes

Spinal fluid changes (Shashina, 1985) (Hartelius, 1952) (Donald B. Tower, 1948)

Further consequences, those that are subtle and pervasive and often not noted by a medical professional who doesn't spend twenty four hours a day observing their patient, are usually caught by a patient's family:

The patient seems "changed" somehow.

Clumsiness, dropping things frequently

Lapses in thought

Inability to find the right words or express thoughts

Deterioration of handwriting

Shortened attention span

Apathy

Deterioration of social skills, moments of "awkwardness"

Difficulty focusing

Difficulty learning / recalling new information

Memory loss of a period up to twenty seven months with no return after one year (Squire LR, 1983)

Amongst the many doctors I have seen for one thing or another over the years, some have voiced immediately that it made sense I was having cognitive issues because *of course* I had had ECT. And sometimes I felt like this was a convenient excuse on their part over any actual sound medical knowledge. Though I've never actually said to anyone, *I think ECT caused this*, others emphatically but tactfully said right off the chart that *"ECT doesn't do that,"* case closed. To these I felt like we should at least consider all integers in the equation to save time and visits.

And still others made straightforward, off-hand comments such as *"Oh yes, ECT. Well that gets better and then it gets worse."* These tended to be older physicians whom I would at least trust a little more to have been around the block a few times, but then again, sometimes younger doctors are more abreast of more recent studies. But certainly not always.

So it seems that my husband's original observation still stands: no-one is really certain about anything in this business. And this doesn't perturb me much. After all, who really knows anything about the brain when you get down to it? We are only as intelligent as the questions we think to ask, the desire we have to explore and the tools we have to answer.

...

If cognition has to do with the unseen thought processes going on inside of us, *where* in the brain do the tasks of what we think of as the mind or consciousness take place, anyway? As we've learned, the brain uses many of its structures to come together to take in information, encode it and recall it as memories. The same is true of how it produces what we term self-awareness and consciousness.

One might say that the bulk of our conscious human experience begins in the *frontal lobes* of the brain which sit right behind the eyes, as this is the area responsible for the many processes that come together to create that awareness first of self and then of our environments, as well as new ideas we generate.

A multi-tasking superhero, the frontal area of the brain also helps us concentrate, plan the week's menu, judge which outfits in your closet should have stayed in the '70s, and create projects for our kids' school assignments even when we think we're totally un-artistic (Carter, 2010). The frontal lobes are our *imagination* center.

Underneath the frontal lobes sit the *temporal lobes* (think *temperament*) which influence our emotion, sensory input, memory functions, powers of observation and ability to put things in order, how we perceive music, and how we display aggression and sexual behavior. The left temporal lobe also takes care of what we perceive through hearing and how we understand spoken language. You can think of the temporal lobes as being where the information you *hear* is processed.

The regions directly behind the frontal lobes and in front of the occipital lobes are called *Broca's Area* and *Wernicke's Area*, where language comprehension and speech articulation take place, respectively. Both have to work together to allow us to speak, read and write. Problems with speech (aphasias) and some types of Dyslexia are thought to occur when these two areas can't communicate with each other.

All areas of speech, reading and writing come together thanks to the help of different brain structures but reading and writing are newest to human beings in evolutionary terms and so these areas are "newly" developed in our brains. The spot where the *pituitary gland, parietal lobes* and temporal lobes meet neatly down within the center of the brain is the *angular gyrus* and this is also an important spot as far as cognitive functions go. This is where the work to help us recognize words in reading and be able to speak them, such as in reading aloud versus reading to ourselves, goes on. The angular gyrus runs relay between the eyes and the other parts of the brain responsible for language recognition and speech.

The *occipital lobe,* sitting at the back of the brain, is chiefly responsible for interpreting information coming in through the *eyes,* so what we see and judge as pleasing or ugly, familiar or frightening, for example, all happens through the occipital lobe. Turning heel and taking off once the occipital lobe has identified that cobra as *stranger danger* is the response attributed to the amygdala, a small structure thought to be a remnant from our early days of evolution responsible for getting us the heck out of dodge.

Speaking of that parietal lobe (let's!), within it is located the *somatosensory cortex* which helps us determine information about things around us from their attributes we can feel through *touch*. So, when you go to a museum and come across one of those *"put your hand in the box and guess what the object is"* activities and you tentatively put your hand in hoping it doesn't have teeth, the sigh of relief you give after realizing it's only a cotton ball is thanks to this area. Without the somatosensory cortex you wouldn't be able to determine the weight is too light to be a jackal, the object too soft to be teeth and the surface too smooth to be a bed of nails.

And what unsung hero is responsible for those awful dance moves you break out in the kitchen while doing the dishes (that might just be me)? The *cerebellum*, located at the back of the head where it joins the neck. You can thank it or blame it.

Because the brain is cross-wired so to speak, it must transfer sensory information from one side of the body to the opposite hemisphere of the brain so that the *cerebral cortex* (the outermost layer of the brain which houses its lobes) can interpret this information for us to use. So as we can see, the amazing brain works constantly with all its parts and processes to produce all the components of consciousness. And while the functions might begin in a specific part of the brain, like memory encoding, most require the cooperation of the whole brain to carry those functions out properly. If only we worked as well with other people as our brain already knows how to do within itself!

When the brain experiences trauma of some kind and it loses consciousness, these various processes are going "offline" until the brain is able to "boot up" again, much like a computer. Computers have become a favorite method of comparison to the brain in recent history and rightly so; the similarity of the brain to a computer hard drive is uncanny. The last time you turned on your hard drive, tablet or laptop and your desktop was missing icons you observed something very similar to what happens in the brain while it is recovering from an injury. The parts and processes are all there, but like the missing icons, the brain has to rebuild the pathways to its directories in order to access that information.

So it stands to reason that the theory that ECT causes a full shut down so the brain can gather up its files, shed old information and start afresh isn't outrageous at all. The thing about theory though, is that is doesn't always bear out in practice exactly the same. It's also sensible to keep in mind that cognitive changes are also caused by several disease processes such as Alzheimer's Disease, Multiple Sclerosis and Depression outside of concussion, though in some of these cases structural damage such as lesions are also noted on MRI scans.

Except, of course, where it is not.

As medical science has pinpointed where in the brain certain processes reside, what happens when these areas experience delays or deterioration is also well documented and can be truly fascinating.

Damage to the Broca region causes *Broca's Aphasia*, producing both written and spoken deficiencies. *Broca's Aphasia's* kissing cousin *Wernicke's Aphasia* is produced by damage to its namesake region and affects the understanding of both written and spoken language. Similarly, adverse changes in the angular gyrus also affect reading and writing.

Other types of damage around this area produce different versions of language and recognition problems such as being able to read to one's self but not aloud or losing the ability to recognize the meanings of letters by sight but retaining the ability to read aloud. In this instance the brain uses its other structures to help match up meaning and symbol, thus losing one aspect of the process but not the whole.

K. Rose Quayle

An interesting cognitive disorder involving language without a clear cause is stuttering or stammering, which shows up on fMRI studies as featuring a more active right hemisphere when the patient is reading aloud. It is theorized that perhaps the hemispheres are vying for dominance so both fire at once because in developing humans both hemispheres have language processing duty until about age five when in the vast majority of people that task switches over to the left hemisphere and continues developing on that side. Interestingly, when a person who stutters or stammers reads aloud with others, the stuttering stops. This is possibly because the brain recognizes the incoming sounds of the words being pronounced in its environment and switches to that process rather than relying on sight word recognition alone (Derek S. Beal).

As in memory processes, because so many functions of the brain happen simultaneously in several areas to control what we experience consciously, where one part is damaged others can lend a hand in performing the same tasks that part was responsible for, though they may go about this in a different way or form brand new pathways to the end result.

Recent studies have shown that the capacity of the brain to regenerate new pathways after structural damage and learn new ways of doing old tricks (called *plasticity*) is present at a much older age than used to be thought. In other words, previously scientists believed if you broke it, you lost it unless you were a kid and still growing your original neuronal networks. Turns out that's not always the case. If you're a grownup and the damage is to the right place, you have as good a chance of being able to recover some, if not a lot of what you lost. The catch is you may feel a bit different doing it. In some cases vision is affected by cognitive issues. We think of vision as occurring in our eyes but the eyes are just the windows to which visual information enters the brain. If something is structurally wrong with the eye, that incoming information is compromised.

If you wear glasses for nearsightedness and you take these off, you can't see far-away objects clearly. The *objects* haven't changed, the information about them coming into the brain has been altered by looking through a lens. In disorders where the occipital lobe is affected, the information coming in through the eyes is misinterpreted. Your eyes may have 20/20 vision but if the occipital lobe is damaged just right, you may experience a manner of blindness because to the brain, the information from the eye either isn't being read at all, or not in a sufficient manner to tell your brain what it is seeing.

There are numerous variations on this as well, ranging from colors not being picked up to objects having a certain slant or showing as being one-sided. Eye surgeon William Bates cataloged an interesting cognitive vision problem called *inadequate central fixation* in people fixate only on a small area in front of them rather than taking in the entire scene and this is most striking when reading (Norman Doidge, 2016). There may be a wide expanse of text but in inadequate central fixation only the middle of the page would be read because the eye can see the entire page, but the brain is only focusing on a particular part.

This is noted as happening more and more in the general population as we read electronic screens and headlines of articles on mobile devices or tweets and our brains get used to taking in whole passages without actually reading them. The end result of this is that is affects our far-sightedness overall. Still other problems in the brain cause cognitive delays and physical problems all in one go. In the case of having a "noisy brain" there are too many signals firing at once between the different lobes of the brain.

This is like being at a loud party by the door and being unable to hear your date sitting at the bar calling for you. The "noise" saturates the brain, making it too "full" to take in any more information or focus on the task at hand. It's thought that neurological disease or damage messes up the brain's natural balance, allowing that noise to sneak in. But when the brain is quieted, things overall improve from balance to sleep and speech.

And like vision, hearing doesn't happen all in the ears either. Dr. Alfred Tomatis, a French Ear Nose and Throat specialist during WWI, saw singers in his practice who'd lost vocal range and discovered it wasn't from vocal cord damage as had always been thought but hearing damage on the surface which affected how the brain "hears" pitch and reproduces it. He developed an extremely effective treatment called the Electronic Ear. This helped singers filter sound and retrain their brains to hear the information and sound of pitch no longer coming in through their damaged ears to enable singing again as they had before the physical damage.

This is an excellent example of the brain again using its other parts to do the job of something no longer functioning in the same capacity. The brain normally fires neurons in time to the music it hears (keeping in mind we *hear* music through the ears so to speak, but we also *feel* the beat) so literally, uplifting music uplifts our mood, slow and sad music saddens, loud and angry music lends to a volatile mood. We can train our brains through the right music to all manner of good cognitive effect but music is powerful to the brain and particularly fast beats have been known to cause seizures. Mozart's compositions have been found to have a universally positive effect on the brain and his works modified electronically have been found to help sensory, learning and developmental disorders such as Autism, speech disorders and balance problems (Norman Doidge, The Brain's Way of Healing: Remarkable Discoveries and Recoveries from the Frontiers of Neuroplasticity, 2016).

In cases of *mild traumatic brain injury*, many disruptions have been documented throughout the brain with effects including issues with filtering extraneous information out of thoughts, problems focusing in the midst of visual stimuli, focusing the eyes as well as tracking, hypersensitivity to light, double vision, changes in peripheral vision, vertigo and dizziness, changes in attention span and focus, fatigue with mental tasks because the brain is having to use more energy to function at the same speed, changes in the ability to perform tasks that require steps, changes in coordination and self-awareness (Kandel, In Search of Memory : The Emergence of a New Science of Mind , 2007).

That all sounds very clinical, mysterious and rather boring to someone not particularly interested in Neurology. Brain damage, to me, always denoted a total vegetative state. It was something kept away in hospitals, not locked up in psychiatric hospitals where the brain was noisily crazy and half-possessed but quietly put away in white-walled, serene medical hospitals where people whispered around the beds of those who had no hope of ever coming out of comas and the like. You may have a similar vague notion of the same. And as there is so little down in publication to link ECT and brain damage, we may ask ourselves what do these fascinating brain conditions even matter?

What does the experience of the *patient* matter?

Is that not the outcome of what all the research and the testing and the treatment are for? When you prepare for an emergency surgery does the surgeon talk to you thoroughly about how you're going to feel during recovery or does he tell you to count back from ten as he places the gas mask over your face? Having had a couple of major surgeries I can say that it wasn't anyone's concern about how I was going to get along afterwards; the concern was whether I was going to survive the surgery, which is as it should be in that moment.

The same seems to hold true for ECT. Once the critical period is done, patients are handed off to the next level of step down care. And this wouldn't be such a bad thing if parity was indeed enforced equally across the country so patients had adequate step-down care to begin with, and they were educated as to what to expect post-treatment, and there was actual verified knowledge available for those staff at those levels of care to spot problems to begin with.

What follows ECT is as much a testament to the shambles community mental health has always found itself in as it is to the myriad of diverse effects not spelled out plainly in patient packets or waiting room magazines that ECT patients nonetheless experience with consistency.

But what does that *feel* like? What is it like to have a functioning brain problem that exists now, in real-time consciousness, and what is it like to live on past the moment of crisis and intervention of that type of issue?

K. Rose Quayle

What does it feel like to have your thoughts irrevocably *changed*?

# How Brilliant, the Dark

*It's as if the whole world's gone dark, and you're the only who knows.*

Whereas the brain's structures are ascribed as belonging to Neurology and the mind is attributed to the world of Psychiatry, the intangible circumstance of awareness that bridges the two belongs to the realm of Neuropsychology. It is in this world that experience becomes memory; understanding becomes fact. It is also here that some semblance of a bridge may be made from the opposing nature of the brain, that which is simultaneously physical and incorporeal. And while the standards of both sides may be measured, what lies in-between them is both undiscovered country and forbidden territory. For even if we could see another's most secret thoughts, thoughts are not flat words read out in our own voices, but the nickelodeon-like culmination of all the senses. In the end, no one but ourselves alone can truly say when something has gone asunder.

In Kara L. Swanson's memoir *I'll Carry the Fork: Recovering a Life After Brain Injury*, Ms. Swanson breaks down her journey through mild traumatic brain injury after a car crash with humor but also a great deal of insight into what it's like to have an invisible disability still not well understood by modern science. Luckily she had a lot of help in the forms of therapy, a good lawyer, supportive friends and employer and the benefit of rigorous testing. Reading her story three years after my own ECT gave me a great peace that someone else knew exactly what I was going through regardless of how we both arrived at the same end.

Ms. Swanson describes the difficulty of being in a sort of diagnostic purgatory, not in the hell of severe neurological disability but not in the heaven of her former function either. It seems she is doomed as one of the "invisible" disabled; those whose limitations cannot be quantified under a microscope but are nonetheless very real and life-altering. The difference here is that while Ms. Swanson is completely correct in saying most of those outside the Neurology department have no idea what cognitive brain injury entails or its symptoms or types, in a *trauma* to the head there are doctors and therapists to aid in recovery and unquestioning lawyers ready to defend. In cognitive injury due to ECT most patients find themselves standing in silent accusation of making up symptoms from the medical community, flat-out refusal to acknowledge symptoms by doctors because "*it doesn't happen,*" and misunderstanding by family and friends who don't understand how they could exhibit such strikingly different behavior.

With so many unknowns, lawyers think twice about representing someone who, by all official reports has received perfectly safe treatment on perfectly safe equipment. With ECT-related brain problems, patients find themselves in a purgatory of one.

It often seemed afterwards that someone clinical should have noticed what my husband and I noticed at home. It seemed sometimes as if we'd awakened from a long dream only the two of us shared and we've discussed this often; the when and when not of the cognitive issues that came after treatment. I knew that there were some issues I kept from everyone such as just how severe the problem of balance had become and what I thought was causing it.

I knew there were some things I simply didn't have words to describe at the time which of course went unreported. I knew many things which had changed were things only I could measure as changed because I didn't make it my business beforehand to discuss my thought process to anyone; hence how would they know? But my husband strongly felt that those issues didn't suddenly appear once treatment was over, rather, they started during it and just didn't never stopped.

Here is where we differed fundamentally: I believed things had definitely improved all around. Not gotten back to *normal*, no, but improved from what I could internally observe.

Interestingly, five years after treatment ended I underwent neuropsychological testing because I was having new sleep and memory problems and was upset to find that during the testing I still wrestled with remembering details and following directions. Which I knew was an issue, of course, but doing so in front of a trained professional was just humiliating.

I felt stupid and in trouble as if I were a child when the clinic asked my husband to come in with me to speak with the doctor. In this type of testing, this is often done so the doctor can get a balanced report of anything a person with memory problems may unintentionally be leaving out or be unable to observe themselves. But routine or not, I dreaded being labeled as a complete idiot on paper, no matter how intelligent otherwise I may be. What seemed like being called in on the carpet turned out to be very informative and the doctor put to words what I had struggled with and struggled to explain for five years: I was having trouble with *steps*.

He also assured me my IQ was still in the gifted range; many brain injuries leave intellect intact. On paper, I wasn't an idiot. But I was also deemed disabled. So, now I felt like a complete fraud. Smart, but not *able*.

My husband wanted to know how I felt about it. "*Stupid!*" I bellowed and he assured, "*You know that's not true. He just told you that's not true!*"

Yet nothing made me feel better. I knew how my mind had changed. Now others had a much better insight into what I didn't have words for and it felt worse. Before ECT I wasn't the type of person who avoided doctors in the hope that if I didn't think about it, it would go away.

After? I watched silently as I did just that; unable to force my own hand to pick up a phone and call; unable to find the words to describe what the problem was. *Steps.* Oh yes, I hated directions. *Just show me what to do!*

As I'd noted after treatment was switched to bilateral:

*Trouble recalling steps- what to do after putting soap on washcloth, etc. Unable to remember which (face) cream I used. Sat for a while unsure if I was done.*

There are many tasks we find ourselves doing every day which require the brain to do things in steps. While your brain is determining what the next step in a task should be, it's reviewing the steps you've already completed while keeping track of what you're doing in the present. This is easily observed when following a recipe; something that people with certain types of brain injuries find daunting. While reading and following a recipe, there are several processes going on at once: recognizing word forms and interpreting these as directions, determining what step goes first, physically carrying out the steps, and so on. With a brain injury any or all of these tasks can be jeopardized, making it difficult to move from one step to another without repeating some of the work or getting lost altogether.

In the writing of this book the greatest challenge I met beyond research or figuring out what to say was simply structuring the chapters and formatting the text and bibliography on computer. Figuring out what order the sections of the text naturally fell into was nothing short of a nightmare and I completely tore apart and rearranged everything several times before settling into the uneasy compromise of what you see here. I realized it wasn't going to seem natural to me no matter what I did; that's just how my brain works now.

Kara Swanson also noted the exhaustion that accompanied trying to figure out what came next in a sequence, the giving up in the middle of a familiar task because it was so daunting to have to consciously choose to perform the unsung tasks that make up the brain's silent repertoire. The frustration that strikes me as I realize I've forgotten the first ingredient in a familiar recipe by the time I get to the fourth is one I cannot describe.

With the exception of one grandfather, my grandparents and great-grandparents were blessed with cognitive clarity right to the end of their lives so I lived in dread of the great unknown of losing my faculties as I aged. But after ECT I began to feel a sort of uneasy peace about the future as if I'd seen a reflection of my self years ahead of time. Struggling with the tasks I'd mastered in childhood and becoming resigned against my supreme stubbornness to learn how to ask for help gave me some small comfort that when the day came, I would have one less battle against myself to fight.

*Which way is this way?*

I was very fortunate that necessity had made me independent as a child and I was taught early enough to cook that though following a recipe had become an exercise in futility, I knew the basics of cooking and how to fix a recipe if it went really awry. Likewise, I had been taught wayfinding by my grandfather so once signs and directions became an opaque soup of confusions, I knew when to stop and what to do to get to a point I could safely get to the next step to get back. So though there were many new challenges, I had my old memories and a good base to start to get back up on.

One of the biggest stumbling blocks I encountered over and over again was an ill-defined perimeter and a lack of language, and this continued to be a problem no matter what the occasion or whom I was facing challenges with. Simply, at first I didn't know what was wrong, then I didn't know how much was wrong, and then I didn't know how to describe what was wrong.

Language. *What a trial.*

Previous to that disastrous episode of Depression that landed me at ECT's doorstep, I had worked with small children in a day-school. These were toddlers, all under age three and not only in the trials of potty-training but that devastatingly emotional time of life predating adolescence when everything is unbearably monumental but the ability to recount it, severely limited.

No wonder toddlers scream a lot; they're perpetual forty year-olds with the language grasp of puppies.

I would be asked how I was feeling, what was wrong, how was I progressing? And I could not pull the descriptors together to give anything close to an actual portrayal so I fell back to the all-American *fine*. Every doctor I saw must have thought me a pathological liar from the door. Even to those who knew me well and knew something wasn't right I stuck to that mainstay because combing through feelings and thoughts and sensations was like being a cork buffeted on ocean waves. I had no traction, nothing to hold on to; no direction.

I cried. I flapped my hands, a childhood gesture that came to prominence again in adulthood during times of extreme frustration. I whined. When the children threw out this sort of behavior, we told them to use their words. This became a mantra in my house. *Use your words.* The problem was, I had lost them.

Though I was often thought of as shy in public growing up, I had a very silly side and did not have trouble thinking of what to say or write. Being made to continually endure my dad's ridiculous but brilliant spoofs on every television theme tune gave me lots of material to regurgitate if I couldn't come up with my own. For the first time in my life I found myself struggling with both.

I came out into the world an early developer. From growing teeth to speaking, to reading and writing, to height and puberty, I seemed to constantly be on schedule two years ahead of my age group. Intellectually, I had some help in this. My parents didn't speak in baby talk to me to begin with and my mother always explained words to me, even the expletives.

I spent a lot of time as a young child with my WWII-veteran grandfather who watched as much Charlie's Angels, John Wayne and the ten o'clock news as he did The Three Stooges, Tom and Jerry and Looney Tunes. And because I spent a good deal of time on my own during my elementary school years, I immersed myself in books of all sorts I lugged home in huge piles from the library in the next town, subsequently spending most of my allowance in their late fees. It was before the internet and I was growing brain cells as fast as I possibly could by speaking, listening, watching and reading. And yes, I loved reading the dictionary.

*Words fascinated me.*

Before I learned to read I was extremely good at memorizing and reciting and I would repeat words to myself just to hear the sound of them and tell stories to other children I was babysat with. My mother sometimes wrote my little poems and such down, though these are now lost forever but as I grew I would take to writing poetry, songs and stories as it was very easy and self-entertaining.

After learning the basics of reading I began to notice that words had a particular weight in my mind, and while the trend of spelling children's names in myriad ways to make them look different on birth certificates annoyed the devil out of the grown folk around me, it enchanted me because each tiny letter change, even written in different handwriting, made an entirely new word with new weight and sound and shape. Poor spelling, however, simply pissed me off like nothing else. I was an excellent speller and felt how very dare someone pare down a precious word, taking away its weight and worth by garbling it?

*How very dare!*

So I used my words all the time. Not being able to find them to use them was a loss unlike that I could have been prepared for. I felt stupid, cumbersome, slow. And that was the annoying part. The treacherous part lied in not being able to describe what was mentally going on for me inside. Perhaps it wouldn't have been such an uphill battle if I had known how to say what had changed.

Losing words wasn't the only language headache. Speaking them had its own unique pitfalls for quite some time.

I had never stuttered previous to ECT but it came out after bilateral both in speaking and reading aloud. Inwardly, it felt like my mind and mouth were out of sync as it had in my head alone when my memories returned; as if my mouth was way ahead of my mind in terms of what we were going to say. If you've ever watched a streaming program online and there's even the tiniest lag in audio you know the compulsion to stop and restart the program to allow it to catch up; it's just irresistible. The red-hot frustration that accompanies when it has the audacity to do it *again* is just as predictable.

Our brains are hard-wired to notice the most subtle of changes in this manner to root out what's true and what's fabricated. These tiny differences seem, in the big picture, not to matter. After all, we're still seeing the show. But they niggle at us in a way that recalls our evolutionary past. *"Something's wrong!"* our cognitive processes scream. *"This is danger!"* And suddenly, our muscles are irrationally poised to pick up the computer and throw it if we can't get the audio working.

Within me, this odd match-off came out in strange ways. For example, attempting to pronounce new words before I'd thought them through resulted in every word starting with a long, snake-like *sssss* as I puzzled it out. This was not a conscious effort, rather it seemed my mouth had its own ideas on how to speak and would chug along fine without me, thank you very much.

As a child, I didn't lisp or stammer or find things difficult to pronounce. On the contrary, if I could visualize the word in my mind, my mouth followed suit, even sans-front teeth or with heavy-duty braces. So, imagine my surprise when I began to lightly lisp and stumble on the *l* and *r* sounds. My tongue seemed to have become too large for my mouth; too unruly and uncoordinated to wrap around such words as our dog's name, *Orry* or my least favorite candy, *lollipops*.

Words over two syllables sometimes came out in novel ways and my husband would slow down and pronounce so I could try and mimic him until I'd get much too disenchanted with his bemusement and end it with a much shorter alternative.

*"We can't waste time in the store, remember there are rel–igables in the car."*

*"What?"*

*"Rul–ig…"*

*"What are in the car?"*

*"El-iga-bles."*

*"I didn't catch that. It's a what?"*

*"Elergables. Efligables. Reregabals! Cheese."*

*"Look at me: Re-fridge-er-a-bles."*

And this was from me, a former nine-year-old who would read her mother's nursing textbooks aloud on car trips so mother didn't get car sick trying to study! Given my love affair with verbiage, it's not surprising that I was one of those little know-it-alls who found joy in pointing out the incorrect usage of such meme-worthy grammar gaffes as *their/there/they're* and *you're* versus. *your*. While the adults around me seemed often surprised by my vocabulary, I knew the truth was far more mundane. I didn't know mass troves of words; I was simply clever at being able to suss out the meanings of large words by their context in a sentence.

If you've ever woken up from anesthesia or a particularly hard nap, you've probably felt the tongue-tied effects of a sleepy brain trying to put syllables together with thoughts. After the rounds of shock therapy were over it often felt like those first few minutes of post-anesthesia had become permanent. Putting words together was just that, putting them consciously together like stepping stones across what was formerly a continual and effortless stream. Writing, as well, became an exercise in tedium.

When my words began to break down, so did my spirit. Something happened between my mind and my spoken words, my mind and reading, and the vibrant lives and stories that words had always told to me. They no longer spoke. Their voices silenced into whispers so slight I could no longer hear them above a faint sigh. My world became silent; the sound sucked out of it like a vacuum. That's not to say I *couldn't* speak at all or write at all. No, *I* hadn't been silenced. Only, despairingly, my network to the world had been diminished.

During ECT before treatment had switched to bilateral I noted the blurring of thoughts and the lengthening of time it took to find the right words and

K. Rose Quayle

express them. At some point near the end of bilateral I began to mispronounce words more often, mixing prefixes with suffixes and concocting altogether new words with bits of unlike terms. Alphabet soup, in a sense. *Po-tay-toh, po-tah-toh*, squash.

My speech arranged itself into a strange pattern which eventually evolved to what it is now: more or less normal with a few idiosyncrasies thrown in for good measure. For some months after I had a difficult time discerning direction and this showed even in my speech with directional words as well as other descriptors. I mixed up sensory words, substituting *see* with *hear* and *hear* with the "see" which we take to mean to *understand* or *know*. To me, hearing and seeing and knowing were all the same sense to be used interchangeably and this caused a lot of confusion for other people listening to me.

*"Don't ignore me!"* He reached over to touch my arm. *"I asked you what you wanted me to order you?"*

Pulling back, I scowled and slapped the menu down in frustration. *"I don't know."*

*"You don't know? You've been looking at it for ten minutes now!"*

*"I can't see it!"* Meaning, I can't *understand* this.

The word *know* as in something already learned came off to me as the action *remember*. So I would become very emphatic that I *knew* while my husband would puzzle out how I could possibly know when he'd just told me, but I was conveying that I remembered him telling me the same fact in another time; I had a static memory of this I could see in my mind. The original incident could have happened the day before or the decade before. Or it may be that I was remembering right there at the time he had just the moment before mentioned this fact and there was no past tense at all to it. In my muddled brain time was diffuse, yet confined.

I had a poor distinction in speech between *before, now* or *to be*. It all ran together and when I'm stressed things merge just as easily with my snags being *this/ these, this/that, here/ there,* and *where/ what.* There were particular sounds I found quite tricky; those that children often mix up in elementary school. *Ch* and *tr* melted together to make a sort of *tchhhh* sound. *Gr* and *dr* and *tr* formed some new and awkward consonant. *B, p, br, pr, pl, pr, sh, ch* pushed each other noisily out of the way to make room for themselves in my mouth. *D* replaced *th, c* with *t, r* with *l.*

The issue with doing things in steps had its own unique spin that showed up in speech as well: parsing out asking a question required thinking of what I wanted to ask and formulating the spoken words. It took me about three years to recognize that I wasn't asking *"May I ask a question"* I was asking, *"May I have a question?"* And asking a question or explaining something I had recently learned or was not altogether familiar with took on an awkward dance that continues today. I find myself repeating *"this" (dis)* as I try to form the words and hear the thoughts. It's akin to juggling for the first time.

We'd both reached the remote at the same time and he snatched it up first.

*"Gimme!"* I whined uncharacteristically like a toddler but he held it out of reach.

*"What do you say?"* He prompted and raised his eyebrows.

*"Can I have'd it?"*

If I was interrupted during speaking everything went back to square one. Sometimes I forgot and found my thoughts later (which could be in a minute, a quarter of an hour or later on in the day) or my thoughts got completely turned around. Or I just, *forgot.*

*"Can we... can we, I was going to ask you..."*

*"Yes?"*

*""Um, can we... see, dis here* (pointing to a box of cereal), *if we went and...-"*

*"Spit it out..."*

*"Can— nevermind. I lost it... yeah it gone."*

*"Okay."*

Twenty minutes later: *"Ah hah! Can we go to the store? We need milk."*

I wasn't a person who ever relished apologizing or was natural at it and indeed, I cringe when someone says *"I apologize"* in customer service the same way my Manx and French relatives cringe when they hear the American *"have a nice day."* It is the height of insincerity and at times, an out-right lie. To apologize is to mollify; not to feel grief over your actions. Growing up, I was taught not to say sorry unless I actually was, else others would know that on top of erring, I was also lying about it to look better.

However, after ECT I found myself apologizing often. I was aware my speech wasn't correct, maddeningly so, and as such I felt continually in the wrong for always bothering someone to help or taking up time to ask a question or forgetting to mention the milk before we leave the store. I was angry most of the time with others for being angry and impatient with me. After all, if they'd had patience and let me think things out, misunderstandings wouldn't happen. If they let me find my words rather than tap their feet and distract me, we would have cereal *and* milk during the same trip. If questions were encouraged and not met with eye rolling and audible sighs, I might know the first time around I wasn't doing something right.

But nobody gets very far with a case of the *if onlys*, so I betrayed myself and learned to apologize in order to get quickly to where I needed to be. Only much, much later would I work on my own viewpoint and realize that no, it wasn't my fault but yes, others are valid in their feelings as well. I learned to say sorry and mean it: *"I'm sorry, I couldn't figure it out. We don't need milk right now We can go tomorrow if that's all right."*

If spoken language was a chore that must be practiced over and over, reading it seemed an unending task that started with one of my favorite book series as a child: the *Little House* books by Laura Ingalls Wilder. During ECT I began to find it harder and harder to concentrate on reading even in short magazine articles and experienced no small amount of stress over it. Subsequently I was put in partial hospitalization to finish treatment as an outpatient and it was there that the first actual reading issues started to come out.

The hospital I was in used DBT (Dialectical Behavioral Therapy) skills training and we were given printed sheets from the *DBT Skills Training Manual* by Marsha Linehan. I had previously been in DBT groups multiple times before and frankly didn't think it did too much so I was quite familiar with the material. But I began to have trouble reading the pages.

It was almost imperceptible at first, but it seemed I wasn't reading all the words printed, much like I might not if I was extremely tired. I didn't think to mention it to anyone because it made sense during treatment that these things would settle down and be done with. And anyway, no one knew anything for sure, nor did I know what was actually wrong, so why even ask?

Nonetheless, ignoring things didn't make them get easier. Near the end of treatment, I found I was unable to read anything in a grid or table of sorts. Following the timetable for the bus with my eyes, reading insurance forms, looking at a checque book, reading a grocery receipt; all of these everyday things were suddenly difficult. After treatment ended I discovered that somehow the left side of the page had become blurred in a sense. I could see there was printing there; I knew I was seeing words. But I had to concentrate very hard to pick up what was there. For someone who had been asked at six years old to help teach the children in remedial reading, it was far more frustrating than frightening to have to sound it out. It became a matter of course to launch my books across the room in complete resentment.

I wasn't sure if I wasn't seeing accurately (which didn't make sense, because I could see my own face on the left, the left sides of doorways and objects) or paying enough attention or losing touch with reality. I put down books and picked up photo-heavy magazines. Strangely, the right half of the page began fading and bizarrely, eventually my field of vision sort of narrowed to the midsection. This seemed not to do with peripheral vision, just with actually comprehending what was written there. But like my memories, which returned from so long ago in the beginning of treatment to eventually catch up with themselves, so my reading did as well.

I began with the Little House books, of which I had a beautiful anniversary printing of. I've always enjoyed those stories so sitting down with them again was a treat during my recovery. Reading them for very long, though, was nothing but frustration. The hours and hours spent with my best friend as kids perusing the naughty bits in her mother's Harlequin paperbacks were a dim, glorious memory now crowded out by hours of slogging through large print chapters in a child's book. I was so ashamed. I could understand the words in adult books. I had no *vocabulary* loss, and that didn't hold me back in writing words at all. But it seemed to take too long to read in my head.

Where there were many words, my brain seemed to skip over things. It didn't create its own visuals anymore as I read, which had always been the charm of reading to begin with. Now, it was simply taxing to match meaning to word, and this made everything flat and tedious and *meaningless*. A big fan of carefully constructed literary worlds such as in *Harry Potter*, *The Tales of Ulm*, *A Wrinkle in Time* and the *Neverending Story*, I now preferred films over books. I simply couldn't revisit those worlds from the page anymore.

A gate had swung closed; a shade had been drawn. How was I going to get back to Camazotz, or Hogwarts, or Fantastica? How would I find Windy Mountain? It was more a practical problem than anything that pulled me out of mild self-pity to work on befriending books again: I was having trouble reading the Bible. While the format of the Bible is now easier for me to read than most texts because of its narrow, stanza-like printing, the small print and Old English did nothing at the time to help me stay on the correct line and progress to the end of a chapter.

Many people are attached to a particular translation of the Bible and while my husband spent his growing-up years learning the modern Message version, it was all Greek to me. My grandparents had brought me up in the King James Version, and this was the formal language of prayer used in our house. To be tripped up by *thee*s and *thou*s as a grown adult was unacceptable to me.

When I picked up Little House it was to practice, to become more and more familiar with reading left to right and reading longer and longer passages so I could catch up on what was never as much Bible reading as I'd like to say I'd done to begin with. I read the whole series of Little House, went on to the Wrinkle in Time Trilogy and on occasion, back to younger children's chapter books on the bus to and from work as needed when I became exhausted. As time wore on I found that reading online was far less productive than it had been in the past primarily because there was just too much else on the screen to sort through. Offline, I progressed to Amy Tan's works and found these took me a bit longer but were well worth the time and over the course of a year I got through *Pride and Prejudice* (and was nothing but pleased I'd finally read something by Jane Austin) and then *The Neverending Story*. Which does, in fact, end.

It was then that I felt it was time to start researching for this book. And there were tears, tossed books, torn up papers and ripped up notebooks but slowly, it got done. Early on in the research process, however, my husband and I discovered the bad business of reading had taken another weird turn. At some point I'd tried to share some information with him and discovered quite by accident that I'd somehow stumbled off the skill of reading aloud, which I hadn't had any occasion to do in who knew when.

We were baffled. The speaking issues I'd started off with picked right back up again when I was reading to someone else. As I spoke my eyes would roam the page unbidden, picking up word bits and putting them together, running sentences on as if there were no punctuation or mashing up sentences from various lines. I would add words in which weren't even printed on the page, stutter, add extra syllables to words and trip up mightily on words with *l* sounds.

I was much better with speaking, I was fine reading to myself. Putting the two together was not so fine.

If I was embarrassed before, nothing compared with the sheer panic I felt at ever having to read something aloud at *work*. For the most part I didn't and wouldn't need to present anything to anyone so it was largely an unfounded fear. At home, my husband and I began practicing in the evenings. As he would work on web design on his laptop at the other end of the couch, I'd read aloud from a library book with the dog at the other end.

Sheer exhaustion often kept me from going on very long. It was strangely depleting to both read and speak at the same time, something neither of us understood but my husband could always tell when I needed to break. I found that for short things such as a list of trivia facts I had to come up with on occasion for work, if I read these aloud to myself over and over during the ride to work I still became very tired but was able to get through it none too shabby in front of others by rote memorization and rest unnoticed at my desk.

When my job and bus route changed, I no longer had the time to read ahead during the ride and asked my new supervisor to read for me. She was gracious and did so. Meanwhile in her office, my therapist patiently encouraged me to slow down and try again while reading through notes for this book. But outside of this small sphere I was most reluctant to let anyone hear my voice in that manner. Only the computer help desk employees who had to ask me to read out screen errors thought I was taking the mickey with them and I was tempted to let them.

*"One headache please, hold the coffee,"* I laughed as we approached Starbucks.

*"Try getting that in decaf,"* my husband smiled.

*"It's in the secret menu."*

The look of panic on the barista's face when I got to the counter and clearly had no idea what I wanted with fifty college kids clambering behind me was matched only by their ever-growing agitation and my total frustration at not being able to read from one menu board to another as well as formulate the order. "*I'm good*," became my usual answer as I slipped back out the door without coffee. I walked out of quite a few sushi bars for the same reason.

Menus were one more piece of printed material to hurl but they didn't have the same weight to produce the same satisfying *thwack* of a book's spine. Learning to load an order on my phone and show it to the waiter solved this situation, though my husband always felt it was cheating. This multi-tasking dilemma spilled over into another point of contention: space.

Reading maps and bus schedules shouldn't have been too daunting given that there aren't a vast amount of words to be dealt with but they're both very spatial. Likewise, formulating a grocery list and finding the items in a store is both a task that requires one to internally figure out where in the store something is and go to get it, preferably in the order it's laid out in rather than going back and forth until you hunt down every single thing.

No matter how I tried to accomplish this, I ended up doing the latter and found myself in a couple of different predicaments: I would get lost, I would pitch a fit in the middle of the store in exhaustion, I would cry, I would walk out and leave it all behind. When our local chain-store grocer remodeled, I took this as a blatant act of war. Picking out something in a display of, say, salad dressings, would begin as a nuisance and progress quickly to a tear-producing situation my husband would do just about anything to avoid. He became my shopping chaperone, an activity neither one of us relished and one I fought him on pretty often. It was because of my chagrin at having to be tagged along with that I figured out how to pace out looking at a circular (a chore that gave me particular anxiety), collecting coupons and making a list to make the actual shopping run as short as possible. I'll never be a coupon mom of any sorts but I'm now pretty good at saving a buck, which I was terrible at before ECT.

The other problem I would find in stores, malls or new places was the overwhelming feeling of "darkness." There was so much visually going on that

K. Rose Quayle

my mind would somehow darken, as a computer screen does when going into power-saving mode. I would be unable to pick out anything in particular, and like with reading aloud, the exhaustion at trying to find something to visually hold on to didn't exactly encourage me to try. It took some time to decipher ways to find something to focus on to keep the lights on. But I was so driven to be once again regarded as independent, adult and competent I found myself surprised at and resigned to my willingness to try just about anything.

# Singing Stories, Chasing Sound

WHOSE decision it was to end treatment first remains up in the air, as all parties weren't in one place at the same time most of the time to even discuss such a decision.

My husband had his misgivings all along and wanted it stopped early in. My therapist had concerns before treatment started. My notes indicate I wasn't keen on continuing but didn't ask formally for it to be stopped. My hospital outpatient record notes that I didn't "show up" for treatment at some point so it was discontinued but other treatment team notes indicate they had decided I was at a plateau and needed to be put back on medication. It always seemed odd to me that I was put back on the same medications deemed ineffective when the whole process started, not in regard to the medications themselves but because of the dosages. One can't simply begin full-tilt on anti-seizure medications without some serious side effects; this is why it takes so long to get to a therapeutic dose on psychiatric medications to begin with.

*The sweet stink of spring...*

These concerns notwithstanding, I began to encounter some of the physical effects that are thought of as classically neurological during this time of transitioning off of ECT, each bringing its own unique distress.

On and off I would smell a horrible odor in the house, something so putrid at first I thought the sewer was backing up. My senses have absolutely no tolerance for stinky stuff so I began a one-woman campaign to root out the cause and sterilize the hell out of it. The pipes checked out, the garbage was cleared, drains all ok, no piles of rotting laundry or shower scum or wet stuff to be found and nothing lying about dead. I naturally blamed the animals.

One animal, in fact, who had become irate that we'd picked up and moved to a new house. I knew cats were territorial but the fit this one pitched could only be called epic. She must be peeing somewhere and sure enough, we caught her at it at one point but the scent was much different than what I was smelling. I bought an immense amount of enzyme cleaner and bombed the carpet with it; purchased one of those Feliway dispensers to calm the little beast and lived with the windows open in spring to air out the house. And that would have done the trick if it had been the cat.

I had no other logical explanation than the cat so I turned back to the cat. Again, cleaned, aired and dried the house. The smell came back. Begged the cat to stop. The smell came back. For the first time in my life of living with many animals I threatened with aplomb that we would take her right back to the shelter and I meant it, so bothered by this scent was I.

The thing was, nobody else smelled it.

I had my husband sniffing carpets and linens trying to get him to corroborate my findings but to no avail. Soon I began to believe it was me who smelled and I upped my hygiene game, dousing myself in cheap perfume wherever I went until the headaches I gave myself convinced me to take it to the doctor. The verdict? While she probably thought I was gone away with the fairies, I was treated for an infection I didn't have, just to be on the safe side. I didn't mention the sharp metallic taste in my mouth which had me pulling back my lips in the car mirror and in windows to check for the blood I thought must be there. No. I was not at all going to a dentist no matter how bad things may taste.

And that might have been the end of it had I not taken a walk down to the church one day that spring and come back running, my nose full of a pong that put the French Quarter in mid-August to shame. I rushed into the house and happily exclaimed, "*I can smell them! I can smell the stinky trees!*"

The high street where we lived was lined with trees the local residents referred to as the "stinky trees." My husband complained of them one day on a walk some years previous and we argued over whether the smell came from the trees or not. For whatever reason the town had planted the things and one could not get through May without hearing the colorful depiction of their rotting perfume from shoppers and schoolchildren, church-goers and business owners. What did they smell like? *"Like crap." "Like dog-doo." "Like something died."* I absolutely could not smell them and was probably the only person in town who couldn't. *"Maybe I can actually smell them, they just don't smell like something bad to me?"* I suggested but was met with an extremely dubious look from my husband. *"Well I guess if you like the smell of manure."*

Still, we bantered back and forth about the possibility of cultural conditioning. Being both from a different country, we had seen many times that what seems delicious to one group of people can, in another culture be just as obviously revolting or likewise, a lullaby sweet to one child's ears may be nothing but shouting to another's. Perhaps the trees' scent was close to something else that wasn't considered to be offensive in my home frame of reference. If that was the case, then things were about to get shaken up because that spring I suddenly smelled those trees and no joshing, it was like some ancient ritual involving a rotting carcass had taken place along the sidewalks of Main Street. I marveled at how anyone could have stood standing near one of them long enough to plant them in the first place. Had something changed in me? In my perception? No-one knew, but as soon as I began to smell the stinky trees, the phantom smell of death that kept following me began to fade.

*Say it again, in American...*

From early on after treatment ended, I experienced a ringing in my ears that raised and lowered without much rhyme or reason and I was none too sorry to say goodbye to that when it finally faded. It began as a sort of high, continuous tone and then flattened out to something not unlike the flat song of cicadas in high summer. Mostly just a real annoyance when watching television at night, it happened less and less often over time until finally becoming silent. But while my hearing itself hadn't changed that I could ascertain, my perception of sound had.

As a child I was surrounded by music. My parents always had on a radio in the car or the stereo record player in the house. We took five-hour long trips to drive to my grandparents' and always sang all the way; usually whatever music the absent parent detested. My mother, a gifted songstress and pianist, was the choir director for our church but also played for several small country churches who could not employ a regular organist so she practiced on our antique upright nearly every day. Teaching *me* to play was an unsuccessful campaign she waged for years.

While I was an enthusiastic car stereo tuner, being dragged around to sing in children's choirs and entertain myself during the adults' practice session ranked well on the bottom of things I felt should be on my agenda. But my mother did manage to teach me to harmonize to her soprano with my alto and I picked it up quite well. I wasn't keen at all on being an alto; it was far more desirable to have a clear soprano voice in school and be picked for a solo. I didn't even need to bother feeling sorry for myself; the music world had pronounced its judgment on altos everywhere before I was even born. Everybody knew altos never did solos because no such things were written for them.

When my voice did eventually deepen to a more steady alto and I began to use it enough to stretch it out a bit I discovered in crooning along with Wilson Phillips (badly) in the '90s that the harmony was much more important than I'd once thought. Without harmony music sounded thin and gaunt. It became flat. I had found my calling as backup singer. Too bad I hadn't ever learned to read notes during all that time on a piano.

Career ambitions dashed, I still had learned to "hear" harmony and was able to sing in choir as an adult by listening to the soprano line and memorizing my own part. And once you learned to hear, you never forgot. They say that about riding a bike too but you know how that goes.

After ECT I didn't forget how to harmonize, thank goodness, but a curious thing happened in that I could no longer sing the melody line without great concentration and then not for very long. This had nothing to with my scratchy high notes, but more to do with being unable to pick out the original song. Strangely frustrating, this wasn't a tragedy as I wasn't scheduled to perform at the Met or anything, but this sort of sound-astigmatism affected me in odd little ways.

Because my parents are very musically talented people and I grew up surrounded by many different genres, I was, like my father, able to identify a huge litany of songs by their first few notes with dead-on accuracy and it only took me one or two listens to memorize song lyrics. And not that this was anything that ever came in use for on a job, but it was something I had in common with my parents and was important in that fact; I was born the visual artist with no-one else to identify with.

Losing this ability affected me more than I could have predicted because it was indeed that one ability I identified in common with my father whom I'd grown up away from. As a teen, I obsessed over little things like being the only brown-eyed one on that side so any little resemblance like the way I stood with my arms sligLhtly out and this memory for music gained all the more importance to me. These things validated that I belonged to my blood family.

The really strange thing about this was that after ECT I found myself often in a bad mood in the car as we listened to the radio. I didn't feel singing along was a skill anyone had to work at so forgetting lyrics was a particular blow and forgetting what song I was listening to halfway in spelled *idiocy* to me. The only consolation with this was that somehow when I sang with a choir I could still pick up harmony by listening to it over and over with other people and in singing, I didn't seem to have the problems with cadence I did reading aloud by myself.

Strangely, my discernment of accents in others seemed to have diminished as well at that point. My husband is from the Isle of Man and it had taken a few years to "adjust my ears" to his mild dialect after we married and particularly the stronger one of my father-in-law and once I had, I found I rarely heard his accent afterwards, though people often pointed it out and tried to guess his country of origin. We watched about 90% mainland British shows on television and though I could never pinpoint where a person was from in that area with any candle to the dead-on accuracy he could, I no longer felt that tiny lag as my mind caught up with what I was hearing. English speaking had become simultaneous with my own American thinking.

We noticed it one night watching *Only Fools and Horses* when my husband remarked I must be in a bad mood because I wasn't laughing. Confused, I said to him that I couldn't understand what they were saying. He looked more than slightly put out because this was one of his favorite shows but didn't say much. The next time we tuned in I caught myself squinting at the screen trying to follow along, as if narrowing my eyes would help me hear better and in turn, understand better. Again, I watched along without so much as a chuckle. It took me simply too long to listen and interpret. The strong English accent reverted from being the second mode of pronunciation it had become to an unintelligible foreign accent. I no longer spoke with my father-in-law on the phone; I was too ashamed at not being able to "hear" him without seeing him.

*Arise, take up thy boots and walk ...*

At times I would be listening to someone speak but would be unable to respond; it was as if I suddenly had no comprehension of what was being said to me. My head would nod seemingly of its own accord or shake from side to side in a manner suggestive of trying to knock something loose from the ears and I'd become aware I was rocking slightly, forward and back again. Coincidentally, back during unilateral treatment, I had been writing about an "electric marble" in my head:

*Dizziness back full force, feels like I have little shock waves going through my head at the base of my skull and on the right side of my head. Actually it feels like my head is a cardboard box and a little child is swaying an electric marble back and forth (in it)- when it hits the box sides it gives off a little 'spark'. That's the best I can describe it.*

*It started off across the back of my head back and forth, back and forth from ear to ear. Then it shot up to my forehead, back and forth, back and forth between my eyes, then over to the right side of my head and kept on that path for hours. It was painful but not unbearable.*

*Still having little 'zings' in my head.... I feel like spring has begun to infest my brain.*

But after ECT ended, the little marble ricocheted through my head for another few months. All of these symptoms didn't occur constantly but more in bursts or fits of sorts. I can't imagine what it must have looked like and I certainly avoided leaving the house unless necessary to dodge being seen.

Involuntarily shaking my head vigorously made me feel like a nervous horse and rocking felt somewhat comforting but I completely drew the line when my eyes began to dart back and forth spastically. That sort of thing just was not at all conducive to reading and the nausea I felt from the world shaking before my eyes didn't lend too much to anything either.

Drawing that line internally was essential to movement. If I let myself get too overwhelmed I'd literally become bogged down and just stop where I was. I had a large fear from earlier in my life of not being able to move freely as I watched my mother wrestle with Psoriatic Inflammatory Arthritis and lose her freedom to walk and consequently, work as a nurse. Anything that kept me still for too long made me nervous, so I was all too keen to get up and walk around freely.

During the first year after ECT I had a great deal of problems with balance which certainly interfered with my independence.

I had always been a somewhat clumsy individual to begin with. A child covered in little scrapes and bruises much of the time, no one could have called me *Grace* by any stretch. Now, when my muscles weren't weakening into melted into gobs of jelly so that I flopped right over to the floor trying to get out of bed, my entire sense of my feet relative to the ground shifted so far I wasn't sure where to put them. Wrestling with myself to put one foot in front of the other was one thing, and coordinating that movement with staying upright and moving forward yet another. If I hadn't had previous bouts of weakness in the legs on anti-seizure medications such as Tegratol, I'm sure I would have been much more worried. Those effects were never high on my list of such to be desired, but they weren't the worst things to have happened either.

The thing that scared me most of all and stunned me into a total silence from any doctor or my husband, was that I couldn't *see* below me.

My side-to-side peripheral vision was ok. I did seek out an eye doctor under the pretense to get some new long-distance glasses and was told my vision was unchanged but a new pair of unscratched glasses could still be got. But still the thought of something being wrong somehow with my eyes absolutely kept me quiet. I fell, stumbled, and even hit the pavement so hard I knocked a kidney stone loose (which had to be surgically removed) but still I said nothing about not being able to see below. Where there had been ground and grass and the outline of my toes, was now the odd fading that had happened in the same way as the left side of a printed page. I knew something was there, but I couldn't make it out. Something in me was scared to death of going blind and even after sorting out that the reason I wasn't walking well was that I couldn't see where I was putting my feet, I would not talk. I would have to figure something else out. The simple and immediate solution was to look straight down to walk. This did work, of course, but was highly impractical when walking near, say, trees or poles or signs. Ouch.

By chance, the *something else* presented itself. I'd bought a pair of winter fashion boots, something I never did because I'd been raised by hard working and practical people who made me wear duck boots until I got old enough to see the value in them and stop being embarrassed by them. Well, my fashion boots did what I'd always been warned about- they pulled apart from their pretty soles as I was treading in the snow and when my husband picked me up from work later that evening, I demanded we go to the twenty- four hour Wal-Mart and buy a pair of snow boots so my feet could warm up. It was after eleven pm when we arrived and there were no women's boots on the shelves but I was not leaving the store without something warm. We walked out with an oversized pair of men's steel-toed work boots I had to double lace around my ankles to keep on but they did one vital and unsuspecting thing: they weighted my feet down so that I learned the feel of stepping down hard enough to regain my balance.

In fact it was being thrown off by the weight that caused me to step down harder where I couldn't quite see and lose my constant fear of falling. Being afraid to fall is a pretty common fear but it reached abnormal heights for me after my ankles gave way twice while walking and down I went. Stepping lightly not only helped me feel like I wasn't going to collapse, it kept me from getting anywhere very quickly. With my new boots, I tromped and stomped 2-3 miles a day to and from bus stops to practice walking. It may not have been the smartest move but taking the alleys in low light helped because the footing was uneven and I shuffled, being unable to perceive how high my legs were picking up. I couldn't use my eyes to cheat; my legs and feet had to get the feel of stepping down hard on their own.

I waddled like a toddler with my arms out to the sides, stood almost bow-legged and picked my feet up way too high at first. This was a total failure on stairs where determining the height of the stairs and how high up I needed to step made every trip up or down fraught with the possibility of banging kneecaps or breaking my pride. Any type of stair with a tread on it made things all the worse. A darker tread seemed closer to me and I stepped higher, often missing a stair going up but not quite catching the next one. A lighter tread screwed me up going down for the same reason but the lighter it was, the more dizzy I became. My husband soon had me either holding onto his arm like an old widow or onto his hand like a young child.

It was only time and practice that sorted out walking. Full of falls, stumbles and headlongs, it only got truly better when the sand covering my vision started to wash away. You couldn't call me a ballerina now, but I stay on my two feet. Most of the time.

*Just give 'em the finger, kid…*

One of the more upsetting effects involving coordination had to do with my hands. It seemed that many of the after effects were only truly noticeable when I was bumping up against them. Of course I didn't notice the wobbliness of my legs until I tried to go anywhere. I didn't realize I wasn't able to decipher accents until we turned on a show. Nothing would have told me my taste had changed until I tried plopping a favorite old food into my mouth just to spit it back out. That is, like I didn't know what I didn't know with memory loss, I didn't know anything was different until I tried it out.

But sitting quietly, minding my own business accomplished its own problems. Without relationship to anything else, it seemed were the contractions in my hands. These conspicuously random spasms would cause my fingers and wrists to curl inward at rest, causing me to truly feel freakish. I sat on my hands when they misbehaved, probably inadvertently drawing more attention to myself but at the time hiding them appeared the only tolerable thing to do.

I've never had beautiful penmanship. I'm a function over form man in that regard. I was decent at calligraphy as a teen but calligraphy uses more motion in the wrists than the fingers. Writing heavily employs the movement of the fingers; drawing combines both. In high school I had an art teacher who looked well on me and gave me extra lessons on the side. Imagine my disappointment when I was given a pencil and told to draw circles, and only circles, by swinging my arm round and round at the elbow. Over and over, never touching the page until he deemed I'd made a wide enough arc and then *tick!* pencil onto paper for a "perfect" circle. After a week or so of this I thought I was done but no, we progressed to the wrist. Another week of sheer boredom went by. Then onto the fingers. What was the point of all this?

One, I was laying down the physical memory of drawing for later when I would paint. It takes a good deal of control in the arm to stand and paint at an easel as opposed to drawing at a table where you can rest your hand and balance a pencil against that. Two, I was learning to control my movement and save strokes by drawing the circle a few inches above the paper repetitively before touching it with the pencil. It's something I've never forgotten and illustrates well how practice makes perfect. It kind of goes without saying that my hand-writing went down the tubes during those months after ECT and this had little to do with hand-eye coordination; it was all in the hands.

Like curling in on themselves, my fingers cramped and clamped around pens and pencils, making it nigh-impossible to write for very long with any legibility. Indeed, anything that required a lot of dexterity with my fingers made me feel as if I had somehow aged. I'd never understood how it was that elderly people found picking up their pills such a chore. I should have been more empathetic; now I knew exactly how.

Cheerios eluded me. Buttons went undone. Zippers gnashed their teeth as I struggled with coats and pants. Wrappers refused to unwrap, shoelaces ran away free. And I perish to think how much money was wasted on pills that ended up lost forever between floorboards. While perpetually feeling as if I were picking everything up with mittens was irksome and awful, struggling with drawing, which I'd been praised for all of my life, plunged me into a sort of despair I felt would never lift. There was so terribly much going on, so much to deal with, that if I hadn't had to deal with it all and keep busy trying to figure out how to outwit myself, I well may have laid down and given up altogether.

When I was three years old I looked at a carton of Donald Duck orange juice in my grandparents' kitchen and drew a large, sloppy Donald replete with his sailor's cap and tag. My grandmother pronounced my future as an artist on the spot and from then on the one thing I always heard I did well at was drawing. I never particularly liked my own style, but I could at least be assured someone else would. Other children were good at sports or singing or acting (I was not!) but I had my own talent I could at least fall back on that was something I found very easy to do. I studied the techniques of traditional animation and spent a good deal of free time as a child painstakingly reproducing Disney film art in the attempt to ready myself to join the House of Mouse as an inbetweener and work my way up. I went to a vocational school for Commercial Art during high school, earned an Associate of Graphic Design and then began my Bachelor of Fine Arts in Communications Design / Illustration. Unfortunately, I had to leave school and was never able to earn my Bachelor's degree.

Nonetheless, I worked on freelance projects and taught myself new techniques as I worked in much less creative jobs to make the bills. Not working in the arts had its drawbacks, namely, no one knew I was alive artistically. But, it had its advantages too. I could do as I liked on my own deadline and create art for my own interest without being afraid I wouldn't collect for it.

Being able to create my own world from my own imagination got me through a great deal in childhood and during years of hospitalizations. Finding myself suddenly all thumbs as it were proved a stumbling block I just couldn't get past until those old lessons in making circles came back up in my memory. They didn't help my handwriting at all; my husband doesn't believe there is such a cure for that save employing my own scribe. What they did help with was drawing from the wrist and later on, using old techniques in new ways to paint using both wrist and fingers that I was later able to apply to a weekly comic strip I emailed out at work for more practice. As a former boss of mine used to say before going out to wage war in customer service, "*When in doubt, just give 'em the finger.*"

*Hello, who is this?*

It wasn't just muscle problems that interfered with my art and writing, nor was it only the cicadas taken residence between my ears drowning out my own thoughts. I recognized my own voice when I spoke, and my own face in the mirror. It took me a while to recognize my own style in clothing but after some time I got the feel of what I liked to wear down in my memory: bandannas and stripes.

Despite this reacquaintance of myself with myself, somewhere within the space between thought and written word grew a chasm in which that essence of my own creativity had soundlessly slipped unnoticed. I had never before had any kind of problem coming up with ideas, or brainstorming, or simply telling a story without prompts. I required very little reference material when it came to creating artwork or new characters for writing; I was naturally suited to poetry and derived great enjoyment from composing it. I didn't write *about* fictional creatures, rather they appeared in my mind and told me their own stories to catch on paper.

Though my writing was never affected in any way near to reading and speaking and in fact came off pretty much intact; I wasn't able to hear the voices of the characters in my novel any longer. Why had they run so far beyond me; what had I done to frighten them into silence?

It was the deafening silence inside my head that scared me to death. It took much longer to find words, to run across the vast plains, sort through the prairies and pick through the deltas of imagination for just the right expression. In speaking of course, I stumbled on words in various ways; the brightness and movement of words sloughing off into a swale of impenetrable grey. It wasn't just difficult to find the right ones, it was difficult to find any words at all. It's hard to describe but writing was almost a reflex. Perhaps writing was akin to riding a bike. Perhaps it happened with other parts of the brain, bypassing speech altogether to bring a more pure product right from my intellect. That's not to say it was entirely effortless. Poetry, which I had previously written en masse and with complete ease, became an exercise in tedium and arduousness.

I often wrote poems as gifts to friends, teachers, therapists, classmates. It wasn't uncommon for me to write several a night when rolling into a manic phase and when things cleared back to normal I'd print little books of them to hand out. After ECT, the short structure of poetry proved very accommodating to reading, yet it was equally sticky to write. In the next three years I would labor greatly to write less than 10 new poems. My sentences lengthened into wild, tangly things lacking in any definite structure and peppered with plain, repetitive jargon. At first I wrestled with what to say. Then I became equally baffled in how to say it. For the first time in the better part of my life I sat down to a blank paper which remained blank under the best of my efforts.

I was still good with word definitions; figuring out vocabulary from a word's root or context remained easy and confirmed to be much easier than reading its definition. Knowing what word to use was now a test I only passed with the help of an online thesaurus. Using such a tool will certainly get the job done, but it doesn't do much for one's voice in writing.

The book I'd been working on prior to ECT was one I had been working on for years and those around me all knew about the characters of this long and complicated novel I was bound and determined to have published. In 2009 I did a major re-write and began the very long process of narrowing down an artistic style and medium for illustrations. At some point when I became depressed I stopped writing and editing; a clear sign things were going very sour.

About a year and a half after treatment I had started back to work and had to take a medical leave for abdominal surgery. I knew I would be off for several weeks and thought it would be the perfect time to do a final edit on the book and get it out the door.

I recalled the main points of the story but something about it wasn't right.

We all lose memory of something gone past that we hear others tell stories of all the time; usually embarrassing stories of childhood from our parents.

Outside of our own sphere we hear personally- retold stories all the time. The lunchlady at our child's school tells us a story about her neighbor, the bus driver shares a story about his minister; our boss entertains with a yarn about themselves in high school. We all choose what we take away from these stories. We decide what we think is true because we weren't there as a firsthand witness to write our own account. The same is true when hearing the stories of our own forgotten memories. By rights, they are largely untrue due to being told by an outside observer without access to our own personal thoughts, just like we know our parents tend to overtell certain aspects or push aside others.

But for those of us born before the explosion of video technology we all live under today, the only hard evidence of our pasts outside of ourselves are either photographic or written witnesses. This holds true for those born before the widespread use of photography as well: where there was no written evidence people made use of other forms of more permanent recordings of memory such as in art and textiles or even by recording events in song verses and pantomimes.

With this in mind, my therapist, husband and best friend broke out what they could find to show me and fill in the gaps or jog my memory. Photographs intrigued me, even when unpleasantly so. I recognized myself in them but where I had changed hairstyle perhaps or been somewhere I wasn't previously familiar with, my mind couldn't quite reconcile and felt uneasy. There was only one instance of video taken of me during the time of my amnesia and after watching about a minute of myself speaking in front of an audience, I turned it off never to see again. I felt extremely fake when compared with this recorded version of me and I wasn't sure which of us was the copy.

Much more disturbing though were those things I'd *written*. The novel I'd sat down to edit was completely familiar to me in several aspects. I knew the tone and feel of the world the characters lived in. I knew their names and personalities. I knew what they looked like and sounded like in my mind. But what didn't carry over from the last edit in 2009 was the sound of my actual writing. There was also the business of their language which I had tinkered with and revised to translate my writing into. Reading this for the first time after ECT, I was shocked at how poor I perceived the writing was.

I couldn't understand the story as mine. To my post-ECT eyes it seemed disjointed and inconsistent. The characters' language was impossible to follow; foreign to *me*, its creator. It felt very much like reading someone else's diary; like someone else had broken in, stolen my manuscript and rewritten it in their own hand. I was well beyond disturbed. I had somehow been robbed by myself.

Trying to be helpful, my therapist offered to give me letters I'd sent to her over the years when in hospital to look over. I can't describe the revulsion that came over me at the thought of this. If I felt like an imposter watching myself in sixty seconds of video, it was something akin to straight voyeurism I imagined in regards to the letters. The suggestion to read those letters angered me in the white-hot way suggesting an offensive act to someone often does and after three years of gentle invitation, I still steadfastly refuse.

*It's oh....so quiet...*

It was something I liked to ask my therapist, not because I liked to hear the answer so much as I didn't always believe her. "*Isn't it lonely?*" I would ask. We had established that inside my brain there was a sort of television set which never turned off. From the earliest times I could remember I heard music inside my mind accompanied by visuals of all sorts. The music could be varied in genre or stuck on the same song for hours. The video may be bright swathes of popish color, random shapes or small movies complete in themselves. For those growing up in the 1980s the best thing I can say is that I was born with MTV in my head; during the golden age of actual music videos, that is.

While most of the channels on my little set were funny or beautiful or fantastic, there were a few that showed movies meant for grown folk and these were mainly frightening to a kid not even permitted to watch a PG rating in the real world. But regardless of the content, my TV was *always* on. My childhood was marked with sleep problems because I was afraid of the dark to the point I couldn't bear to close my eyes in case I missed something I couldn't see anyway. But I also didn't want to fall asleep and miss what was playing on screen one.

I wasn't consciously thinking of all these things; rather, they transpired right along with my usual thoughts. One of my hallmark symptoms of hypomania would be the increase in busy-ness inside my mind. Racing thoughts, loud music, and saturated images foretold a certain stretch of sleepless and incredible nights I welcomed until sound became too loud to hear; thoughts too swift to catch.

"*Isn't it lonely?*" I asked of her. Because I knew what I saw and heard was from inside me and not real, I wasn't considered to have psychotic hallucinations. Unsure what exactly to term them, she referred to them as *visions* and assured me most people did not in fact have a TV living inside them. This baffled me at first and I wasn't eager to believe it. But once I saw that she was right, the people around me weren't always busy listening to something inside them, I became quite sad about this, quite sad for *them*. Thus, my eternal question.

Creativity wasn't something I had to work at with this continual feed of images and sound. If it wasn't already knocking around onscreen, I could effortlessly splice something together to devise a new movie to fill my thoughts. During ECT I still wrote and drew until later on during bilateral when it appears my inner thought-life dulled to some sort of swampy approximation of what they'd been previously.

I'm not sure how it happened exactly; how it was I faded away. Did it happen in stages? Did a part of my mind disappear in one go or by bits or perhaps it dissipated like mist? I suppose it can never be discovered if I myself don't know it. While I don't know how things shifted, I do clearly recall what I thought *like* before. This is a tortuous business, this *knowing*. I should think it happens to us all one day in the far future when we consider how it felt twenty years before when we could run without pain and walk without stumble. Easy to remember, impossible to do again.

We take it for granted that our thoughts will always be uniquely ours; that is, they will take the same shape they did all of our lives. I'm not sure what makes a person solely their own self. It is their appearance, their talent, their emotions, their heart, their thoughts? It is all of these in our own unique combination which make up the fingerprint of our souls. But it's tempting to panic when something is removed. It's irresistible to think when one part is diminished or missing, we too are diminished or go missing. How much so when memories are lost because the past is gone. But all of us have forgotten out first years. Would we say to another, you cannot recall being born, therefore you do not exist here in front of me? Of course not; no one recalls being born.

And questions of reality and meaning aside, what about those who do have Alzheimer's or Dementia, or those who have had other personality-altering illnesses or injuries? It's sometimes devastating to comprehend the change but it is still just that; a change, not a death to self but an evolution of it. Perhaps we must work to graft devastating experiences into our timeline rather than seeing them as a death and end to a previous existence.

That was not what I wanted to do. Naturally, I wanted to sit down and think out a new chapter of my novel without picking up a pen. Naturally, I desired to forget the thesaurus and return to the time of ruling my own imagination rather than sneaking in through an unlocked door like a thief. My drawings dropped off in quality and certainly quantity as I sat with a pencil often staring into space, waiting until my tea had long gone cold for the old friends of my mind to remember me and visit.

Curiously, after ECT my visual imagination greatly diminished but my inner monologue seemed to take over. I no longer heard music in any comparable way; my television had turned into talk radio. The upside? The upsetting visions of violence I could do nothing about but stand by helpless and watch as a child vanished, but so did the beauty. For this reason, when I was younger I tried to skirt around medication to deal with these in treatment; I knew instinctively I could not have one without the price of the other. To me it was too high a price to pay for now I knew how lonely it truly was without them. I was stranded without a country, alone with only myself. My therapist tried her best to assure me that most people felt alone now and again and this was completely natural, they simply didn't have all the extra noise going on in the first place to miss. Yet there was simply something that didn't translate in those comforting words; some sort of essence lost.

The solitude was bizarre and unfathomable and I often lay in bed long after my husband fell asleep listening for the voices of my book characters, thinking over and over, "*Where are you?*" But no answer came. How sharp, this loneliness. How bright unto blinding, this dark.

*I was always me…*

As creativity was always a big part of who I was prior to ECT, it remained after but in different ways. I couldn't simply produce the amount of material I could before as everything had slowed to a sort of clumsy crawl and my head now had space to rent. It was surprising but (surprisingly) not disturbing to find that my thinking itself was changing in structure. Though I fought against and mourned the loss of my direct route to my own stories and their characters, it seemed almost a given that my thinking modes would be altered and this was a much more natural progression. That in itself would have bothered me before, and I cannot explain why it didn't after.

Thoughts had a very physical quality to them for me. I recall growing up experiencing my thoughts as very visual. Concepts were bright and diffuse. When I "got" something the insight travelled around my mind in a circular fashion, picking up related items in my understanding like a bird fluttering from one ear to the back of my head and around to the other ear picking up bits to take back to its nest. Overall, thinking was circular. As I got older it became brighter as well. Important concepts presented themselves somewhat like movie stills flashing by, intersected by a sparkling silver thread which traveled around the back of my head and through those related ideas up to the front of my head where they came together to form a whole theory. Understanding was always an "*Ah hah*!" moment, an explosion of myriad points of light. It felt something akin to a cross between an extremely powerful Lite Brite and a Van de Graaff generator.

The lights had not gone out totally. They dimmed; they lost their path. Thoughts now did not travel around, they came directly through from the back of my head right to the front, unadorned, without added embellishment. It was now the whole concept, not the details which made it to the forefront. Even traveling the straight and narrow had its pitfalls. For one, I made associations of things that often seemed unrelated to others. This was something I'd always done, but in the time before, I was able to trace my little bird's path from one concept to another to explain. For example, thinking of *birds* when someone mentioned *cake* went like this:

cake – sweet—dessert –pie—four and twenty blackbirds – birds

Without the extra stops along the way for my thoughts, cake went to birds and trying to figure out the path brought me right back to the muddy ocean sprung up in my head. Wading wasn't possible against its waters and nothing could be seen. Where insight was once very physical, now forming the thoughts felt very much like trying to wade against a current. It was exhausting and frustrating.

For this reason my temper, always hot and quick to flare, seemed to always be up and ready to go when I was asked to use my mental capacity for anything I knew I was going to struggle with. It wasn't that I didn't want to do the work: as soon as I found it difficult to read and work I began taking out child's math and reading books and worked at these to help my handwriting and adding, etc. What brought out my worst side was the fear of being seen as stupid and as such, incompetent. My pattern was one of denial and anger. *"I don't want to and I don't need to!"*

My husband maintained sadly that I'd changed. In my own mind only my thoughts had really changed. I was much too busy dealing with the physical things to bother about my actual self too much. I was too busy pushing people away and hiding what had happened to really sit and wonder who I was now until several years after ECT. I'd never particularly liked myself, so I didn't see what was wrong with my changing. No one seemed to be able to put their finger on it exactly. They said my taste in food had changed, my preference in television shows. Beyond these minor likes and dislikes, the big, bad disparity everyone alluded to was never named. Like my aunt who had had ECT all those years before and countless others, I was believed to have passed into the obscurity of psychiatric history, to have simply *"never been the same."*

# I Only Come for the After-Party

*So, did it work?*

While they are wont to tell everyone in the neighborhood if someone is having shock therapy, the same people will prove very reluctant to ask such a question aloud about ECT of said person. This tells me two important things:

*Regardless of the resurgence of its use in modern times, the stigma of ECT is still very much alive.*

*Mental illness is still largely misunderstood.*

To be able to speak freely about ECT we must first be able to speak freely about mental illness with the same parity as we do with the traditional physical illnesses. In 2013 with the 5th revision of the Diagnostic and Statistical Manual of Mental Disorders (DSM-5) it became apparent that the old fight over who treats the mentally ill, what constitutes a mental illness and whether or not mental illnesses deserve the same treatment has not died at all but rather come right back around again to fulfil the destiny of history to repeat itself. The main argument today centers over biology and mental health and the empowerment of patients over the symptoms of their illnesses, with the battlefield littered by those who believe mental illness does not exist (but is rather a natural consequence of coping or not coping with circumstances) and those who believe mental illness must be treated with outside remedies such as medications. It's a fierce issue that I can recall being fought as I was first coming into the mental health system when parents of schizophrenic patients were being told they did not cause their children's illness; a complete turnabout from the generation's belief before me.

In my mind this will never end. Until the mystery of the mind versus the brain is solved, mental illness will always remain segregated, feared and ridiculed.

ECT doesn't show up in women's magazines or the sports pages. Many patients are only presented with ECT during a crisis when it may not be the best time to make judgments. If we can put this treatment option on the table as prosaically as medication, it would start conversations before an acute event in which there is no time to make a well-informed choice. Perhaps the problem in ECT is not so much the amount of information as the timing. Can you imagine a prime time pharmaceutical ad for electroconvulsive therapy? I can imagine a Super Bowl halftime ad spin but then again, I know how humorous memory loss can be. For the average person in the U.S. watching evening telly with their family, it's cliché but acceptable to be informed of a medication's side effects ranging from split ends to hemorrhaging but try to sell memory loss with electroshock and watch any progress against stigma backslide a good sixty years. Those who want big pharma out of the doctor's office don't tend to want ECT to replace it either.

What's even more ironic is that Schizophrenia, the original target for the development of ECT, is little more an open topic of conversation than it was then. ECT's return has really ridden on its success with Depression. It's interesting to note that in the same vein, cancer has come more and more into the public conversation as the percentage of incidence increases in America. But though we're made aware with early detection and treatment the survival rate increases, we don't see ads for types of chemotherapy or radiation as these retain their own sort of taboo. What's abundantly clear is that there is *no clear answer*; questions must be asked and we must become willing to ask them. Mental illness is incurable at this time in medical history. It is maintained, it is abated;

its complications can wane or be subdued. But it refuses to vanish no matter how far we look away from it.

Looking at a person and making the assessment that they are free of mental illness because of ECT or any other treatment (therefore making the answer to the question self-evident) proves a lack of understanding. People with mental illness on the whole are excellent at hiding their symptoms due to the inheritance of centuries of stigma as well as the natural inclination of the beast to cause sufferers to *withdraw*.

*So, did it work?*

This depends on how we define *success*. I survived the depressive episode that led me to treatment, so yes, in that sense, it *worked,* it was *successful.* I'm alive, but it seems rather green to say one round of treatment continued to keep me alive when we are strongly cautioned that ECT is a maintenance treatment that must be repeated at some point if not using medication to manage illness. I have not had any repeat ECT since 2012, have been in therapy and have used various medications to manage my Bipolar Disorder as well as made changes to my diet and exercise routine. What we attribute to ECT past the initial survival of a depressive episode, etc. is, I think, largely personal.

We make an untold number of choices in our lifetime, some great, some seriously misjudged, some essential and many just extraneous. A portion of us spend a lot of time trying to get out of making a choice or in a prison built from choices we made in the past. We can't change the past but we can choose to keep moving and keep making choices to bridge present with future.

It's simply the truth that at times human beings are faced with two equally bad choices, or what appears to be. So many times I hear the maxim "*choosing the lesser of two evils*" but in some instances there are just two equal evils; there is nothing more. Then what can we do? These are times when faith kicks in. Whether it be in G-d, or in oneself or in loved ones, a person can only take a leap and hope to heaven when they come down they get off with a broken leg. Legs do heal.

I feel this is what I must have been thinking when I chose to undergo ECT. In that respect, yes, it *worked*. I didn't die from either my own hands or the treatment itself. When I consider the portrayal of recovery given at the office of a medical doctor I am struck by the difference in words and tone as opposed to that in the psychiatrist's office. I don't mean for this to be a slam on psychiatrists or those who work with them because they are a product, after all, of their training and social environment. I also don't mean to excuse them, because we all are responsible for our own actions. I only propose that we all also have to earn a living and don't always have the luxury of doing the right thing and the lucrative one *together*.

The glaring difference in these two worlds is the "recovery" bit. While recovery as a final freedom or overcoming does get bandied around in the psychiatric illnesses such as addiction or eating disorders, it's often considered a temporary state with an underlying expectation that it won't last. This has roots in practicality due to the nature of such conditions. Until they are cured, they are not cured and it is prudent and essential to keep in mind that they do wait for an in to wreak havoc. Would it kill anyone to have some unbridled hope that they may *not* do this?

For the major illnesses such as Schizophrenia, Bipolar Disorder, Obsessive Compulsive Disorder and others there is no such "recovery" and rightly so; they are presently incurable diseases. The language used around them and the regimen aimed at them are at best the role of a lion-tamer: one who beats the beast back for a short time, not one who frees the lion of being a lion.

ECT did not cure me of mental illness. I didn't expect it to. In fact during the writing of this book I had several depressions and felt at times I simply could not go on; that learning the dark history of mental health's past was too much to know or that reading my medical records and diaries were too much to deal with. So in that respect, it didn't work.

*So, it didn't work?*

I don't think it's ever wise to give completely black and white answers when questions in themselves are often not black and white. All the world is relative. I asked to try ECT and signed an authorization to do so. I was given all the safety exams prior to having ECT and passed these. I had no neurological disease or injury at that time. I showed many of the same symptoms as a person who has had a concussion or mild traumatic brain injury during treatment and thereafter. These problems largely resolved themselves within five years and those that didn't had no traceable cause otherwise.

It seems obvious to say ECT did *not* work for me. This would be entirely true if we were basing success on the *absence* of any negative effects. For many, this is a crucial factor of success when choosing a treatment method. After all, you're trying to get better from one problem, not trying to cause ten more, and ECT causes many undesirable side effects at least in the short term. For myself, I'd had so many undesirable effects and reactions to medications over the years I knew darned well ECT was not going to be scot-free. Knowing myself, I am fairly certain I would have looked at memory loss and thought *"Hey, if all I forget is the treatment forever I will be a pretty lucky toad."*

What helps in determining if something went the way you expected it to or not is to ask, *has it accomplished what I set out to do?* Let's be honest, most things don't occur in a nonstop flight from point A to point B. This is partly what makes humans so enduring; our flexibility to adapt to challenges we didn't foresee as well as our capacity to learn lessons from adverse situations. While ECT did not in itself teach me the following lessons, it did bring on all-new challenges I wasn't expecting, there's no doubt about that. But it also augmented many past experiences to bring with those challenges new and novel ways of living.

*Confidence.*

I grew up one of the least confident people I know and I wish I'd known the magical quality of confidence as a teenager. I wish I'd known the big secret that carries people through their self-doubt and shines off on all those around them. *Confidence*. It's a quality that defies society's stereotypes of who we are and who we are limited to be. If we have it, it doesn't matter who thinks we don't fit the part. Confidence opens doors we never thought possible from our own restraints.

The effects from ECT incapacitated me enough at first that I didn't have the time to worry over how awful this must look. I wanted to be independent enough that I began to be willing to ask for help. How did this give me confidence? Frankly, I wouldn't have thought I had the right to ask beforehand; I thought I had to do it all or risk someone thinking me incompetent. As time went on I saw that when I asked with sincerity and explained why, people listened and wanted to help. As I became more able to do things for myself and work with others to find solutions to the situation, I found other things I could be good at outside of art. Though not a direct effect of ECT, the total *experience* of ECT gave me confidence to carry on with me years after that initial incident.

*Empathy.*

I could usually be prevailed upon to show kindness. Empathy in the face of someone getting my goat *was not at all in my vocabulary*, particularly in regard to my marriage where I was going to take the first shot in any argument. Being knocked down to the level of a child after treatment somehow showed me just how fragile, ridiculous and lovable we must be to G-d.

When one has children they begin to understand things their parent did. It makes complete sense that these crying, selfish, boorish little tyrants are not at all what we think they're going to be when the shower commences and the sweet little dresses and sleepers come out of beautifully wrapped gifts. After dealing with these creatures day in and day out, we see that our parents were totally justified in losing their tempers, giving us nothing but tee-vee dinners during the school week and *trying but trying but trying* to sit down somewhere without us for five minutes. No one questions this. No one questions either the fierce love we have for children and its magical way of smoothing over all the messes they made in between the bathroom and bedroom doors.

It was in that light that I realized just as G-d loves my mess of an adult self, so I needed to start remembering that everyone else around me, like them or not, had a period of being knocked down in their life. Shouldn't I treat my fellow adults with the same care I would children?

*Faith.*

I was raised by strong Christians when I was small who left a lifelong mark on me as far as prayer and Bible study. I am terrible at both. I want to be faithful but I struggle with it, finding that modern everyday life fills me with doubts. I feel sometimes forgotten by G-d completely. I struggle to praise and worship and I feel much more at home with the LORD in a forest, on the street, even in a psychiatric hospital than in a church.

Having an experience like ECT has strengthened my ability to have faith. It was always there and it has been tested in a multitude of ways during my life but not in *this* manner. This was in a way, an ultimate inspection for me because after my thinking changed and my coordination went and my words dimmed, I didn't wonder what I had left; I found a certainty that if I took what I had left and leapt G-d would catch me and we'd walk together through what was coming.

I don't say that to be flippant. On the contrary, I watched myself go from the neatly trimmed hedgerows of popular Christianity to the wild tangles of desiring more faith.

*Willingness.*

I had a therapist once who would ask those of us in treatment if we thought we were being willful or willing. I never deigned to answer so she'd pronounce me as willful. Fair enough; I knew very well I wasn't willing to do what I was supposed to. We've all heard *"What doesn't kill you makes you stronger,"* and while that's a lovely sentiment for those who have gone through a lot and it's one I'd like to believe.

But I'm not sure that I do.

There are plenty of awful things that happen to us all the time that don't manage to kill us and we don't search them out again to test the theory. They remain awful blips on an otherwise stodgy radar. And of course we all know (and may be) a person who goes through an inordinate amount of terrible things and comes out bitter and resentful, no better in the slightest for having survived.

The key is willingness. Are we *willing* to gain from a negative experience? Before ECT I was certainly not. I recall being extremely vengeful of my husband's employer when he lost his job; very bitter at the various losses we'd gone through as a couple and devastated at not being able to finish my degree at my dream college. After ECT? These concerns became stepping stones to making the world a better place in a way only I could. I was willing to pick these things up and send them on before me; to speak of them to people who may benefit from the bitterness I'd already gone through. In some ways it seemed much harder to do, but if I could spare them living the same angry life I had, I was now willing give it my best.

*So... I'm confused. Is that a yes or a no?*

Put it this way: the main criteria in success when we're talking about a treatment is in reference to the symptoms of the illness it is used for. Depression, the mainstay of today's application of ECT, is largely felt emotionally. It isn't a completely emotional disease; Depression affects sleep and eating and energy as well as many cognitive functions. But if you're suffering from Depression the main and doggedly determined issue is with the emotions you feel imprisoned and murdered by.

I had sailed by even that point by the time I elected to have ECT and was now in the danger zone of feeling alternately suicidal and completely apathetic, but not caring about getting there. A very dangerous line to be standing on, the only thing that brought me to asking for intervention was a vague sense of guilt that I wasn't *more* concerned that my emergency-dispatcher husband would probably get the terrible call to send out an ambulance to his own address. People who have been depressed for a long time sometimes feel that same sense of guilt turn on them and declare them not fit to live because they aren't doing anything about it. I was not this sort of person; I felt guilty for not doing anything about it and I knew I had a very tiny window to act on before I too would also be swallowed by the same thinking.

After the heroics of saving someone from suicide attempt, whether it be the dramatic and painful process of pumping one's stomach after taking pills or surgery to correct damages done by more physical means; the business of coming back into the world is painstakingly slow and does not move in leaps. It moves in the tiniest of steps and events and sometimes it starts off seeming like the morning will never come again.

*More talkative.*

*Pretty groggy though I smiled a little to myself at lunch which was progress. I answered a question or two in the table game too – I usually have a rough time getting out of my head enough to talk very much unless I'm really focused.*

*Feeling very irritable this a.m., angry. Shouted at a few people, very impatient. Feeling raring to go through. I feel like there is a little image of the future trying to bubble up in the very edge of my consciousness. It's galling because I can't reach it to examine it but I know it's there.*

*Hopefully in the next few treatments the rest of my mind's clouds will start to burn off and I'll be able to plan something and really believe I can do them. Wouldn't that be nice... it's been so long since I've been excited about my life.*

*Having a hard time concentrating on anything today.*

*Very dismayed I can't focus to pray my morning prayers. Tried to nap a little but mind won't slow down enough to sleep. Feeling pretty down today too- have been crying all morning but not sure what over, (I don't feel anything). Guess this is a part of my brain getting its files in order. In a way it feels hopeful though because before I came in I couldn't cry and it's such a release. It's just very uncomfortable and very overwhelming. ....I feel like a crumb floating in the ocean of my thoughts just getting buoyed about by the tide- very lost. I guess this is good though... better than feeling nothing at all.*

*Right now I am feeling fearful about continuing treatment and I want to quit. I guess my goal for today will be to talk myself into continuing because I am only halfway through and there is a tiny wiggle of excitement in me towards my new life without struggling so much with depression.*

*It feels as if there was a filing cabinet of old memories I'd long since filed away and it just got tipped over and everything's flying out of it around my mind. I think my mood's lifting just enough for me to get out of that numbness into extreme loneliness. I (didn't make a treatment goal) so they wouldn't let my friend and husband visit and half of my bawling was (over that) so I think this stuff might just be working.*

*It's very hard to describe but my mind, at the edges, feels this little bit of crinkly light like it's trying its best to glow. I think it's trying to feel better and it wants to. It's almost a little exciting.*

*Today I have been plotting out my garden this year and filling out seed order forms. This is awesome because I can focus on it. It's taken me probably 3 times longer than usual to get done but I'm able to do it and want to.*

*Dr. says this is progress and I agree. I said to him that I'm not a huge fan of crying but considering before I came inpatient this time I wanted to be able to for (some) release, I think I'm starting to even out somehow.*

*I can't wait to see my husband tomorrow. Feeling better emotionally this morning, Was able to read a chapter in my book- Dr. commented that It's good I am able to read; that's some progress.*

*Still feeling overwhelmed though and I don't want to go to treatment. I know those people won't let something happen to me but all the same, I'm terrified when I wake up. But that's good in it's own way- you have to be able to cry and get through sadness. It's like being tried by fire- it burns!*

*I did talk with staff about my suicidal thoughts and fears and hopelessness. I wanted to know how many more treatments I had to have but they're not sure. I rather hope they don't just give up because I'm not going to make it at home in this state.*

*Dr. gave me some extra Ativan to take–I don't like the stuff but I know I do awfully when I'm off meds so I guess the nurses are right– since I'm off my (other meds) I'm bound to be feeling worse before I do feel better– it's just hard to keep that in mind when all I do is cry.*

*It was slightly easier eating today though– I guess that is improvement. I feel like spring has begun to infest my brain.*

Those tiny leaps one makes in coming back into the world are miniscule but profound.

*Then, would you recommend it?*

No. What I *would* recommend to a person contemplating ECT is to do their own research from several sources that are for and against the procedure to formulate questions. I would recommend you talk to a trusted physician about these questions. I would recommend you talk to others who have gone through the treatment before making such a decision. Just as I wouldn't tell anyone to chuck their psychiatric medication without a lot of thought or in the event of an emergency, I wouldn't tell anyone to take them either because I am not a doctor. Same goes with a big decision like ECT. While I don't know that I would have made a different decision had I had more information when I sought out this treatment, I know it would have made the transition afterwards much smoother.

While ECT is considered a last-ditch treatment still and may be administered when a person is at their lowest and not necessarily in the best place to make decisions, determining ahead of time if this is a treatment option you'd want to pursue is best. If you are able to choose ECT as a front-line treatment, getting the facts and mentally preparing yourself for the experience and possible side effects is best. There's no one best way to do this; it's impossible to really know beforehand what your personal experience will be.

In that regard, ECT is no different than any medication prescribed for mental illness; they all have possible side effects. When altering brain chemistry there will be effects in other parts of the body because every chemical in the brain controls much more than just emotion. Finding out what may happen and being realistic about this and the manner in which these things will be dealt with takes some work and is the least of what you owe yourself.

It is unfortunate that we are so closed off to the progression of mental illness that we must make treatment decisions on the fly when a suicide attempt presents itself or an act of public violence occurs because these are ends to a long path of symptoms internally, invisible but profound. It's heartbreaking that this is how we get involved with mental health; that we are blind to that person no one says hello to at work or who sits by themselves on the bus or who always smiles and chats at the lunch counter but somehow seems alone. No matter what sort of treatment you feel is best for you or your loved one, or how you believe the illness came about, the point is that is it needed.

To those I speak to who don't wish to have any treatment I say this: I completely get it and neither do I. But make no mistake, mental illness hates you and wants you dead. That's a fact. Though the rates of illness and risk factors vary by race, gender, sexual orientation and country as well as cultural perception and reporting, mental illness is, to borrow a phrase from Saint Peter, "*no respecter of persons.*" That is, no demographic is spared. (SAMHSA, 2016) (NIMH, 2015) (US DEPARTMENT OF HEALTH AND HUMAN SERVICES) (Fish, 2016) (DeAngelis, 2002) (World Health Organization, 2017)

It's also a sobering fact that some of us just won't survive with 800,000 deaths by suicide per year worldwide and 7 people in the U.S. dying per hour (World Health Organization, 2014) .

Now, are we going to sit and anxiously wait until our number is called or are we going to start fighting?

# Part IV

# Support

# Look Left, Walk Green

"Look *left*...walk...*green*.."

I breathed this, my mantra as it became apparent nobody was going to let me cross the street at the busy intersection outside work.

Many pedestrians complained about the unsafe conditions of this particular crossing of two major city streets, two ramps and the exit off of a busy parkway. Despite the hundreds of employees, students and tourists who found themselves at this unfortunate corner every day trying to get to lunch or the bank or the bus stop, traffic never seemed to take into consideration human beings aren't well equipped against the speed of an automobile.

"*They don't get it!*" I overhead someone exclaim one day after a particularly close call. *No*, I thought, *they do. They're just jerks and that's the end of it.* It may sound illogical but there was something liberating in the realization that some people just don't give a rat's ass about anybody else's safety. It was like a big, ancient secret had been pulled out of some moth-ridden drawer, dusted off and shared.

I didn't have to worry about those idiots disappointing me by breaking rules and putting me at danger because they would do just that by nature and I would avoid them to keep my limbs intact as was my own nature and we would all go on in our separate orbits. This is not to say that I agreed with the driving habits of these nameless people who seemed to have no issues at all with running down someone's grandmother, but once I got it into my mind that this is how it is I was able to focus on my own issues in crossing the street.

*Look left, walk green* is what I tell myself when I cross a busy street. I am a shameless jaywalker and always have been, but after ECT I found my judgment of distance had changed along with my sense of direction. When I got back to my regular, walking self I still wasn't tip top with directional sense so I began telling myself before crossing to look to the left and check for traffic and walk a towards the green light, as one faces the green light when safely crossing a street.

Not crossing the street *wasn't an option*; I had to get to work in the morning and back to the bus stop at the end of the day. Even if I managed to avoid Hell's Corner I'd still have to get myself across traffic at some point in my life. Having been hit by a car once while crossing the street, I knew I needed a good and foolproof strategy because frankly, getting hit by a car really hurts. The foolproof part came in the timing. If someone jumped the gun or I wasn't totally sure I had the light, I had two options: I would either cross with a crowd or just wait it out until the light changed again.

Before you have ECT there are a ton of things you have to think about but there are a couple of things I think are essential extras: Before you begin treatment try to prepare by having a collection of familiar photographs of family members, friends, pets, happy events and your home. You may have trouble recalling these things directly after treatment and it's good to get familiar with home before you return there. This may also be a time to arrange for a visit from a clergy member from your place of worship as an extra support as many people who have had ECT feel separated socially after treatment and talking about this may help the transition back into attending your place of worship.

If you're in the process of going through a round of ECT you may experience all kinds of tasks and situations you will have to rethink. At first you will be overwhelmed and it's really paramount to surround yourself with support in the way of family members, friends, therapists and doctors. If you're one of many people in the mental health community whose supports aren't always that *supportive* for various reasons, following up treatment with partial hospitalization, an intensive outpatient program or some type of therapeutic or skills group can help fill in the gaps of your support system.

Non-treatment groups can be helpful too in just keeping you in touch with your community. Libraries, colleges, places of worship, fire halls, community civic centers, JCCs and hospitals host all kinds of special interest groups and classes and you can always find like-minded or like-minded souls on social media outlets by searching for tags in user posts and profiles. Looking for fellow patients with schizophrenia? Try searching for *Schizophrenia (#schizophrenia)* or *mental illness (#mentalillness)* or *Schizophrenia groups (#schizophreniagroups)* and see what comes back. You may end up with a whole new group and type of friends!

With the type of mild brain-injury symptoms that crop up with ECT treatment, one can find oneself feeling alone and totally disconnected from self. Everyday tasks become so overwhelming there always seems to be a fresh set of tears and a bright, crisp tantrum ready to go around every corner.

Dr. Diane Roberts Stoler noted that after an accident, even doctors didn't know how to help during her bout with Post-Concussion Syndrome, neglecting to totally explain what she was going through or give her answers on how to handle her symptoms (Diane Roberts Stoler E. a., 2013).

With so many of the same symptoms and the same sparse education on what to expect and how to manage the unforeseen, it's helpful to have some practical solutions to try before throwing in the towel with ECT. By all means, *first seek medical attention.* Hard as it may seem, speak to the ordering psychiatrist first about any problems you may be having.

This can sometimes be intimidating for two reasons:

We tend to shy away from confronting doctors because we either fear them and don't want to bring any further suffering on ourselves or,

We trust them implicitly and feel questioning their judgment to be taboo.

Either scenario isn't beneficial in helping us in the long run. Doctors are human beings. They make mistakes on occasion just like the rest of us and they operate on what information they have, just like the rest of us. They are not gods that we cannot question them. After beginning with your physician, you may feel you need a little more than what you're getting or, if you truly don't feel you can go back to the same doctor, you're going to need to go to the appropriate place to be evaluated for your symptoms.

A neurologist is an excellent place to start (you may need to see your GP first for a referral depending on insurance) as they can order brain-related tests to help narrow down what's going on and take an appropriate course of action. I always saw Neurology as rather stuffy but after a few years of putting it off myself, I realized there's no use going to see a foot doctor if your sense of smell is gone.

Likewise, a neurologist may give you a look over and refer you to a neuropsychologist for cognitive testing or a physical therapist to start working with that lopsided gait you've taken on. This doesn't mean the doctor doesn't know what they're doing, or that they're sending you off; it means that they are also not going to waste time seeing you for something they are not the most qualified to treat.

Now with ECT- related symptoms, physicians are not always sure what do or who to send you to. I think the best approach here is to be logical about what's going on. While it's certainly true that some doctors turn right off the minute those three letters are mentioned, many are receptive to at least holding an entire conversation with you if it's not the main focus and others really have no idea about it. It may seem counterproductive to hold back a bit; after all, ECT is what brought you to the office to begin with.

But I'm here to tell you that if you calmly present your symptoms and mention that you also had ECT and wonder if it is contributing to those symptoms rather than going in with an accusatory manner in regard to your treatment, you can get much further. Because even if your doctor has never heard of shock therapy, as a human being they're going to naturally become a bit defensive when faced with your assertions that one of their fellow physicians may have done you a wrong turn. You may feel this is watering down what you mean to say. Maybe so, but that old adage about catching more flies with honey never gets old.

When experiencing side effects from ECT it's important to get as many facts as you can to determine what's a normal side effect and what may be due to other causes such as medications. Because the jury's still out on whether or not ECT directly causes brain damage, I suggest we look to the definite symptoms of mild traumatic brain damage to form a plan of attack in getting back to a functional normalcy, because they so closely mirror the effects ECT patients experience.

The difficulties listed here which may arise during or after treatment are all things I have personally experienced to some degree. Many resolved themselves in the first 18 months after treatment but some linger on and are daily problems. I have organized these tips and suggestions so you may take what you need or quickly reference to come back and try something new. While I have tried many of the suggestions here, there are also things new to me and you will want to experiment to see what's right for you.

*Sleep.* Changes in sleep patterns are pretty normal during a course of electroshock treatment and those with mental illnesses know that insomnia is characteristic of these disorders. During and after ECT it's completely normal to feel like you've never slept in your life and now must make up for lost time. They say nobody ever sleeps in a hospital but I felt like all I could do was sleep and once I got home my routine went something like this: sit down, fall asleep. Use the restroom, fall asleep. Take a bite of something, fall asleep.

But because the brain requires all five sleep stages to make daily wear and tear repairs, it's extremely important to make sure you are getting enough sleep and good quality sleep. It cannot be stressed enough how important sleep is to a psychiatric patient's well-being because of the direct link between poor sleep and symptoms of mental illness. Insomnia can also show up after ECT, though it may seem almost impossible to even think of staying awake at times. The mind naturally goes over the day at its end so practicing mindfulness and doing your best to highlight your accomplishments during the day (making it to the corner store and back when last week this seemed a herculean task) and blessings received (disability checque came in time to pay rent) or pray a prayer of gratitude for what you do have helps the mind let go and not ruminate because most people with a psychiatric disorder and sleep problems report not being able to settle their mind down while their bodies are exhausted.

**Practice deep breathing.** This is a perfect time to concentrate on further relaxing the mind and body to get the deep rest the brain needs in order to repair from the day's learning. Remember that it takes more power to do the same tasks as before ECT so you need to rest when your body blatantly tells you it needs rest.

**Take a mid-day nap** to help fatigue. Just a short one! Sleeping during the day routinely can also interfere with sleep.

**Prioritize ahead of time** what needs to be done during the day and delegate this to either a less busy time to allow rest or hand off to someone else. Normally, thought processes are most effective between eight am to twelve pm and then again from six pm to eight pm. Try to schedule a nap between these times and before mentally taxing activities (Diane Roberts Stoler E. a., Coping with Mild Concussion and Mild Traumatic Brain Injury, 2013). Work in extra rest times if you have a busy week ahead of you as mental fatigue can be disabling.

**Don't fight fatigue.** Rest if things become too much. Don't be mistaken that fatigue and exhaustion mean a person will sleep well; patients with mild brain damage often can't sleep at night.

**Use a meditation technique** such as Guided Sleep Meditation, Body Scan Meditation, or Zen Worry Meditation to help relax and prepare you for sleep (Emet, 2012). Try deep breathing exercises such as the 4-7-8 Relaxing Breath exercise to help calm down and release stress.

**To help with lingering lethargy,** attempt the Stimulating Breath Technique (known as the Bellows Breath (Dr. Andrew Weil, n.d.).

**Proper exercise** can help both fatigue and insomnia. If you are physically able to engage in regular exercise make it a priority to do so.

**For those with a more limited range of movement,** the Chinese practice of Sleeping Qi Gong (also called Chi Gung) can be used. The Japanese technique of Reiki can also be utilized to aid sleep and can be done either on one's own or in consultation with a Reiki Master.

**Insist on proper sleep hygiene in your household.** Keep your bedroom for sleep only.

**Keep the bedroom cool** and set the thermostat down overnight; keep feet uncovered if you can. Make sure bedtime and wake time stay consistent even on days off work or holidays.

**Remove** televisions and electronics from sleeping rooms.

**Stop work and activities** one hour before bed to signal to the brain it's time to slow down and wind up for the day.

**Keep a bedtime routine** as religiously as possible, even if it's just smoothing out your pillows and turning off the light. Be mindful of your movements as you do this; your brain will pick up on the repetition and associate that routine with slowing down for sleep.

**Check with your doctor** to see if you are deficient in any vitamins or minerals such as Iron, Magnesium, Vitamin B12 or Vitamin D which must be adequate in the diet for healthy sleep.

**Check with your doctor** to see if you should try a Melatonin supplement to help get your body back on a regular sleep schedule.

**Cut out sugar before bedtime.** The body burns through sugar quickly, elevating temperature during the process of digestion and keeping you awake. Have a high protein snack earlier in the night to avoid this.

**Because dreams and nightmares** are often bothersome during treatment, and certainly can be after, try journaling about your dreams. It can also be helpful to check out the *nightmare protocol* (Romeo Vitelli, 2015).

**Meditate** on the phrase *"I've done my best"* at the end of the day before retiring as a closure for the mind to begin setting for the night (Emet, Buddha's Book of Sleep: Sleep Better in Seven Weeks with Mindfulness Meditation , 2012).

...

*Coordination and Motion.* While balancing on your own two feet seems to be the biggest issue in muscles and motion after treatment, there are other much more subtle effects on coordination that can cascade into larger problems. If you've ever seen a newborn colt stumbling around in its first hours you've got a good idea of what it's like to do anything gracefully for a while after ECT ends. Walking is a complex process which involves many different factors and requires immense communication from the brain to the muscles and nerves. It's not just the arms and legs that cause us to stay upright and go forward, our eyes and visual perception contribute to balance and anyone who experiences vertigo or dizziness can tell you how even pressure on the sinuses near the eyes can make a room spin. If imbalance or weakness persists past the end of your ECT schedule, make absolutely sure to be seen by a physician to rule out any additional problems.

**If it's decided that you need physical rehabilitation,** make sure to get it done and *stick with it*. Repetition is the hallmark of PT so *do not skip*!

**Consult a doctor or chiropractor about posture.** Good posture helps us balance and bad posture can lead to more than just balance problems.

**Traditional Chinese medical practitioners** can help with balance and vertigo with *acupuncture*. Scared of needles? Ask about *acupressure*.

**Take care of your sinuses and nasal passages.** Simple nasal washes are available over the counter to keep the nose clear and clean and adjusting the humidity in your home can help a lot with sinus pain. If you use a prescription spray or inhaler to reduce inflammation in your passages make sure to take this as prescribed.

**Move slower!** It may seem like it but 95% of the time you don't have to get there as fast as you would to an emergency so take your time. Getting up and down quickly from laying or sitting can drop blood pressure too quickly and bring on dizziness to the point of passing out. Again, slow down a bit.

**Take your time turning around.** Any time I would turn in a public restroom to latch the door I would lose my balance completely. Turn *slowly*.

**If you ride an escalator or on elevators,** try to keep your head straight and choose a focal point at eye-level rather than looking down or to the sides. This also goes for those times you take a shortcut up a broken escalator instead of finding the stairs and when you try getting off a water ride onto a stationary platform. Research shows that the rate at which we need to move in reality to get where we're going and the rate that our brain perceives it needs to direct us to doesn't match up (Daily Mail, 2004). I have a great deal of difficulty with this at amusement parks and I find looking straight ahead at a fixed point helps my brain sync up much better.

A similar type of vertigo can occur when the light changes. For example, when looking at pulsing light or the moving shadows of cars against the highway or walking out of a dark house into bright sun.

**Wear sunglasses in bright light,** look at a fixed focal point away from moving light and certainly don't look into pulsating light. If you cannot cover your eyes or escape moving light, sit where you are until it passes and cover your eyes if you can to stand before moving again.

**Using writing utensils with a larger circumference** or pencil "grips" can help tame sprawling penmanship and typing over writing ensures everyone can read what you're trying to say.

**Two-handled mugs and pans** act as insurance against dropped cookware and overfed pets unless you're me and then *nothing* keeps teacups unscathed.

**Buttons, shoelaces and zippers** require dexterity you may not have right away. Besides delegating these to others you can use some common objects to get back into the swing of things. A child's lacing shoe or lacing cards can help with lacing, as well as oversized buttons or beads you can string together. An old shirt with large buttons can serve as practice and clipboards work well to secure papers if paper clips are too unwieldy. Resealable bags gave me all kinds of issues so I switched over to washable zipper bags and washable Velcro sandwich wraps for lunches. You can get these online and in some stores in the lunch box section, as well as plastic or glass storage boxes and lunch kits. If you have trouble prying those lids off you may consider the type which have snap sides. Personally, I do a lot better with those and I think the seal is better. If you're sold on resealable bags though, try the freezer bags; the closures on them are bigger and color seal types let you know if you did in fact get it closed. Lastly, *double zippers.* I don't know who ever thought those were a good idea but avoid those if you don't absolutely have to deal with them!

**Poor balance and vertigo** are formidable, to be sure, but are not reasons to stop all physical activity. Exercise helps regulate hormones and improves flexibility and range. A physical therapist or personal trainer can give you appropriate exercises to try and there are a great many routines you can do sitting or while in water. You can also check out exercises for seniors such as the *Sit and Be Fit* program to get you started.

**Yoga** is also an excellent tool for learning balance. There are many, many disciplines of yoga and all use breathing and awareness as part of their moves. Don't be fooled: yoga is a serious tool and uses muscle groups you probably didn't know you had. I read a book about a world champion bodybuilder once who said he worked out tirelessly to keep his title and when he tried yoga he'd never been so sore the next day in his life. While yoga is all about balance, be certain to consult with a physician, physical therapist or holistic practitioner before jumping in.

**And the most effective tools** are often the simplest and most intuitive. A heavy pair of boots can indeed make the difference in feeling where to step and old-fashioned repetition and hard work will never let you down.

...

*Vision.* Visual changes can come in many forms and bother people to varying degrees. Because these changes begin in the brain and not the eyes, wearing your reading glasses is not going to help much. Light plays a big role in whether or not visual changes get you down or not so try adjusting light exposure before giving up! As with balance changes, any visual changes that persist after treatment should be promptly evaluated by a physician as these can be indicative of problems in the brain.

It may seem extremely obvious but people usually need to be told anyway: if you are having blurred or double vision, have a seat. This is not the time to elude police in a high-speed chase, fire up the wood chipper or practice walking the tightrope over your neighbor's pool. Fatigue will bring on all sorts of eye troubles so do the first logical thing and rest. Glare and reflections can confuse the most healthy of brains at the best of times. When you're not at your top, glare can make you lose your footing and sense of distance.

**Wear sunglasses** in outside light, when working near water or shiny surfaces and indoors where glare is more likely such as near store makeup counters and in public restrooms. The glare from your computer screen is not exempt either.

**Set your phone and device screens a bit dimmer** than the factory setting and set them to dim to a sleep mode during the hours you shouldn't be on them anyway or turn them off completely at night.

**If you work on a computer** try to look away from the screen every fifteen minutes for at least sixty seconds. Set a timer on the computer itself or on your phone or watch or yes, an actual egg timer.

**Believe it or not, that ugly wallpaper** in your mother-in-law's living room can throw your brain for a loop. *Visual overstimulation* happens when your brain can't sift through and process information it acquires visually. Busy patterns, optical illusions, doubles and multiples and even closely packed type sometimes overwhelm. I am prone to this type of overstimulation in particular. Busy patterns make me quite tired and optical illusions such as those found in funhouses have caused me to become so inundated I've just shut down where I was, unable to take one more step. As soon as I was taken to a dark room or somewhere visually blank, I was fine within five minutes.

**Hell no, just don't go.** To combat this, try to avoid places like funhouses (or perhaps your mother-in-law's), look away from intricate patterns and if you do get overstimulated or suddenly exhausted, stay where you are until it passes. Because visual overstimulation isn't just limited to amusement parks and ugly ties, you can always just sit it out. Grocery store displays give me a headache, restaurant menus have made me cry and I can get lost *on* a map before I get lost *with* it.

Others may think you're antisocial when you decline shopping at the mall on a Saturday night or going out to a concert or watching that 3D movie you promised to take your nephews to. The sheer number of items to look at, the colors and the signs and lights can leave you extremely nauseous with more coming in than your brain has time to sort through.

**Wear your sunglasses inside.** Try attending films with- you guessed it- lightly tinted glasses or sunglasses. I try not to bother with 3D films but if I go I do not use the glasses as they're just a recipe for a frantic trip outside to find the washroom.

**Go to a different show.** There are many cinemas now who have show times for families of children with developmental disorders that keep overstimulation down to a minimum. You may not find many "grown people" titles offered but you can at least still take your nephews to the show and have a good time yourself.

**Wear headphones.** Sounds like a waste of a concert ticket but noise-cancelling earphones or plain old wax or swimmer's earplugs can free your brain up to hear what's going on. It certainly makes or breaks a concert experience for me. The music is loud enough you're not missing anything except maybe someone rabbiting on behind you.

**Make a list.** Shopping is best managed with simple lists either by good old-fashioned paper and pen or using list apps that keep everyone in on list changes in real time wherever they take their phone. Some of these organize the list by general store layout and making a plan of where you will and will not go that day beforehand makes the trip less likely to derail. Be careful of the paper you use for a list whether it's being made on real paper or the digital version. Use or set your device to plain paper with clean lines and double space your list to make it easier to read.

**Shop late.** So many grocers are open late or twenty-four hours now so you can go when the store is less crowded and fast-acting anti-nausea medications are available to keep on your person to help get you through your sister's graduation. Family reunions? Well. I think the rule is you can skip every fourth year at least.

**Lay low for a while.** Depth perception is one of those things you tend to have or not have naturally and if you drive you know just how important it is. If you do normally drive you are not permitted to do so through the duration of ECT rounds but it's a good idea if you are having lingering effects to see a physician before you get back on the road. Even if everything is ok you can still be a little more prone to overstimulation when driving so if you start getting too tired, pull where it's safe to do so and take a break before getting back on the road. Make sure if you feel drowsy that you do not fall asleep with the car running due to carbon monoxide risks!

**Ask for directions.** If depth perception continues to elude you, use other cues in the environment such as landmarks to tell you how close or far away you are, where it's safe to turn, or when it's safe to cross. Memorize these clues so you begin to look for them automatically *(Look left, walk green!)*. If you still get stuck, ask for directions.

**Get on the bus.** You may need to take public transit or a taxi, walk with a friend or get a ride rather than risk yourself and others in a car.

**Bag the GPS.** But if you are driving and you're going somewhere new, refrain from using a GPS. That's a bit much for your brain to follow, so go over your route before you go, just like we all used to do before Garmin.

**Get out a Sharpie.** If you have trouble recalling your things such as clothing or personal items like I did, it may be wise to mark these with a sharpie or tag of some sort. Blue Painter's tape with your initials in marker works well and comes off without a mark. Sewing and crafts stores also sell tiny clothes tags for people who have home sewing businesses. Tacking these onto your stuff is a cinch.

**Read short books.** Reading can be a challenge in several ways but don't let that stop you. Reading short passages for shorter periods is a good place to start. Larger type such as that found in books for the sight-impaired helps as well as children's or young adult chapter books where the lines tend to be more widely spaced.

**Using a bookmark** to move down the page line by line can help with eye tracking. Sometimes the problem has more to do with focusing the eyes and eye fatigue. And make sure you mark your place with the bookmark!

**Don't read in low light** and try adjusting the font online or choosing reading material with a bolder print. I know it's much harder for me to read for very long online but if I dim my screen I can go for longer. At work, I have the background and text colors reversed in some of our software screens and there are many computer programs you can do this with. Ask your help desk or IT coordinator before you change settings!

A final word on visual disturbances: your field of vision may temporarily change. Peripheral vision may become dim or one side of your vision may seem to disappear or "darken." In some visual and neurological conditions the source of input needs a rest. The *Feldenkrais Method*, developed by Moshe Feldenkrais, is an interesting low-tech treatment used to integrate the senses through awareness and gentle movements. The Covering the Eye technique of palming over the eye to allow its nerves to rest from hyperactivity is a recorded lesson one can order online as well as the Bell Hand Lesson which targets hand eye coordination (Susan Dillon, 2012) . As with any visual disturbance or before trying any new remedies, see your GP right away to determine if this is a brain concern or limited to the eye. If in doubt, get checked out.

...

*Hearing.* With brain injuries we don't normally hear much about hearing as being affected but it certainly can be and is not just annoying, it drowns out other sounds so that a person can't hear conversations or softer sounds.

**Put the subtitles on.** Ringing in the ears or hearing a continuous tone is often reported and while there isn't much one can do about it directly, using subtitles and captioning on televisions and mobile devices can at least ensure there is less to miss.

**Pick up some earplugs.** Like in true hearing loss, sometimes people have a hard time picking out sounds in a crowd and this can be helped by using noise-dampening ear filters. The ER 9, 15, 25 ear filters or Hear Plugz-DF which are used by the military and by musicians, can be obtained by an audiologist.

...

*Pain.* Unsurprisingly, headaches and migraines are part and parcel of ECT and outside of over-the-counter painkillers, there are several other simple things you can do to combat head pain.

**Get rid of triggers.** For one, know what your triggers are. For some, specific foods trigger headaches or changes in the weather or fragrances.

**Cool it.** For others, temperature can bring them on. Cool compresses on the forehead are helpful particularly if you suffer nausea with headaches.

**Push back.** When I get bad headaches I find counter pressure is the only thing that helps. To do this, I roll up a towel and press the side of my head being affected into this or lay it on my pillow and press it laying down.

**Heat up.** If you are prone to sinus headaches be sure to take a decongestant or take a hot shower to breathe in the steam or conversely, hold your head over a steaming bowl of hot water with a towel covering your head and the bowl to make a sort of tent.

**Drink it off.** My husband swears on the power of Jamaican ginger beer to clear the sinuses and pressure. Look for (non-alcoholic) ginger beer in glass bottles in a grocer or import shop.

**Use your fingers.** I have found recently that the Shaolin practice of dredging the channels (combing the scalp) does wonders to relax the scalp and lessen pain (Ming Lu, 2011).

**Listen to your doctor.** There are plenty of migraine medications and vitamin B supplements you can consult your doctor about but it's also wise to look into pressure points to help quickly bring down the intensity of a headache (hint: your ears can do amazing things!).

Even after ECT I still had a lot of leg pain and sometimes those who have had a brain injury also report bodily pain. Any type of sleep disturbance will increase pain so do your utmost to get enough quality sleep. When you begin ECT you will stop most of your medications, particularly any anti-seizure medication. The neat thing about anti-seizure medications is that they can be used to treat neurological pain such as that in fibromyalgia. If you're still having pain after getting back on your meds, talk to your doctor as they may just need to be tweaked.

...

*Cognition.* As discussed earlier, cognitive issues are extremely varied and everyone is unique in how their brain works but there are some general hallmarks in regards to what patients having ECT report. Extreme fatigue, confusion, speech problems, memory problems, differences in sense of smell and taste, differences in personal taste, shortened attention span and issues with learning are amongst the most common and the most alienating. While it often seems like things will never get better, they can and you have options to help you get on in your everyday life.

If you had to stop in the middle of that last paragraph and start over at least one time, you may be having some problems with your attention span. Don't feel bad, I did that a couple of times as I wrote it. Attention span is quite possibly the most far-reaching and damaging consequence of ECT I have experienced because it influences so much. It's not just listening to instructions at work or watching an entire half hour television show or getting through a test but the little things like being present to remember your kids asked for omelets for dinner today because they made their own in school last week or focusing on a recipe for those cookies your stomach has been thinking of all day.

Being able to focus is vital to driving safely, operating any type of machinery, keeping an eye on young children, reading, memorizing information, following directions, and performing any type of skill. We tend to think of attention span only when it's short and often when talking about children who "can't sit still." But attention problems plague adults as well and ECT can interfere with this. It's mighty frustrating to sit down to read or write or cook or play a game and get absolutely nowhere with it because you just can't keep your mind on it. Apply that to your whole life and you can imagine what little you'd get done in a day.

After experiencing an injury, the brain may have trouble filtering. What this means is that normally your brain filters out the extraneous things in your environment so you are able to focus your thoughts on what's important. When your brain is trying to recover it's not particularly vital to filter in order to function so the extra stuff around you from sights to smells to that cat fight last night in the alley are extra-distracting to the point you truly cannot concentrate on anything except each new stimulus as it rolls in. That being said, you may ask *"How am I going to fix this attention span problem if I can't concentrate long enough to listen to the directions on what to do?"* Well, you don't necessarily need to.

**Meditation** is an excellent tool to help with concentration and focus and it seems very daunting to begin but the nice thing about meditation is that there are a million forms of it and you start with very small, manageable exercises. Meditation is something you practice so there's no need to worry about not doing it well enough.

**Mindfulness** is sort of like mini-meditation and the practice is used to improve the skill of non-judgmental observation for all manner of things. There is basically nothing mindfulness can't be applied to and if meditation full-tilt seems too much, try small mindfulness exercises like just observing your breath or the texture of your food.

**Timing your activities** can help you focus without being overwhelming. When I used to look at the clock I'd try to figure out how much time I had to complete something and I'd stress about "only" having that amount of time. Recently I noticed that I'm really only good at doing anything for about fifteen minutes at a time. If I need to get important work done I set a timer for fifteen minutes and at the end I must do something else for another fifteen before coming back to my first task. It's truly the only way I get anything done and I find I'm more productive over all that way.

**Resting enough** is vital to attention span as is drinking and eating properly. Anything your body needs is going to take its utmost attention away from whatever you'd like to be focusing on. We never seem to give our brains the respect they deserve; it takes a vast amount of energy to think normally. When your brain is not at its peak that amount of energy needed to do the same tasks raises dramatically. Listen to your mind and make rest a priority.

**Medications** for Attention Deficit Disorder are on the market which may be helpful. If you're not having luck with anything else and your attention issues are truly disruptive, talk to a doctor about medication options.

Other cognitive changes can be annoying, disabling or humorous depending on how you look at them. The key is to figure out what your end goal is and how to get there. For example, the left side of a clock face baffled me for quite a while and my husband attempted to talk me into getting rid of the analog clocks in favor of going all digital for a couple of years. I felt like getting rid of the clocks was admitting defeat so I learned what positions the hands needed to be in for the last possible minute I had to get out the door for the bus to work and put stickers along the rim so I knew what the clock face looked like when it was time to go. The problem was, I wasn't able to switch to digital well so I ended up turning my alarm off when I didn't mean to or setting it the wrong time altogether over and over. Finally, I gave up and got a smartwatch though I kept it on an analogue face I couldn't read for a while! Eventually I saw how impractical it was to wear a big expensive watch I couldn't read and reset it to digital. Now I get the time, weather and date on my watch but I still keep wall clocks for the nostalgia of it.

**Write it down.** Figuring out what you want to begin with can be very challenging, tiring and frustrating. A friend of mine keeps various notebooks and binders with pens all over the house and in her car for ideas on just about everything. I've seen people keep a pack of index cards for the same purpose because they fit just about anywhere and you can shuffle them to organize by priority and of course, reorganize when you change your mind! It also helps to keep asking yourself what the most important thing is. It may take you several rounds until you whittle down to the *most* most important thing and that will be your first step to moving towards what you want. Remember, the smaller you can break down your steps, the more manageable they will be.

**Make a list.** I'm a list person. Lists make me feel like I'm *going* to do something. They're great because I certainly can't remember what I need to shop for, set the DVR for, tell my husband to pay on the electric bill, etc. There are all kinds of humorous list-making pads available from office supply stores you can get as well as the humble Post-it pad which has saved many a meeting. There are also apps for your mobile device you can use alone and add to from a web browser or your family can add other family members on to maintain a community list like with the shopping. I use one with my husband that either one of us can also strike items off so we can pick things up as we go and not buy twice. We also customize lists for bigger things such as home improvements that need done or weekly errands.

Speaking of remembering what to do, there's remembering to keep your memory healthy.

**Take care of that brain.** Do everything you can to keep your brain healthy with sleep, exercise and good nutrition.

**Tell them to scram!** Make it a priority to cut down distractions and work on focusing so you are able to encode important information into memory. Turn off the phone, put down the book and focus as best you can to build this skill up. Surround yourself with people who actively support this because you'd be amazed at how even loved ones will unwittingly sabotage your effort by wanting you to look things up, show them photos, check out their Facebook post right *now*, etc.

**Make notes, take notes.** Many people find taking notes helps them remember even if they never read the notes again. Dictating notes into your phone to listen to later is a study trick you can put to good use.

**Snoop a little.** Use environmental cues to help you remember. It helps me remember when it's time to take a break at work if I pay attention to what my coworkers are doing at the time. This helps with eating, drinking and taking medications as well.

**Touch things.** I know, germs are everywhere. I'm not saying go lick stuff but touching things gives your brain one more facet of something to encode in the memory. When I go for a walk I often touch permanent things along the way (the metal railing on a retaining wall, the lion sculpture at the end of a drive, the large tree trunk across the street) to help me recall where to go. It's kind of like playing tag or scavenger hunting. I'm pretty crap at audio directions but I'm way more likely to remember the way if I see what I've already touched.

**Make technology work for you.** Smartphones have built in alarm utilities you can set to chime, vibrate or activate a smart watch when it's time to do something. The haptic alert on my watch is the only thing that successfully keeps me on track with meds every day; I just need something to tap me and say, *ok!* There's also an egg timer, an alarm clock, or the voice-activated home assistants such as the Amazon Echo. Voice activated assistants have several handy uses. Following a recipe is a notoriously taxing thing for anyone with a brain injury but with an assistant you can have them read the recipe to you. Conversions need not be a mystery either; you can simply ask.

If that's not your cup of tea there are untold videos online to show you how it's done without all the reading. Don't stick your nose up at this; I learned how to fix a busted freezer in the middle of summer from a guy on YouTube!

As reading can be a challenge, follow a few simple suggestions to get more out of what you can do.

**Don't read when you're tired**; this will only frustrate you and tire your brain further. Read in enough light and when you have time to take breaks and go back to it. I keep books around the house in spots I like to sit in and I make it a goal to read at least one paragraph every time I sit down. There is no shame at all in reading children's and young adult books to "practice" or train the eyes, though I certainly wrestled with this preconception for a while. These books are typeset for beginning and intermediate readers and depending on where you are in your healing journey there's sure to be something enjoyable for you. And who doesn't like illustrations?

...

*Communication.* This can be a true challenge after ECT at times. Stammering, stumbling to find words, mispronouncing and running words together are astoundingly disheartening. There were many times I sunk into silence out of defeat.

**Slow down.** Slowing down and deep breathing are two of the most effective things you can do for speech. I found tapping the words out with my fingers on my leg helped me keep rhythm as well. It's hard to slow down if you feel the person you're speaking to is hoping you hurry up but rushing will only gum up the entire works; *slow down.*

**Ditch the Bics.** Likewise, there are simple helps for writing to communicate besides typing over handwriting. In most jobs, you are required to use some manner of word processing software and writing can have its own special challenges.

**Get online.** Making use of spell check and an online thesaurus or dictionary can really get you through a pinch. Thesaurus.com really helped me with writing *Look Left, Walk Green* because I get stuck on what word I want to use so writing is a stop-start affair and reading an actual thesaurus is exceedingly difficult for me. With online reference, you only have to input your search terms and the exact query is brought back. No thumbing through pages of type. Spelling and grammar checks as well as rulers to help with margins make word processing your best friend in the business world.

**Get offline.** And if penmanship is your goal, few things beat the lined notebooks elementary schools hand out to practice lowercase and capital letters. If you're like me and do better writing than speaking, use email and instant messaging to do the bulk of communicating.

**Grab a book.** *Abstract thought* is what we use to comprehend time, mathematics, humor, music, symbolism, and is often a problem for those experiencing brain injury that can make them feel stupid and frustrated. Because abstract thought is something developed in mid-childhood, it's smart to borrow some of the methods schools use to foster this.

**Count it out.** It might be impossible to comprehend amounts but using an abacus or piles of beads to count out amounts can help us connect the number symbols with amounts. Illustrated books of idioms and puns as well as comic books can be gotten to visually figure out complex expressions.

**Talk it out.** Talking through thoughts aloud or with someone else is greatly helpful in following concepts from beginning to end. I do this all the time at work when I get stuck and I figure if nothing else my coworkers get a chuckle out of it.

**Move.** Movement also helps; just like some people naturally "talk with their hands," others think with them and still others do best on a walk or while doing chores where their whole body is moving while their brain makes the connections. Some things, however, have no clever workarounds or shortcuts but simply take determination and practice to improve.

**Communicate however you can.** It would be dishonest to tell someone there's a magic way out of brain injury or a quick return to the self they remember being after memory loss. No lie, there is nothing that can accurately describe the complete isolation one feels in this situation. As Kara Swanson tell us, the injury is invisible and the effects are sometimes so alienating because no one can crawl into your mind to see what's wrong. Brain injuries rob us of the words to even express what's wrong sometimes, locking us into a prison not only do we rot in alone, but that only we can see. It is no wonder many people experiencing cognitive problems become depressed at some point.

Let me be straight with you. Sometimes people around you aren't going to understand. Car drivers will yell at you to hurry up across the street, neighbors will mistake your wariness around them is from being standoffish, not the uncertainty of amnesia. Strangers will think you strange when you tap things to remember them or gaze fixedly at a corner to gauge distance. Family will wonder why you were fine yesterday but today can't remember to tie your shoes up. Coworkers will assume you're antisocial when you don't recognize them outside of your office. The running commentary you overhear will surprise you in its breadth and misconception; there will be little others don't notice and judge yet little they will bring up to your face.

You will feel a part of yourself has been cut away and worse than losing it will be the vague sense you don't even know what you've lost. You'll learn to wish for the sharpness of grief so it can be over with. You will feel the world has abandoned you to the asylum. It has not.

You must learn to speak a sort of pidgin to reconnect to others. Few will have the time or inclination to learn what you're going through but you must find ways to show them that they can understand. It's not easy.

You'll feel ungrateful for wishing you'd never done this. You'll feel guilty for asking, stupid for doing and lonely in the midst of all. You will be angry. There's no easy way to bring ECT up; there's no corner to hide in from it. There will be no going back. You cannot erase, you cannot undo. But you can go forward. You can go on.

And you must, because no matter how you came to have treatment, it was for the purpose of going on.

Try your level best not to hide. I know that's a lot to ask but it's best for all involved. I made this mistake for years, hiding what I was struggling with from friends, family members, my husband and even my therapist because I felt it was a weakness and that I should have sorted these things out l myself. This was a mistake and I hope it's one you don't make. Tell your doctor, your therapist, your family. Be aware they may be taken aback or not quite know how to handle things. That's ok, they're new to this too. Attempt to assume they want to help and go from there. Remember they may have seen a million people go through the same thing or maybe none at all but they haven't seen *you* go through it until now.

Whether you experience one or all of the issues discussed here, someone else *is* going through it too and by the nature of the treatment is probably suffering alone. Online groups are unique in that they bring together people from different demographics who might not connect offline normally or who are separated by distance. I'm all for them in moderation (you can't spend all your time online and maintain health offline) and you can find many others out there who have gone through ECT who can totally validate what you're going through and have tons of awesome tips and thoughts on this.

Now here's my disclaimer on that. While ECT groups can be very powerful, please be selective when choosing one. Like offline, many of these groups tend to be either very pro or anti-ECT and that's natural as like-minds attract each other. If you come across a group that is not very open to an opposing viewpoint to their own, I'd look a little further. Offline, educational groups through a local NAMI chapter, addiction recovery groups and health classes at local hospitals can also be a good place to feel out who might be in the same boat as you.

A final word before you go: by and far, memory loss is likely going to be the biggest thing you have to deal with directly after ECT and I'm going to be frank; it's *terrifying* and can fill you with despair. Like any kind of medical treatment, you have to decide for yourself if this is an acceptable risk and if the benefits outweigh it. I thought it was, yet the reality is that nothing could prepare me for the ways it would express itself in my life. Please know that you are indeed in good company and you have many tools to get through this and go even further than you ever imagined. It may be through a different path, but the view ain't half bad from this side either.

# The Singular Burden of Remembering

EVEN less known than positive personal testimonials about ECT are the voices of the families and friends of those patients receiving the treatment.

What about their joy, their apprehension, their fear, their bewilderment, their loneliness? FDA docket 82P-0316 is chock full of stories such as one woman's lament that she couldn't recognize her family, none but one son. How devastating for that family to hold such hope for relief from the ravages of mental illness and be rewarded with the devastation of memory loss! How equally horrid for the lone son who would shoulder a sort of survivor's guilt for being the only one to inhabit his mother's present mind.

As a psychologist compassionately said to my husband years after ECT had taken place, *"How terrible for you, to be alone in the burden of remembering for the both of you."* What an accurate observation, one that was so validating to my husband it allowed him for the first time to voice concerns he'd believed that no-one else would believe or want to hear. I suspect this is much more common than can possibly be known.

Why do we not hear more of the stories of the supporting cast during the education of patients before treatment, in the media surrounding it and the artistic works portraying it? I can scarcely recall anything I've ever seen go deeper than a stereotypical "deer-in-headlights" look on the faces of husbands and wives, children and parents as their loved one is wheeled away to be shocked, or alternately, the outbursts of anger as the same cast of characters send same said loved one off to be punitively shocked. It's not a very realistic vision of the immeasurable reactions and experiences to the multitude of outcomes that may occur after ECT.

The odd mention here or there is often confined to bodies of evidence against the usage of ECT but these too are sparse. Otherwise, one would have to turn to such neurological narratives as those of the likes of Oliver Sacks or the pleas for help and understanding on the plethora of support groups online to realize that anyone outside of the patient themselves even exists in this unconventional sphere. And while mental health has been slowly recognizing the vital importance of a patient's home culture and family in as a support in their recovery, it is much more backward and blatantly stubborn in the case of the experience of ECT.

Witnesses to memory loss know this: it takes no prisoners. It is torturous to think that your loved one remembers your ex-wife's birthday three years ago but not your son's bar mitzvah last summer or even more prosaic yet somehow poignant, sitting on the porch swing together on a Tuesday night. But this isn't how memory loss works. In *encoding* memories, emotion plays a part in how things are encoded, but when it comes to the loss itself, here there seems to be a set of archaic rules only the brain in its own unique wisdom knows. And this becomes even more devastating when we think, *"Don't our lives, our loves and heartaches together mean anything in the end? If we are only to be forgotten, what are we but disposable collections of random points in time?"*

Perhaps memory loss attempts to teach us that we must allow it to mean something *now*; we must detach ourselves from continually escaping the past and preparing for the future. We are, without pause, moving *towards* or *away from*. Perhaps the loss of memory whispers, *"Be still."*

Nevertheless, while there is time enough to ponder the lessons learned from loss, in the very here and now where loved ones await the sentence of cured or damaged or something in between, it is crucial that we hear the voices amidst the anger, the sorrow, the fear. In talking about including a history of mental health treatment in this book, my husband pointed out the desperation of those families and patients who would have consented to lobotomy before ECT is the same as how he felt about me consenting to ECT at the time, it showed how horrific mental illness is. But on the part of the responsibility of therapists, doctors and hospitals, more care and judgment should be placed in evaluation still today, because often the patient is not relying on the expert opinion of whether or not he or she should receive life-saving treatment that his or her family is.

He likened this to asking someone severely dehydrated if they would like a bathtub of water to drink? Of course they would, how could they say no? Yet we know from hard scientific evidence that consuming such a volume of liquid would dilute any sodium in the bloodstream, throwing off the balance of electrolytes enough to kill, making the very thing they need a means to their death. Accordingly, those taking care of the patient receiving ECT should be supported as well, before, during and after.

What can a carer do for their loved one and themselves during ECT?

Take care of yourself. You've heard it, I've heard it and we all ignore it: if the plane is going down, put your own oxygen mask on before you put on your child's. And this goes against all logical sense. Except it doesn't.

Think it through a moment. You know you're not good to anyone unconscious. That's totally logical. What it is not, is *emotionally* coherent. You know you'd rather die than take care of yourself over your child in an emergency, yes? That's emotionally obvious. If logic and emotion had a knife fight over your loved ones, who would win? Emotion wins every time.

Which then makes *logical* sense that you need to *take care of your emotions* before attending to anyone else's, including whomever your taking care of. This sounds rational, easy, and for some, a bit self-centered. Surely two and a half out of three ain't bad. It *is* logical, it *can* be easy, and yes, it *is* self-centered. Not *selfish*, self-centered.

There's a great difference here. Self-centered just means you are focusing on taking care of *self*. Selfish is putting yourself above others. It's more *"We're watching this show all night because it's my favorite and I couldn't care less that I said I'd help you do the dishes."* Clear?

And I want to make sure that's clear because it trips people up left and right when it comes to being healthy while caregiving. It keeps them from asking for help so they can do the job right and asking for empathy from others while doing it. Make no mistake, mental illness not only hates the person it exacts itself upon, it hates everyone around them too. If you're going to be up to fighting, you've got to have your house in order first.

Put your mask on first. There are several ways to do this and I suggest you take a few that work for you and keep them in your arsenal of daily practices for your *self*. Or you know, all of 'em.

...

**Therapy.** Ah, it's not just for the crazy I assure you. There seems to be a per-vasive feeling in society that consulting a therapist is a sure-fire way of broad-casting to the world someone has lost their mental faculties. Let's be honest here: anybody can fill the role of a therapist. If your insurance is crap or you don't have access to a therapist where you live, tea and biscuits and your auntie can do much the same thing as long as you are not having thoughts of harming yourself or anyone else (that's a red flag and a half to call a professional). Not everybody has an auntie, or a best mate or a gaggle of girlfriends to do this, and therapists do have some unique attributes that make them a good resource to tap into for several reasons:

*A therapist is confidential.* By law, what you say to the therapist is confidential. Unlike Auntie Queenie, a therapist does not have your mother on speed dial to tell her you just bought that dress at retail. What you say to a therapist doesn't leave the room. Except in the case you may be plotting something akin to murder. Then, you know, someone has to tell.

K. Rose Quayle

*A therapist is objective.* What that means is a therapist is a human being. You're going to say things that anger them, sadden them and probably put them off like any other human being. A therapist is trained to keep those reactions out of the room so you can safely prattle on about whatever you need to without fear of being judged. They're not going to roll eyes or suck teeth or give you the hand.

*A therapist doesn't tell you what to do.* This is a huge misconception people have about therapy! You're not going to be told what to do with your life. A good therapist helps you discover within what you should do. Basically, we all have the answers within us, but like most other situations, we're complete experts at telling others to do what we should actually be doing ourselves. Why so hard? Because most of us lack a great deal of insight into ourselves. Therapists help us gain that insight so we can make good decisions: *our own.*

*A therapist isn't just for bad stuff.* Another misconception is that therapists are only there for the bad times. Untrue. Do we only have bad times in our lives? I hope not! Therapists love to hear about future dreams, plans and accomplishments. They're proud of our triumphs and want to hear that stuff along with the trials we face. Sometimes you're just bursting to brag and everybody's too busy to hear. A therapist is a listening ear you want to keep on staff for yourself.

*A therapist is a good resource.* Many therapists these days have a degree in social work (LSW or MSW) or are working within an office which has someone in a social work role. They can give your referrals to other offices or for other services you may not realize would help you. It saves a lot of Googling if you ask a therapist.

*Therapy is much more than sitting in a chair.* It's work. There are many types of therapy most people aren't even aware of outside of the mental health community. Some popular therapies are Cognitive Behavioral Therapy (CBT), Dialectical Behavioral Therapy (DBT), Radically Open Dialectical Behavioral Therapy (RO-DBT), among many others.

The caveat with therapy? Well for one it's not free. Sometimes people feel a therapist is always going to agree with you since they're being paid. Ahem, that's not what they're being paid *for* so don't be fooled there. Others feel that a therapist won't care because again, they're being paid. Reality check: most therapists have a degree in social work. People don't go into social work for the salary no matter where they work so if they care, you've got a decent therapist. The other thing is that a therapist is a human being. The relationship between you and your therapist is exactly that: a relationship. It has rules and expectations and sometimes someone gets disappointed and even the best therapists will piss you off at some point. That doesn't mean anyone did anything wrong.

You don't just find a spouse on the first date and sometimes you go through a few therapists before you find the right one, too. Expect that. Therapy is individual; it evolves over the course of treatment. Some people also need a psychiatrist for medication, but many just see a therapist. Some people see them through a hard time, some see them for years. There's no right or wrong as to how long or how short your time with a therapist is. Just don't give up if you're not finding the right fit; after all, you want to be able to trust this person right? NIMH publishes a nice online guide to finding a therapist you may want to check out.

...

**Meditation and Prayer.** To start, meditation is not for sissies and you won't sell your soul to the forces of darkness doing it. Rather, meditation is a skill one must learn and an exercise one must practice. There are all manner of useful things meditation can help with that most could use a little help with anyway.

*Meditation helps with sleep.* Who gets perfect sleep other than infants? Meditation helps cultivate a more restful state overall and lowers overall need for sleep, probably by raising sleep quality.

*Meditation helps with pain.* It's no sin to take an aspirin on occasion but so many people wrestle with chronic pain that doesn't go away with an occasional

Bayer's or even a non-occasional one. From fMRI study results its indicated that meditation aids the brain in perceiving less pain (allowing it to achieve mind over matter). In other studies proper meditation technique has been found to reduce pain at a better rate than morphine. Those who experience chronic pain disorders can benefit too: Fibromyalgia patients have more good days with pain overall when trained in meditation (Dienstmann, n.d.).

*Meditation helps manage stress:* In the modern world it's impossible to escape stress of some kind and chronic stress can kill. Meditating before a stressful event lowers the effects felt mentally by that event. Meditation also helps the body's immune system, so the body is better able to cope with stress. And as a bonus, regular meditation also helps manage the stress response that raises blood pressure.

*Meditation is for everybody.* There seems to be a style to suit everyone from every corner of the earth. There are meditations that focus on breathing, awareness of the body, muscle relaxation, clearing the mind, even eating. The popular Lovingkindness Meditation even focuses on you focusing on someone else!

*Meditation isn't a religious thing.* It can be, it's used in the five major world religions (Christianity, Judaism, Islam, Buddhism, and Hinduism) and can be incorporated into worship, but does not require any affiliation with religion to use. Meditation is a tool and a pretty effective one at that.

The caveat with meditation? You do have to practice. Meditation is like lifting weights; those muscles don't sculpt themselves. You're not going to get it like a pro the first time out and you may need to try a few different types to find out what's your size. And of course, time: if you're not going to dedicate some time to meditate, don't bother.

**Prayer** is rather like meditation in that there's a lot of focus going on and a degree of quiet needs to be maintained to do it for very long. It can be thought of as a form of meditation on a higher power or the universe itself. For those who are not familiar with the practice of prayer, it can seem a little daunting. What does one say? How does one say it? What's the magic formula?

*Prayer has many forms.* Certainly there are prescribed prayers in all religions, those that we say during worship or at festivals and the like. And there is a more formal language generally used in more organized settings. But the essence of prayer is to open up one's heart to a higher power; to make oneself bare to the universe and all who have gone before us. It is making oneself vulnerable by saying *"Here I am and I need help."* There is no right thing to say; just as we are unique and rare individuals, so too are the forms and utterances of our prayers. Some people sit, some people kneel, some rock back and forth, others hold their heads or clasp their hands. Some close their eyes, some tilt back their heads and some outstretch their hands. I once watched a documentary featuring a little girl somewhere in Asia who said she twirled when she prayed because that's what made her feel close to G-d. If twirling is what does it for you, then by all means, tally-ho.

*Prayer is not begging.* Prayer is humbly asking for the intervention of something far greater than us in our lives. It can be used to intercede on behalf of others and many find comfort in the act of praying for their loved ones going through a difficult time. Prayer requires trust that the prayer is being heard and humility in asking for blessings.

*Prayer is not just for asking for stuff.* By no means is prayer all about asking for blessings. Prayers all around the world are used to adore a higher power, to proclaim that power's greatness and mercy and receive communication back from that power.

*Prayer is portable.* There are cultural norms and taboos regarding where and where not to speak to a higher power and if you subscribe to a certain religion you may feel these cannot be deviated from. But consider that we think every waking moment and prayer is a focusing of thoughts. We were born with the tools to pray wherever we can quiet ourselves and focus.

*Prayer is not just for the faithful.* All religions have a view on this but nothing stops a person from sending a prayer out into creation with the hope it will be heard. Sometimes it's all you can do to stay sane.

...

**Relaxation** is not really an option for health but when you're caring for some-one it's sort of like flossing; you know you should and you know what's going to happen if you don't but *man, who has the time?* Here we have to think back to the oxygen mask. You're not going to be any good to anyone exhausted. Many people think relaxing is equal to laziness. Not so. Relaxing is taking care of yourself and being willing to put an a temporary end to something pressing. Laziness is saying you're on a permanent vacation and you're not interrupting that for anything.

*Relaxation is vital to repair work on the body.* "*I don't have any injuries so I don't need to rest for my health,*" I can hear you saying. Did you know you can be the healthiest person on the planet and part of what makes you so is regular maintenance work the body does on itself? Pretty neat stuff but let's not be unrealistic. If you never give your body time to do that work you can expect exhaustion and illness at some point to take over your life.

*Relaxation is not always easy.* Grabbing a drink and a book and putting your shades on by the pool sounds pretty relaxing but most of us don't have that sort of scenario going on all the time. Finding the time is one thing but what to do is another problem. Sounds kind of sad to think the majority of us these days have to schedule in a good nap but even sadder are those of us who can't name five things to do to relax. This is because in modern times we equate busyness with success and power. If we let ourselves stop for a moment, the need to justify is so strong we have no problem coming up with excuses and apologies.

Slowing down is not a sin, nor will the world stop while you're doing it. I work long hours and I hate going to bed when I could be doing all the things on all those lists I love to make. It's never easy for me to do but I have been "allowing" myself to take a nap on the bus both ways and "allowing" myself to put the lists away at night. Or, "not allowing" myself to take my phone out of my purse or off the charger. However you have to look at it. Find something you can allow or not allow yourself to start with for ten minutes of downtime and work up from there. And yes, that's every day. Soon you'll be *accomplishing* a well-deserved rest.

...

**Exercise and Nutrition** don't seem especially fun but they're not to be missed if you want to get things done in the long-run. Not just tools for fighting diseases and keeping aging in check, getting enough exercise and the right nutrition helps with sleep and since you're trying to relax, sitting at a desk all day and slogging down cheeseburgers and soda will throw the whole game off.

*Exercise doesn't have to be in a gym.* For some reason we have trained ourselves to look for the best solutions online when we're obviously born to exercise wherever we are. Remember those circus strongmen of old? They'd pick people up like flour sacks and show those unbelievable muscles! They used weights and their own body's resistance. Looking like a million bucks might be your goal, but even if it isn't, you've got plenty to work with. Take a walk, ride a bike, run up the steps. *You got this.*

And did I mention that post—workout stretch is really quite *relaxing?*

*Nutrition is not what you think it is.* There's this impression I've had all my life about that nasty word, *nutrition.* I'd think of it and images of mineral powders and hospitals came up. I'd get this metallic taste in my mouth and think, "*No thanks, now hand me that candy bar.*" Seems I'm not the only one so let me set this straight: nutrition is simply the study of the stuff you need to be eating for your body's health. You already know this drill; you need so many calories and such per day split up into food groups. Candy bars, while not something you ought to eat all day every day, are part of that whole nutrition bag as well.

Making it more complicated than it is rakes in millions for infomercials, magazines and best sellers. Many of us are on special diets and this complicates stuff further. But seriously? Once you know *how* to eat, it's not real complicated to find *what* to eat in this country of excess. Don't use time you should be using with other self-care items to shelf-surf. Pick up something and get on with it.

...

**Charity is not just for the holier-than-thou's.** Doing for others takes the focus off of our own problems and puts things in perspective. If you've seen someone extremely active in charitable institutions and thought they were a little goody-goody, you're not alone. Keep in mind though that the more you see someone in this situation the more people there are behind them just like you who aren't seen. It's those people who really get food out to the hungry and shoes on the feet of the poor. The impressions we get about who does charity should never keep us from being charitable ourselves.

You might think, "*My lands, I'm taking care of my brother during ECT and now you want me to go take care of somebody else?*" Well I'm glad your hearing is in good shape because that's exactly what I'm saying. Here's why:

*Charity takes the focus off of your situation.* Unless you want to go spend more time volunteering to take care of someone else in the same situation, and that's your choice, chances are the people you come in contact with are facing totally different challenges. That in itself is liberating.

*Charity allows you to use your talents.* So many of us are in jobs where no-one really knows us and we're not using any of our real talents in the name of keeping our mortgage paid. Coming home to care for someone might make you feel like you're never going to use your skills or maybe you feel you're just crap at this carer business. How frustrating is that? Volunteering your skills where they'll be used can be even more beneficial to you than to who you're helping.

*Charity is a requirement of some religious practices.* Charitable works figure in all major religions with certain seasons inspiring different acts. Some religions consider charity to be an act of worship towards G-d while others see it as a practice of holy life. However, you do not need to be religious to practice charity and you don't need to ascribe to the religion of a charity to give of yourself there.

*Charity doesn't require money.* We all have financial concerns and frankly, money keeps a lot of people from giving to charity. Giving means of yourself.

Look around, find a charity that needs someone to teach painting, someone to watch kids in a daycare, someone to read to the elderly. Sites like Pinterest also have tons of ideas on how you can be giving without using money.

...

**Laughter** is a medicine and release like nothing else. It may have been a while, or not, but think of the last time you had a good, loud laugh. I say loud because when you're really having a good time you can't laugh softly. Some of us snort when we laugh, some throw our heads back, others dip their heads down. As for myself, you know I'm having a good time when I clap. My point being, there's no right or wrong way to laugh and it sure feels good doing it. Why is laughter so important when you're taking care of yourself?

*Laughter does great things in the body.* When you laugh, endorphins flood your bloodstream, making you feel better and better the more and more you laugh.

*Laughter connects us to others.* I'm not the most social person but when someone is laughing, I feel like everything's going to be fine. When we go through sad times or tense times with another person, if we can find something funny to laugh over we can come together again. A laugh amongst strangers is often the most powerful icebreaker as well. Everyone likes to laugh, after all.

*Laughter does not equal foolishness.* When you're under the gun to get a lot done you may find yourself reasoning away fun times by thinking that if you engage in frivolity, someone might think you're being *frivolous* with your time. You can be in the midst of a pressing deadline at work and giggle over something to yourself or come through a life-threatening situation and laugh about something in it looking back. Laughter is just an expression of how we see something and others might not see what's funny in the same things you do. I hope someone told you that your views don't make you good or bad, what you do with them does. If not, you've been told. Laugh away.

You're going to have days when you feel alone. *You're not.*

You're going to have days when you resent your loved one. *Perfectly natural.*

You're going to have days when you'd do anything to go back to things *before. That doesn't mean you're a bad person.*

You're going to ask why did you have to be in this situation. *That's human nature and doesn't mean you're complaining.*

You're might feel guilty that your loved one might find out about these thoughts. *Chances are, they already know and the world hasn't ended yet.*

As noted in the previous chapter, online groups are very popular and have their ups and downs and if you have no other support I'd take a look into those. But let me preface that by saying while full of great people in similar situations, be wary of groups who don't allow a differing of opinion or boot you out for disagreeing. I have seen threads where everyone is commenting peaceably and suddenly the whole group turns on some small thing they pick up on by the poster. The last thing you need is someone attacking you for doing what you know works in your situation. Remember, unless they're in your house they don't have the whole story.

Don't pick fights about it, just quietly leave and keep up the faith as you search for a better place to hang. It's out there.

# Part V

# History

# Before We Were Human

MENTAL health has a long and often dark history greatly misunderstood by the American public.

Cultures around the world see the mentally ill in sometimes completely opposing lights. From the ancient Greek and Roman belief that mental illness was a punishment from their gods to the Biblical hero King David's use of impersonating insanity to protect himself from King Achish (1 Samuel : 21: 12-15 ) to the Dagara Shamans' belief that the crisis of mental illness precedes the birth of a new healer from the *other* world (Gaddis, 2010). On the other hand, Asian and Ayurvedic beliefs view mental illness as being caused by disharmony in the spirit and imbalance of energy and Latino views tend to lean towards a more natural, organic cause, while Native American tradition suggests mental illness is a reflection of imbalance in the wider community. So the world truly has its own split personality on how it perceives illness of the mind. (White Swan Foundation, 2016) (Elizabeth J. Kramer, 2009) (UC Davis Health System, 2009) (Scull, 2015) (Elizabeth J Kramer, 2002)

Whatever the view on its cause, treatments have sprung up since ancient times tailored to these perceptions ranging from the natural, novel, and somewhat silly to the downright torturous stuff beloved by horror writers and haunted house attractions everywhere.

For the ancient Greeks, Romans and Egyptians, the treatment of mental illness wasn't seen as separate from that of bodily illness. For most, if not all, of the history of the U.S. it has always been separated both in ideology and physical proximity. Asylums and Sanitariums were built away from medical hospitals; psychiatric programs and offices are still mostly in their own buildings or have their own separate emergency rooms in well-funded hospital systems. Insurance companies bill and pay for behavioral health services separately and most times not as generously. States are now required to uphold parity in coverage but there is still not a hard and fast rule of just how equal is equal so the coverage of mental health treatments can vary state-to-state. I happen to live in a state which upholds the minimum par, and while for me personally that's enough most of the time and much better than it ever was before, it still doesn't quite represent an equal perception of the behavioral and medical sciences.

In the U.S. alone, there have been tremendous changes in the philosophy of treating the mentally ill, who remained for much of our country's history before the 1950s deprived of the right to own land, marry or have children. Seen by some as possessed and to be feared, others as contagious and to be avoided, still others as dangerous and to be locked away or an embarrassment to be silenced, or even still as a contamination to the gene pool to be sterilized and ended. The population of the mentally ill has been, in this country, something of a sitting duck that, when not a drain on society, could be exploited to aid society's ills. As in all things however, the *outcome*, not the motivation, is what history views as the final judgment of how successful an idea or philosophy is. Let's take a look at how mental health treatment began in America and how it developed to the point of using ECT today.

In the early days of the American colonies there were no facilities or treatments for mental illness. The insane were kept at home, sometimes in chains and sometimes put into prison for lack of anything better to do with them. By the mid-1700s America, new and bright-eyed on the world stage, was indeed a dark and dismal place for the mentally ill. Those deemed insane were sentenced to stay out their time in asylums which, during this era did duty mainly as quasi- prisons, keeping the insane locked away from a society who felt a keen sense of danger in letting their crazy relatives walk around unfettered. This isn't to say no one cared about the ill's woes, not at all. Families of that day worried about their ill relatives and had the same heartaches we do today when faced with the diagnosis and symptoms of mental illness.

But the manner in which medical science saw and treated mental illness was punitive and chock-full of what today we would deem as violations of human rights. Patients in our country's early days were whipped, chained, cuffed and put into straight jackets (called *madd shirts*) and given straw to sleep on in small, partially underground cells. Everything we think of today as being "classic asylum", was the norm in mental health at that time. And while today we watch television shows and shudder in morbid curiosity at the suffering of some poor normal person who has somehow gotten themselves institutionalized as a form of torture, in the 1700s it was a common practice to go to the *actual institution* and have a look at this veritable human zoo in person. Fences had to be put up to cope with the influx of busybodies who needed something to do before cable was invented and at some point these institutions realized they could benefit and began to charge admission (Whitaker, Mad in America: Bad Science, Bad Medicine, and the Enduring Mistreatment of the Mentally Ill , 2010).

In 1783, Benjamin Rush, a man of Quaker background, began reforms to the asylum system that would pave the way for major changes in how mental health as a medical discipline would eventually evolve in the future United States of America. One of the original Founding Fathers, Rush was a signer of the Declaration of Independence and also a member of the Continental Congress. He obtained a degree in law at the ripe old age of fourteen and went on to spend time at Princeton University before traveling to Scotland to obtain his medical degree and returning to his hometown of Philadelphia to become Professor of Chemistry at age twenty-three. A man who could never be called a slouch, Rush also campaigned against slavery, was married and later fathered thirteen children (Biography.com Editors, 2017).

But to Psychiatry, Benjamin Rush was a founding father of talk therapy; the gold standard of mental health treatment across the nation today. Previous to Rush's time, the patient was committed or sectioned by their family or a court of law and treated according to visible symptoms such as mania or hallucinations or the report of the family or other witnesses. What the patient thought and felt hardly came into things. Rush experimented with speaking to the actual patient about what ailed them and listening to their concerns, probably not quite like Bob Newhart or Kelsey Grammar, but something on those lines. He felt that kindness and respect would go far to give the insane at least a bearable existence (which fell in line with Quaker beliefs). Rush's vision of treatment included such therapeutic activities as gardening and walking on the grounds as rewards for good behavior and even beds with mattresses.

Benjamin Rush and all his lofty ideas were a saving grace to the insane at the time. Who could argue that dignity didn't lift the human spirit and benefit one's state of mind? But Rush was also a physician at the end of the day and that meant that the crusade of a physician to eradicate disease called him strongly to continue the search for better treatments. Because mental illness was so poorly understood overall, this proved to be a true setback to the very progress Rush had made up to that point. He fell back to the mode of thinking he'd encountered in Europe during his studies, which was vastly different to that of the Quakers whom he had come from. European thinking on the treatment of insanity was based heavily on interpretation of the textbook *The Practice of Physick: Two Discourses Concerning the Souls of Brutes* published in 1683 by Thomas Willis which examined the belief that the insane were like animals. This came at a time when science was sussing out what made humans higher than animals, with their conclusion being that the gift of reasoning was the great divider. Since features of psychosis and mania include behaviors that were considered animal-like (hallucinations, unkempt appearance or neglected hygiene, unintelligible speech, apparently super-strength or indifference to cold, lack of reasoning), it made sense to physicians at the time to cure such an illness the same as one would tame an animal: through fear. It became quite acceptable and encouraged to beat the illness out of the patient; to terrify and break the wild animal and leave behind the docile man.

This was the common practice during most of the 1700s. By the late 1700s across the sea in France, treatment of the insane in Paris had become truly deplorable and daily featured beatings, starvation and the keeping of the ill in dungeon-like conditions where Parisians, like Americans, went to the asylum for entertainment value. In this context it's hard to even imagine what must have been the catalyst to spur the French government to send Dr. Phillipe Pinel to take over and evaluate the care of inmates at that time. But when he arrived he made the acquaintance of Jean Baptiste, the superintendent on the grounds. Baptiste felt that if people were spared the rod and were given some boundaries and stability, the asylum would have a much better chance of treating the insane in a "make better" sort of sense rather than a "beaten into submission" sense. And while beating into submission and taming the wild were certainly *economical* treatments, their success rate was suspect.

Consequently, the asylums Pinel had charge over began to change in a radical manner for the day. Pinel began in baby steps what today is routine practice: getting a patient history, asking the patient what they actually thought was wrong, believing that the patient was indeed a human being with an illness that needed to be treated. He wrote that in his observations, patients were of all stripes and classes; affected by illness equally and all able to show the best of human qualities when well, saying:

*"I cannot but give enthusiastic witness to their moral qualities. Never, except in romances, have I seen spouses more worthy to be cherished, more tender fathers, passionate lovers, purer or more magnanimous patriots, than I have seen in hospitals for the insane."* (Mrs. Sushma. C, 2016)

Pinel's observations convinced him mental illness was caused by something other than the reigning theories and when he published his vision of a complete "mental health" system in 1801, he envisioned doctors trained to identify and treat various types of mental illness over such garden-variety insanity as was assumed at the time, a thought well ahead of the Diagnostic and Statistical Manual of Mental Disorders (DSM). Under Pinel's direction, patients were kept busy with work and lessons and the thrashings did not commence. This system of respect, productivity and benevolence proved quite popular with patients and with their families.

Yet back in America, because treatments of the day were fashioned on the Western European methods which Pinel had tried to break away from, the common prescriptions included blood-letting, administering mercury to cause violent episodes of vomiting and nausea, blistering the skin with mustard powder rubbed into cuts in the skin, and starvation. It made sense to doctors at that point from observation that pain in itself could shock a patient enough to separate them from the illness and theoretically, more pain was needed to bring a person back permanently to break the hold of psychosis for good. The standard treatment of weakening the body to subdue the illness of the mind was powerfully convincing: pain was essential to saving the soul, not unlike the flagellation practiced among the religious in medieval times for the same end. And pain carried with it a double bonus: even the threat of treatment effected that insanity-curing fear and made the insane more manageable for staff.

Why would well-meaning doctors who put so much into the study and theory of curing insanity resort to what amounted to torture? For some, the reigning science at the time insisted this was the *only way* and this was what they put their faith in. But for others, much had to do with that siren of sirens that calls to all men alike: money. It was, and still can be, profitable for a doctor to stand up in court and testify to a person's insanity if their well-off family paid for a private asylum or to vouch for the insanity of a politician's relative in order to put them away in a less *public*, place. With this new dimension in treatment, physicians were soon touting their harsh but miraculous cures and the public accepted their expert opinions that that tough love to the extreme was the only way they could save Crazy Aunt Mary (or keep her locked up).

Laws to make sure the insane were really insane were put into place in England in 1774, but in 1788 King George III became mad (and *certified* insane) and suffered a long and terrible bout of torture from his physicians which ended finally in a remission. Though historians have gone back and forth about this with some believing his original symptoms had more to do with a genetic disorder and as such, the reprieve was more part of its natural course and nothing to do with the treatment. Others have analyzed his handwriting during his ill periods and believe this is evidence of the King having Bipolar Disorder (Worsley, 2013) (Segen's Medical Dictionary, 2012). Either way, the King held the key to another change in ideals.

Because the medical science of the day hailed curing the King as absolute confidence in the whip and chain approach, utilizing the cure of kings only raised the money to be made. As a result, private institutions grew rapidly into the 1820s. The 1800s brought about new ways to cure the insane. What amounted to waterboarding became quite popular (near-drowning while blindfolded) as well as cold baths and painful blasts of water. The act of drowning in itself spurred on many finer tuned methods and the idea of swinging and spinning a patient caught on. Soon the ill were strapped down to boards and spun around until they lost all of their fluids on one end or the other (or both). It was a terrifying remedy and led to public outcry loud enough to influence parts of Europe into banning the practice (Whitaker, 2010).

I think we can safely say in looking to the past that the *interest* of the public was to cure the ill and not see them harmed beyond the scientific sensibilities of the day.

Meanwhile in America, Benjamin Rush found the success rate of European drowning techniques particularly inspiring and he ran full tilt into establishing his own theories of madness at the College of Philadelphia where he was on faculty. He was convinced that circulation in the brain had a great deal to do with madness and just about anything including the kitchen sink could bring on changes in the blood vessels (he may not have been far off in *theory*; there is great evidence for the changes in circulation brought on by stress and we know now just about anything causes stress!). To cure this, the obvious choice was to bleed the patient to balance out the flood of blood in the brain. Sounds reasonable on paper except that human beings do indeed need a certain amount of blood or we wouldn't run on the stuff at all, and like his European muses, Rush took as much as possible.

Rush did have some really nifty ideas on how to draw blood away from the head to create that elusive balance and he still believed in treating his patients kindly. It's unfortunate that bleeding them to near death was thought of as the sound treatment of the day and fell under that umbrella of Acts of Kindness. Again, being a new science in a new country, water therapies held a special fascination and the thought that with water one could drown out the old and bring about a second birth of sorts free of illness as a sort of misguided baptism became the newest fad in treatment which lasted quite some time.

In the meantime, Rush died, as we all tend to eventually, and with his exit from this world the entrance of what was called "moral treatment' came into practice. Way back in the late 1700s when Phillipe Pinel was championing his new vision of treatment of the insane in Paris, the Quakers, a religious group of outcasts in England, were finding themselves in direct agreement with Pinel's ideas. The Quakers actually date back to around 1650 when they began officially as the Society Of Friends and began their practice of not claiming allegiance to the King of England and other behaviors that had them on the outs with the Monarchy. Like other groups in England at the time, the Quakers made their way to the New World and amongst many other contributions to American culture and government, they also brought great reform to the treatment of the insane based on the ideas of Dr. Pinel.

When the Quakers meant "friends" they meant that humanity was a brotherhood and that included the insane and ill of the world and all in the brotherhood of man deserved respect. Quakers believed in an inner light, that all the peoples of the world from all backgrounds and stations were made in the image of G-d and so therefore were brethren. If they were able to see this inner light they would be able to follow it to the purpose G-d intendsed for human beings. The Quaker faith is naturally designed in this way for the fight for equality (Productions, 2016).

In America, the Quakers opened up their own asylums beginning in 1796 which were veritable palaces in comparison with what was available at the time. The Quakers had already established Pennsylvania as a colony with a radical new vision well before working on the mental health system as it were at the time, though they had become a minority in the state at that time because of their refusal to participate in activities related to war.

The height of the era influenced by the Quakers is categorized by the beautifully-built stone buildings on sprawling grounds across the American landscape. Their belief that the insane were due the common respect of being clothed and treated for illness translated into small, beautifully-designed facilities with educational and recreational activities as well as responsibilities for patients. Though the Quakers had great success in alleviating the symptoms of what were considered the incurable insane, and gave their patients a respectable, gentle life they would not have otherwise had, they did not necessarily believe in aa actual cure for insanity.

As such, moral treatment by the Quakers was more palliative in nature, harkening back to the belief of man's inner light and being able to cure oneself if given the right environment to cultivate it. Therapy as we think of it today in which the therapist guides the patient to overcome problem *behaviors* caused by their illness was nonexistent in that time, so while in a moral sense many of the Quakers' beliefs in their fellow man could be said to be correct, "medically" moral treatment was off the mark by what we know today of what happens in the brain. But it was still a powerful testament to Americans that kindness over the strap in fact helped and made progress. Americans embraced the idea that the insane should be treated well as it was flush with the founding ideas of the Declaration of Independence and Quaker practice influenced many privately-funded asylums to be built and run on the moral treatment idea. One such notable asylum was the Pennsylvania Hospital for the Insane (Penn Medicine, 2017).

Under Dr. Thomas Kirkbride's leadership it was likely the best example of moral treatment in the hospital setting. Dr. Kirkbride's practices at the time of urging patients to stop blaming others for committing them to hospital, to attend to personal hygiene and dress, to work on social skills, to examine their own behavior, seek forgiveness for the acts they may have done under the influence of their illness and repair those relationships is very suggestive of the DBT[3] skills taught today in therapy groups. Of course the moral treatment route took time. Patients had no clinic option, no case managers or day hospital. They lived in care until deemed well and room and board in hospital took quite a lot of money (Kirkbride Buildings History, 2017).

The Quakers themselves were very distrustful of the European method of treatment used by Benjamin Rush and his associates to the point that they did not employ doctors at all to run their asylums but relied on laypersons to staff them. This of course was not taken well by American physicians who could've used the work in all the new facilities. As they couldn't beat the Quakers, they banded together to build their own facilities with state funding largely secured by the lobbying of reformer Dorothea Dix, a contemporary of Ralph Waldo Emerson, whose focus was on the poor with mental illness who went untreated (History.com staff, 2009).

It wasn't Dix's intent to end moral treatment; she in fact had been cared for by Quakers after what is thought to have been a mental breakdown (MS., 2006).

[3]Dialectical Behavioral Therapy, Marsha Linehan

It was upon seeing conditions in asylums on her return to the U.S. after this that sparked her fervor to provide decent hospitals for the poor. As a response to overcrowding reported by Dix, large state hospitals were built for the masses as opposed to private asylums for the rich.

As Psychiatry as a discipline was established, the study of mental illness commenced. It was theorized that the problem lay in the nerves, or more to the point, the frazzled nerves that came from 1800s American daily life grappling with a country trying to divide itself and then a bloody civil war to keep the States together. Today, medical science knows for certain that stress does indeed have the potential to kill us through physiological changes.

Crowding out the practice of moral treatment, the new larger hospitals were just the size to hold the thousands of new patients coming in to hospitals during the Civil War years and this in itself validated the need for a quicker method than moral treatment to its critics and the comforts of that method were lost in the fervor to brick up buildings fast enough to house those coming off the battlefield. Staff were less hired for the skills as much as their reliability to show up to work and strength to restrain a patient when needed. But the general rate of cure dropped steadily across the country and patients stayed in asylums longer.

The Civil War brought another change in philosophy for the treatment of the insane. As fickle as human nature and belief are, it's no surprise by the end of the war moral treatment was seen as a farce and something much heavier needed to be implemented to cure the world of the burden of insanity. My grandfather, a beloved man and WWII veteran, was committed of the truth that war is good business, meaning that war brings commerce and boosts an economy. The growth and establishment of businesses after a war is somewhat a given. It was no different with the state hospital system in post-civil war America. It was good timing that the patient population was quickly rising and doctors needed patients to stay in business. They put forth the new thinking that mental illness was indeed a *brain* disease and so needed to be treated by doctors specializing in the brain. Real doctors. *Neurologists*. It seems that the "real doctor" vs. psychiatrist rivalry has never really died, and now we know where it started. Medical science soberly made its pronouncement and thus ruled out the use of Psychiatry in treating insanity. As such, the old standbys of bloodletting and restraints returned; physical treatments for a physical brain ailment (Whitaker, Mad in America: Bad Science, Bad Medicine, and the Enduring Mistreatment of the Mentally Ill , 2010).

But Psychiatry wasn't through or over. In 1892, the American Medico-Psychological Association was formed (Health, 2008) to begin a new type of treatment far, far from that of what Ds. Dix and Dr. Kirkbride might have ever imagined. The belief that all men are created equal is one we Americans hold so dear to being the fabric of our nationality that sometimes we are blinded to it. It's as if we hold our flag up so close to our eyes it blurs into one color; blotting out the individual stars and stripes. It is blatantly obvious since the writing of these words that men aren't treated as if created equal if they are different from the accepted norm in race, religion, class, status, gender, etc., etc., etc., the list goes on. Equality is an ideal we must always strive for and this is very hard, unending work. There are periods in our history when we as citizens collectively sigh, "*This is too hard in the midst of everything else going on,*" and we give up on a particular group.

In the early 1900s that group was the mentally ill because of a theory proposed by Englishman Sir Francis Galton, a relation of the famous Charles Darwin. Galton was noted for publishing a book in 1869 titled *Hereditary Genius* some ten years after Darwin had published his opus, *Origin of Species* from which we get evolution theory. If Darwin pissed people off, it's a wonder Galton didn't suffer pitchforks at his front door. Though he made tremendous contributions to the study of human intelligence, genetics, calculus, and meteorology (Editors of Encyclopaedia Britannica, 2017), his work in *Hereditary*

*Genius* decidedly announced that humans are not at all equal and the affluent, white-populated areas of the earth needed to band together to make more babies and crowd out inferior blots on the human genome. Galton did not pull these theories out of the air by any means. He was well-learned in genetics and studied the pedigrees of traits in dogs well before moving on to the family pedigrees of humans. In a stunning display of *"you say potayto, I say potahto"*, Galton's travels worldwide convinced him human beings were as racially and intellectually separate as ever, where Darwin's convinced him of the commonality and relation between races.

This difference of observation would be a death-knell to millions in the coming century (Mukerjee, 2016). He believed that mental and physical traits are inborn and so, the more undesirable traits floating around to be reproduced and scattered, the worse off humanity as a whole would be. Now there were many groups around the world who fit the definition of "undesirable" but Galton saw and convinced the American public that the insane were truly at the bottom of the heap because insanity showed up in all demographics, marking its' sufferers as rejected from the legacy of mankind. It was clear to Galton that if society agreed to shelter its insane by way of asylums, it was natural for society to expect the insane to refrain from reproducing. Celibacy: the price of treatment (Editors of Encyclopaedia Britannica, 2017).

Keeping human DNA clean from inferior genes was called *eugenics*, referring to the "well-born", though other monikers were used before settling on this Greek-inspired term. For the first time this way of thinking introduced the theory still in use that mental illness can be inherited. Galton himself was extremely interested in twins and believed he could find the proof for the passing of mental illness through genes in such studies. Horrifically, the Nazi doctor Josef Mengele would *borrow* this idea for his infamous twin studies during the Holocaust of WWII. During the years eugenics picked up, immigration was expanding greatly, bringing plenty of undesirables into the US borders and skyrocketing the its popularity (Mukerjee, The Gene: In Intimate History, 2016).

Though many modern cities were built with the labor of immigrants, the rate at which they crowded those cities, reproduced, filled the asylums and convinced captains of industry Andrew Carnegie, John D. Rockefeller, Jr. and others to back laws made to force sterilization on the insane and prevent them from marrying. It all had to be stopped right at the root (though we all know marriage and babies aren't exclusive to each other, it seems the rich old men covered their bases). Galton's theories came into the 1900s strongly due to his next best seller, *Inquiries into Human faculty and Its Development*. Furthering the eugenics fervor, this volume spelled out Galton's belief that human beings could indeed circumvent the eons needed to perfect natural selection and jumpstart humanity's advancement by pulling out the bad seeds manually (Black, 2003).

Declaring someone insane became part of the norm in the early 1900s in order to take them out of the gene pool, put them in an asylum and forcibly sterilize them. How this passed by the public's better sense is frightening when looking back from an age where gene manipulation is indeed possible and the amount of in-utero information is staggering. At the time, America was empowered with brand new science and threatened by the swelling of immigration numbers into the country they'd more or less just established. The intellectuals and millionaires of the day pushed the idea of eugenics to save the human gene pool, to save the economy, and to save the ideals of America. The final tip to sway the scale of public opinion was biologist Charles Davenport's theory that each ethnic group inherits negative genes specific to that group which influence behavior such as a tendency towards prostitution or thievery, etc. which today we would consider to be a very racist attitude.

Due to this, it was imperative to cleanse the available genes in the world population to keep it safe from future criminals of all sorts who couldn't possibly help themselves from their pre-programmed behaviors. With funding and support from Andrew Carnegie, Davenport researched and figured out what it cost the U.S. to keep their unwanted and pronounced that the sterilization option just wasn't economical. Surely castration was the answer to achieve the goal of bringing order and a docile temperament to the insane so that they would no longer even desire to procreate.

Science went to town with this novel idea in studying genetics and eugenics, studying the family genealogies of the insane and symptoms in any other family members to prove the passing of defective gene matter and establishing a dedicated office to represent this new branch of study, with schools such as MIT, Cornell and Harvard getting in on the science as well as the Carnegie Foundation and Harriman Railroad.

It was being recorded with alarm that white, upper class birthrates were falling and couldn't keep up with the non-white, non-American population expanding rapidly. Sterilization couldn't keep up with the sheer numbers and a new solution was being sought out. But proving insanity and criminal tendencies were passed down proved to be difficult with the available science at the time and soon even relatives of the insane could be diagnosed (or accused) by default because it couldn't be disproven either. Because the science hadn't been perfected, family trees were studied scrupulously for any hint of defect and this was truly grasping at straws but succeeded nicely in convincing the public that insanity was indeed a disease that must be eliminated from future generations. Notice that the goal here was to stop the sick from passing on their illness rather than to cure the illness itself.

As more and more papers were churned out of universities by prominent scholars on the dangers of Jews, blacks, personal of mixed race, the poor and the insane on white stock, the American Eugenics Society sprang up in 1926, made up of scholars, scientists and American Psychiatric Association (APA) members. With a brilliant campaign aimed at convincing the public that they were throwing their tithes foolishly into the fire to support those "...*born to be a burden on the rest*" even churches were convinced of the theory and began to preach on G-d's favor to those He made without biological blemish (Mukerjee, The Gene: In Intimate History , 2016).

Schools followed suit and taught children that some were simply less than and thus unfit to procreate should they ruin society. If that sounds like a load of propaganda it's because by Miriam-Webster's definition, it is: *"the spreading of ideas, information, or \textit{rumor} for the purpose of helping or injuring an institution, a cause, or a person."* (Merriam-Webster, 2017)

Part two of this scheme to shift Americans' views on what constituted as favorable genetic material involved country-wide "better babies" contests in which mothers brought their little ones out to fairs and carnivals to be shown like pumpkins to doctors who would declare their rosy-cheeked progeny to be "better."

Suddenly, it was no longer absurd to pass laws to protect America of their rights to be free of tax-money-sucking burdens to the state. In fact, why hadn't anyone pointed this out before? Even supreme court justice Oliver Wendell Holmes wrote, *"It is better for all the world, if instead of waiting to execute degenerate offspring for crime, or to let them starve for their imbecility, society can prevent those who are manifestly unfit from continuing their kind..."* This infamous quote would be brought up in the Nuremburg criminal trials to defend the Nazi's practice of eugenic extermination (Black, The Horrifying American Roots of Nazi Eugenics, 2003).

Various states made marriage illegal for those identified as having mental illness beginning in 1896 with fines and prison sentences as consequences and by 1933 all states were on board. Sterilization laws were still sketchy and went back and forth because of a clause that only asylum patients could be sterilized by force but that left a lot of degenerates to take care of and America stepped up to proudly become the first country to force sterilization with almost 2/3 of the country in favor of the measure. The law continued to be redefined and expanded with doctors claiming it was so therapeutic patients asked for it. For whatever their personal reasons, there are indeed accounts of patients being grateful for the surgery and requesting it but in historical hindsight with the pressure put on patients to submit to treatment of various severities, it may be impossible to know if this is exactly true. How also can we know which of the treatments and practices we defend today will break our our descendants' hearts as they refer to us as victims who were fooled into giving ourselves up to? (Mukerjee, The Gene: In Intimate History , 2016) (Wong, 2013)

Accordingly, public opinion of the act grew strong in favor with this evidence. But in other countries the reverse was happening as had in the century before. When Benjamin Rush based his treatments on European theory, he had no idea it would come right back around. Europe didn't want to waste time sterilizing people, though killing them outright was frowned upon all round. The book *The Passing of the Great Race* by Madison Grant who was the U.S. leader of the eugenics movement, became a favorite book of Adolph Hitler in Germany and he heavily relied on state-sponsored extermination to end Germany's gene –sullying problems.

So enamored of the American practice of eugenics was Hitler that he mentions it in his infamous tome, *Mein Kampf.* The Nazis believed strongly in the concept of *Rassenhygeine,* or *racial hygiene,* which in laymen's terms is the same as eugenics: taking out all the impurities of the race to pass on only the best traits to future generations. Hitler kept an eye on U.S. experiments such as the practice of sending patients from the Virginia State Colony for Epileptics and the Feebleminded off to eugenic *camps* (Wong, A Shameful History: Eugenics in Virginia, 2013). In 1933 he enacted the *Law for Prevention of Genetically Diseased Offspring,* called the Sterilization Law which furthered the Nazi view that defectives were ruining the great German nation (United States Holocaust Memorial Museum, n.d.). After all, it was mused, *"The construction of a lunatic asylum costs 6 million marks. How many houses at 15,000 marks each could have been built for that amount?"*

By 1935 Hitler proposed extermination as the quickest way to sterilize. At the time in Germany, in order to declare someone unfit to reproduce they had to be taken to a special court and these were simply becoming overrun from trying the country's schizophrenics, manics, physically disabled and those like them. Trials cost money and took time. If this whole process could be cut out, how much the better for the state? But even Hitler knew outright murder would be a hard sell to the Reich. Turns out he didn't have much work to do in the end.

In a move unbearable to think about, a Nazi couple petitioned right about that time to rescue the nation from their defective genes by euthanizing their disabled baby (Zoech, 2003), a child who would for years be referred to only as *Case K*. Hitler took the opportunity to put his extermination plan into action, and from 1935-1939 *preventative sterilization* killed thousands of children and teens.

In 1940, the Nazis had taken French Nobel-prize winner Dr. Alexia Carrel's suggestion in his book *Man the Unknown* that undesirables should be put out of the human race with gas (his idea of the most humane option) literally and sought to begin the master race of the Third Reich with eliminating 70,000 to 90,000 of Germany's insane and disabled in specially constructed gas-chambers (WW2History.com, n.d.). In 1941, Hitler, impressed by the savings of the country over eighteen months of exterminations, ordered the chambers dismantled and reconstructed at the infamous concentration camps of WWII.

The idea in this form of *preventative sterilization* made its way to America and "mercy-killing" as it was thought of was advertised to be done by poison as this was thought to be the least unkind method. I must note here that the method had some serious thought put into it. This was an age where insanity was being recognized as a disease that caused not only suffering in the community and a threat to the human genome but a disease that destroyed lives and could possibly be passed on genetically. Those were some big ideas to grapple with in a short time historically but I do think it should be remembered that to the scholars of the time, mercy killing was a "humane" method already being practiced in Germany. Using this method, it made sense to end the patient's suffering and conquer two aims at once.

While abhorrent and based in deception as Germany's exterminations were, to the public and the families of victims, it is still more thought than was given in times past in regard to insanity outside of the years of moral treatment. American eugenicists saw Germany's practices as the natural answer to their research and wealthy Americans sent funding to German researchers to carry on the work, particularly at The Kaiser Wilhelm Institute (Black, The Horrifying American Roots of Nazi Eugenics, 2017).

In a twist of perfect irony, Galton himself had suffered a nervous breakdown as a young man before his work on eugenics and had to leave Cambridge to heal at home (Editors of Encyclopedia Britannica, 2017). He did, obviously, feel his genes were superior and not subject to the weeding out of eugenics because of the famous names in his family tree. Everyone else with a rotten apple in the tree apparently suffered the whole barrel spoiling. It took only seventy-five years, a human lifetime, from the time eugenics was first proposed to the cold murder of millions under Hitler's hand.

By the end of WWII eugenics was declared a crime against humanity and the American asylums had degraded so much so that former soldiers returning from combat compared them to the concentration camps they'd witnessed overseas. The filthy, poor conditions of the buildings, nakedness, hunger and stark neglect harked back to the French asylums nearly two centuries before. Economic issues during the war years led to deterioration of care but so did the eugenic attitudes remain that the insane did not warrant the money to be spent in tending them. A formal expose in *Life Magazine* in 1946 titled *Bedlam: Most U.S. Mental Hospitals are a Shame and A Disgrace*, by Albert Maisel shocked the country with hard photographic evidence and equally hard accusations of abuses and even deaths behind the walls of modern asylums (Cooke, 2017).

While *Life* had covered asylum care previously, it was Mr. Maisel's article written with the observations of conscientious war-objectors including Quakers and other religious groups who had volunteered their service in low-staffed asylums that brought out true and righteous outrage in the American people. Beginning with the state of Ohio, American eugenics laws were repealed in response and work to treat the mentally ill of America better than Hitler treated his victims of war in Germany began.

After such an uproar, Americans were left with a bad taste in the mouth of Psychiatry. To keep in business, Psychiatry needed a hook of sorts for funding to continue research. Towards the end of WWII Neuropsychiatry was gaining ground and the Neuropsychiatric Act was passed in 1945 (National Institutes of Health, 2017) to research diagnosis, prevention and treatment of mental illness. On paper this sounded like a forerunner to today's outpatient clinic model with preventative care being stressed to keep patients from needing hospitalization in the first place. The pendulum had shifted from preventing the mentally ill themselves to preventing the need for serious treatment for their illnesses. From this shift the National Institutes of Mental health (NIMH) was founded (University of California Press). In the treatment setting water therapies came back for the first time since Benjamin Rush's day, repackaged and with a vengeance to cure.

With new claims of success rate, the classic hydrotherapy images of rows and rows of bathtubs in large institutions was born. Patients could be bound up to black out sensations such as sight and sound and placed in a tub of hot or cold water for hours or days with other reports as from the Pennsylvania Hospital of weeks or months! In the interest of the patient, doctors felt that prolonged exposure to water helped a variety of ailments and the bath was made to be as pleasant as possible, considering. If soaking for months didn't do the trick, the needle shower could always be employed (not like it sounds) or wet packs were also an alternative option.

Though the needle shower and baths were humble enough, most patients were understandably unfavorable towards being wrapped tightly in wet sheets and left to lay for days until the fabric shrunk. Still, none of these methods in the early years after the war held any candle to the new, exciting and horrific field of psychiatric surgery. The theory of what caused and cures mental illness was yet again to take a sharp turn.

# Holding on to One's Molars

As we had previously learned, even in ancient times people thought there was a correlation between Epilepsy and mood changes, with physicians of the day speculating that if they could produce seizures in patients, they could bring on the beneficial effects of them. But a seizure is like lightning in the brain; an electrical storm. How to go about creating lightning inside one's head?

Shock therapy in its earliest form didn't come along until the end of the 1930s and is predated by several other popular tactics to create a state of shock in the body (as well as surgery to correct the brain) during the last years of the eugenics schemes in the United States. As there's more than one way to skin a cat, there was also more than one way to put the body into a state of shock.

Neurophysiologist and psychiatrist Dr. Manfred Sakel discovered the unforeseen use of *insulin* shock when he treated a famous morphine addict who also had Diabetes. After he gave her an accidental overdose of insulin, she fell into a mild coma and on coming out of it, Dr. Sakel observed his patient reported her drug cravings had abated. The correlation was a godsend for those treating addictions and soon a theory was formed that it worked because it damaged younger, newer brain pathways caused by disease so that the older, original pathways could take over and rebalance the brain.

Who was most noted for an imbalanced brain? The notoriously hard-to-treat schizophrenic patients. It didn't take long for insulin-shock to be used on this population and indeed, schizophrenic patients did seem to improve and so validated the 1927 mistake by Sakel and allowed it to last a very long time into the twentieth century as a preferred treatment.

Another form of shock therapy used by Dr. Ladislas von Meduna of Budapest in the 1930s was that of *chemical* shock. After studying both schizophrenic and epileptic brains, he thought he found slight differences in the nerve cells (which since has been refuted) that lent to the older theory that the presence of seizures and Epilepsy somehow prevent Schizophrenia. His work began with trials of camphor, which has been in use since the 1500s as a treatment for a variety of conditions from cold sores to fungal infections. He then progressed to using Metrazole (marketed as Cardiazol in Europe) as a method for shock.

Metrazole is a heart medication which certainly caused seizures in patients but they were generally awake through the procedure. The risk of fractures from the seizures was quite high and the seizures were notoriously hard to control. While taking heart medication until you seize is a horrendous experience on the body, Metrazole shock had good press in the U.S. and was credited with some notable success that lead to various European clinics set up and maintained for the treatment throughout WWII.

Though Metrazole shock therapy was discontinued in many areas in favor of ECT, the drug itself is still available today for its original purpose. With the need for a treatment *like* that of Metrazole being so great during the war years, scientists across Europe quickly looked for something better. And by better I mean, something that caused seizures in a controlled manner and would knock a person out before the seizure actually started. Insulin shock therapy was somewhat easier on a patient but required a good deal of staff to watch a patient's vital signs. Normally you wanted to avoid a coma at all costs because if the blood sugar dipped too low too quick or the patient wasn't able to absorb glucose quickly enough to offset a coma, death was waiting in the wings. It was the sheer maintenance of insulin therapy that drove Psychiatry towards a cheaper and more permanent solution.

What today is called *Psychiatric Surgery* (or Psychosurgery in recent history) was once considered to be high science; a breakthrough in the treatment of Schizophrenia. Psychiatric surgeries encompassed a variety of procedures including the removal of organs and teeth, *leucotomy* and *lobotomy*. These treatments are also still thought of as the most barbaric of psychiatric procedures, perhaps not always in their mechanics but the intent behind them which seemed often to have nothing to do with healing and more to do with punishing someone.

Because mental health treatment and punishment for what was deemed deviant behavior at the time are so intertwined, we will need to be very mindful of fact versus opinion as we wade through an even darker period of history leading up to the widespread usage of ECT as a first-line treatment. Dr. Bayard Holmes and later psychiatrist Dr. Henry Cotton can be thought of as the granddaddies of Psychosurgery in the twentieth century.

Though they never met, their ideas about bacteria causing the infections which brought on mental illness spurred them on to remove teeth, parts of the digestive tract and the sex organs (by Dr. Cotton in up to 80% of his female inpatients) with a death rate of around 25-30%. The practice went something like this: if the symptoms of mental illness didn't subside after the first surgery, the doctor began pulling out subsequent vital parts in the name of keeping ahead of the infection. Dr. Cotton, however, did not stop with mental patients but also did the procedures on children (along with his own, as did Dr. Holmes) in the name of preventing mental illness from beginning. Ironically, Dr. Cotton was never trained as a surgeon; he died suddenly in 1933 (Neuroskeptic, 2015).

The removal of organs to treat mental illness was followed by leucotomy, the father of a later and much more infamous treatment known as lobotomy. Leucotomy is simply the removal of brain tissue thought to be the direct cause of mental illness symptoms. Neurologist Egas Moniz, of Portugal developed it in 1936 based on the thinking that people with obsessive disorders had brains with "fixed" or obsessive circuits and it stood to reason a few snip-snaps in the right place would keep brain chatter down to its usual dull roar. Moniz won a Nobel Prize for his work in this area.

The leucotomy was performed with a *leutocome,* a long instrument with a looped wire at the end that could be inserted through any of four to six holes bored into the skull before the procedure and turned or twisted to sever brain tissue connections. Though it may be difficult to understand why the leucotomy might have been such a paramount development, let's break it down. Physical treatments involving the brain tissue directly at the time besides insulin and Metrazole shock included injections of alcohol directly into the brain as well as injecting malaria-infected blood directly into the brain and also injecting a schizophrenic or depressive's own blood into the brains of others affected by paralysis.

These physical treatments for mental illness were called *somatic* treatments. It was thought in the 1930s and '40s that severe mental illness was caused by a physical condition or defect giving it an organic cause while lesser (non-psychotic) illnesses had an environmental cause such as stress or situation, not unlike the prevailing theories of the late 1800s and not unlike those of today. This manner of thinking became quite popular along with a eugenically-themed theory put forth in Europe that certain body types are more likely to develop certain mental disorders. Today, brain surgery is performed daily on thousands of patients with dysfunction from accidents or other illnesses and no hope of functioning normally or as the case may be, surviving at all without the repair or removal of the tissues in question.

What used to be done with scalpels is now many times done with non-surgical treatments, i.e: medication, chemotherapy, vagal nerve stimulation, etc. But in this part of past history there were no psychiatric medications as we know them today and major mental illness meant continual torment from a non-curable illness, total marginalization from society, many times living out life in an asylum or exiled from one's family if not imprisoned and left to die. In the case of one's choices being:

A. Live out the rest of one's life alone in mental torture unable to better oneself,

B. Live out the rest of one's life tortured in an asylum, or

C. Take a chance someone will poke around in your head and give you a relative shot at something better,

for many people option C didn't look so bad. That is, when it was chosen freely with Informed Consent. Informed Consent, the practice of informing a patient about treatment and getting their permission to administer it, is a practice we believe in deeply today but was not always a feature in medical treatment of the first half of the twentieth century. At that time, it was a widespread practice (thought of as the kinder means of treatment) to keep certain stressful or disturbing aspects of illness and its antidotes from a patient. This didn't just happen of course in mental health treatment; many cancer patients were sent home to die without ever knowing the name of the illness stealing their lives away in countries around the world and shades of this practice still exists as deemed fit.

In 2017 America we believe more or less that the patient should know the name and pathology of their ailment and how to fix it so they can partner with their doctor to fight on the same side. This is the ideology, but many times it does not cross over into mental health. And during the 1930s whenlLeucotomy really got its footing from the focus being to keep people out of the asylum long-term, Informed Consent was virtually nonexistent.

Leucotomy became the favored technique in Europe and Dr. Moniz 's successes with the surgery included schizophrenic patients who became subdued and much more manageable after the procedure. But it is recorded that Dr. Moniz did not do much follow-up with his patients after the initial procedure and as with any other surgery, there is always a percentage of relapse and frankly botched jobs. Let's stick to the facts: major mental illnesses sometimes require serious measures to control symptoms. Mental illness is still quite poorly understood in medical science. When you've got someone out of control right in front of you and nothing else is working, you've got to do what works. In traditional medical practice we're talking cracking someone's chest open to save them. It's not pretty, has lots of nasty effects later and if done right, saves a person's life. Such is also the situation when saving a person's life or those around them from the effects of mental illness.

It didn't take long for the practice of leucotomy to cross the Atlantic and gain an American spin, retooled, shortened and renamed the *lobotomy* by Dr. Walter Freeman. Lobotomy is the procedure well-known as the "icepick" surgery in which a long, thin instrument is inserted into the eye socket to gain access to the brain to sever connections for the same result as a leucotomy. But instead of *snip* and *snap*, lobotomy was more like swashbuckling through tissue in half the time it takes to get to the same areas of the brain. Though Egas Muniz never intended his surgery to become commercial, Dr. Freeman saw the free market potential and through his marketing of lobotomy as achieving the same results of leucotomy in a fraction of the time, American Psychiatry took hold and lobotomy took off as the new in-vogue treatment.

Early on, Dr. Freeman partnered with neurosurgeon Dr. James Watts who had previously learned to perform leucotomies from an instruction kit mailed from Dr. Moniz himself. From this the duo developed the procedure of lobotomy and whittled it down to the world-famous transorbital procedure, *transorbital* referring to the eye socket in which the instrument is inserted. While quick and cheap, lobotomy also had some drawbacks.

The big problem with the procedure was that surgeons couldn't see what they were cutting as they did not have the scanning or monitoring equipment used today. During the procedure, a local anesthetic was given and the patient was made to answer questions or make movements to let the surgeon know if they were in the general area. Today with functional MRI scans (fMRI) procedures are still done in this same manner for brain functions which cannot be monitored as in a famous recent example of musician Roger Frisch playing the violin with his head open and brain exposed during a Deep Brain Stimulation procedure to correct hand tremors (Starr, 2014).

However, lobotomy also caused a lot of brain damage in the process because it was so inexact and because it went into the brain via the prefrontal lobe which controls a good deal of cognitive functions and therefore screws up a whole lot if damaged.

Not trained as a surgeon himself, Freeman even admitted that with lobotomy, patients lost something in their personality and the process itself was quite risky but the result outweighed such risks for those with serious illness and no other hope of cure. Freeman rushed his results to present to the medical community and got into some serious upsets with colleagues but sweeping headlines across the country reporting the miraculous outcomes of these surgeries advanced its acceptance over past therapies. In some cases lobotomies were done as an exhibition for the medical community, putting the mentally ill once more in the role of sideshow as they had been almost two hundred years prior.

Many patients later relapsed, developed seizures they did not previously have or were required to have a second surgery. Some didn't gain freedom from the hospital but rather ended up there for life, unable to care for themselves at all. A different type of blade was used to perform lobotomy than was used in leucotomy and the end sometimes broke off in the brain, requiring the surgeon to go back in to retrieve it. It was swung upward rather than turned to do the severing of tissue and was done from a different direction than with leucotomy, with less holes put into the skull. As would later be the case with early electroshock, if the patient was still awake and responding during the operation, the surgeon assumed he needed to do *more*, cut *more*. (Levinson, 2011)

While many patients were given a local anesthesia, some were not, and these patients did sometimes report feeling an obvious relief from their fear or anxiety as the last cut was made (Valenstein, 2010). Because it was such a quick procedure and hospitals were really gunning to get their patients discharged after years of high-maintenance shock therapies, some worked out to the penny how much they would save per year per surgery with critics in the medical community accusing surgeons of jumping straight to lobotomy rather than assessing whether it would actually be helpful or even appropriate first. James Watts was so confident in Dr. Freeman's technique that in their famous co-authored book *Psychosurgery: Intelligence, Emotion and Social Behavior by W. Freeman and J.W. Watts,* he wrote a short manual with instructions on how to perform a lobotomy anywhere so anyone could manage if need be.

Though Watts was a neurosurgeon, his contemporaries protested this, maintaining that there was a reason why they were required to get some sort of certification in opening up a skull outside of reading a book. But the tome was well received by the public and highly influential because of its self-reported successes with the number of surgeries rising exponentially after WWII with returning soldiers. The push to get patients out of asylums was also heavily socially driven after *Life Magazine's* 1946 "Bedlam" article.

Outraged, the public demanded a solution and lobotomy was right there to answer the call. As time went on, other protests occurred over whether statistics reported were accurate or whether "quieting" patients with the surgery was for their benefit or for their carers, that those performing lobotomies didn't take proper cleanliness precautions, that some patients would have naturally had remissions in the course of their illness so didn't need the unnecessary risk of surgery, and that the follow-up testing at the time wasn't adequate to measure the damage done to begin with so how could it be known to what extent harm had been done alone or with help? A 1948 article in the U.S. publication *The Nation* even referred to lobotomy as *"raping the soul"* (Valenstein, Great and Desperate Cures : The Rise and Decline of Psychosurgery and Other Radical Treatments for Mental Illness, 2010).

The wide range of effects with lobotomy surely had much to do with its imprecise execution; as some patients like twelve year-old Howard Dully went on to marry and write books about their experiences and others like the famous Kennedy sister Rose, reverted to a childlike state requiring continual care (Day, He was Bad, so They Put an Ice Pick in his Brain, 2008). As time went on, the quiet nature of lobotomized patients was likened to that of zombies and became the striking picture of the procedure as these patients certainly had less anxiety but also less care for life, little motivation or emotional response. As had been admitted by its creator, something was lost in the cure. Serious public protest against the procedure began in the late 1940s and though it waned in the '50s, lobotomy is recorded as still being used as late as the early 1980s, replaced by ECT and psychotropic drug usage.

So popular was lobotomy during its high point that it was used by notable hospitals such as the Mayo Clinic and the University of Pennsylvania as well as the Administration of Veterans' Affairs on nearly two thousand returning soldiers to treat a variety of mental illnesses. Veterans returning from duty are very susceptible to Depression and Post-Traumatic Distress Disorder and so require mental health treatment specialized to their needs, which is where the VA system comes in on the side of government-provided treatment for the military. The treatment left many men unable to leave the hospital or care for themselves; some died from the procedure itself. The theory of having a second childhood and growing up with a healthy brain died on the spot with the stark reality that none of us gets to be Peter Pan after all. Realistically, it was later noted that in some instances it was simply impossible to say if the surgery alone helped because many patients had already gone through several shock therapies before even having lobotomy (Newitz, 2013) (Phillips, n.d.).

With even psychiatrists questioning why science hadn't come up with something better by the 1950s but unable to point to anything else with the same dramatic results, the climate was excellent for a novel new treatment, something as bold as lobotomy but that didn't involve ruining any kitchen utensils or messing around with anyone's actual brain matter. Again, it was Europe who stepped up with the next big turn in mental health history.

On that side of the globe in Switzerland as early as the mid-1930s scientists had been looking for a better means to induce seizures than the failed Metrazole method and had been using electric currents on dogs to observe the effects. This was not pretty work and was done in most inhumane ways in the name of providing better options for human beings. In Italy, it had been observed that administering electric shocks to pigs in the abattoir subdued them but did not kill them, thereby making it easier to drain the animal of its blood as part of the slaughter process. This process is still used in commercial butchering today and though regulated (or not, as has been alleged by countless watchdog groups) (Grandin, 2015), it is again, very nasty stuff.

But the idea of electric shocks at a rate that did not actually kill was sparking new theories in the medical world and Italian Dr. Ugo Cerletti and his student Lucio Bini made the leap of electric + seizure = cure. In a sense, they were looking to control lightning in the brain to exploit its curative properties and soon enough they had come up with a machine to do just that. Dr. Cerletti had worked with epileptics during WWI. His theory was that the body produces something he called a *vitalizing substance* or *acro-amines* after a seizure or after engaging in an extreme struggle. Cerletti and Bini would shock animal subjects with a machine Bini built and they found that shocking the animals through the mouth to the rear caused the electric current to pass through the heart. While it certainly produced the seizure they were looking for, it also killed the animals on the spot. When they modified the machine to pass an electric current through the head only, avoiding the heart altogether, the seizure was produced and the animal lived.

In 1938 with a volunteer who had already been assumed to have a major mental illness by the policeman who picked him up at a train station, Dr. Cerletti began trying out his new machine and reportedly to great effect. It is speculated, however, from examination of Cerletti's own personal records that in reporting his successes the doctor may have left out a bit of his initial failures, that the discovery was less an *ah hah!* Moment and more a trial and error process. From other sources, the first round on Cerletti's volunteer didn't knock him out so the machine was amped up. On the second round the subject cried out to them to stop lest they kill him but the good doctors reasoned they weren't giving it enough juice if he was still talking and cranked it up again. Third time seemed to be a charm and afterwards when the subject came to, he was observed to be much calmer than previous to the treatment and did not recall the it in fact at all (Aruta, 2011).

Why keep out this information? Likely because selling the concept of shocking a human being with electricity would have been perceived by medical science as, well, *unorthodox* without incontrovertible proof that it worked with a 100% rate of success. If we are uncomfortable with the usage of electricity today on the brain in this age of safety protocols and surge protectors, how much more so would people a century ago have been!

But there were indeed several improvements to Metrazole-induced seizures with the new electroshock treatment, one being that the patient generally blacked out quickly after the seizure started rather than having to suffer through it and of course it was not invasive like brain surgery techniques. The patient did not have to be opened up to be treated. On that account, Dr. Walter Freeman criticized ECT in the early 1950s as well as the new psychotropic drugs for causing amnesia and suicidality in some patients, yet he used also used electric shock in his later practice to knock out lobotomy patients pre-surgery when the procedure was refined to its ice-pick stage through the transorbital lobe.

With electric shock, one also did not generally fall into a coma as with insulin treatments of old, though ECT, like most treatments of any sort has been known to cause death in some rare instances. The wide usage of electric shock spelled the final death of Metrazole shock because it was easier to administer and caused less fractures from the convulsions at the time in the arms, legs, hips, spine and jaw amongst other areas. Insulin shock, on the other hand, remained a favorite practice in Europe despite its upkeep well into the 1960s. The general idea with ECT was to jolt the system enough to reset the brain and allow it to start fresh without having to "grow up" emotionally again as with leucotomy and lobotomy. It was theorized that to heal the brain it must be broken and rebuilt from square one, not unlike re-breaking a bone which has been fractured and healed incorrectly (as it is still thought to do and how it was explained to me in 2012).

Whether or not this is the actual mechanism isn't known and there are always those who perhaps are too far gone into the depression or other illnesses who do receive *some* benefit but not the full effect as was observed of me when treatment was discontinued to restart medication per my medical records. While greatly hoped for during its development, we know now that ECT is not a cure for mental illness, its continued success depends on subsequent treatments and in many cases, combined with therapy and medication.

After Dr. Cerletti developed that first machine, different models began popping up across Europe and found their way to America where the free market put the technology to use right away. In 1940 the first therapeutic treatments were being done and by the early 1950s ECT was used across the world much in the same quantity as its cousins Metrazole treatments and lobotomies still were, but ECT emerged the clear winner while the drug therapies were being developed that would later become the dominant first line treatment remaining to this day.

What brought it ahead beyond its physical merits? The same old story that pushed Metrazole to the front of the line: Money. Like so many other twists and turns in the road of American Psychiatry, the dollar figured into many treatment decisions and advances because of the cost of keeping the masses housed in state hospitals. A study done in 1954 determined that after overhead costs were taken out of the state allowance for asylum patients, the amount of money on average being spent on daily food for each patient was a reprehensible 16 cents a day. We can see clearly that the cheaper and more efficient a treatment was in moving patients back out into the open was top priority for American medicine (Valenstein, Great and Desperate Cures : The Rise and Decline of Psychosurgery and Other Radical Treatments for Mental Illness, 2010). Being a cheap and easy treatment gave ECT the presence in hospitals across the U.S. of a frontline treatment and soon enough, it was being given to most patients entering psychiatric care.

# Washing One's Brain
# and Other Tales


WHEN we think of the usage of ECT as a treatment for mental illness, one name stands out above the rest: Dr. Donald Ewan Cameron. This Scottish- born, Canadian psychiatrist was once called the "CIA Mengele" for his work experimenting with the practice of depatterning on the mentally ill in the Alan Memorial Institute of Montreal from 1957- 1964 as part of secret CIA campaigns against enemies of the United States during the Korean War (Herculano, 2009).

In the early 1950s just after WWII ended, the U.S. was heavily involved in the Korean War (1950-1953, respectively) and reeling from the damage done to troops during WWII by the Russians and Chinese. The U.S. government was looking for a way to gain information from enemies to help keep ahead of the Russians and Chinese, who were adept at *brainwashing*, as the term was coined during those years. The CIA reasoned that their tactics were so effective against American POWs that they must be using extraordinary methods. But research into this brought the government to the conclusion on the re-education of Chinese prisoners into Mao-ism and the effectiveness of extracting confessions in the Russian Gulag that these were purely psychological methods that worked only within the criminals' own culture.

It was an unbeatable combination and feeling time was running out after American POWs began coming back from Korea having confessed to crimes they didn't commit, the CIA turned to unorthodox tactics to gain footing.

Some of these tactics were explored in covert operations such as PROJECT BLUEBIRD, PROJECT ARTICHOKE and MKULTRA (National Security Archive, 1975) where research was conducted in the mental effects of isolation, LSD, memory loss, hypnotism, truth serum and electroshock amongst others. Conspiracy theorists often cite these three operations and they've come up a lot in popular television series such as the *X-Files*, and more recently, *Agent Carter*, *Minority Report* and *Stranger Things*.

Many records of these projects as well as multiple other related CIA studies were destroyed in the mid-1970s but remaining references are available for public review through the CIA's website and others can be obtained by filing under the Freedom of Information Act (Project MKULTRA, the CIA's Program of Research in Behavioral Modification, 1977). If it was true that the Koreans also had this type of power against U.S. soldiers and spies, in a military mindset the only option would be to gain this power and beat the enemy at their own game.

In war, survival is *paramount*; when looking at how our own existence is dependent on the victory of past campaigns it can be tempting to justify any means, but method can become fuzzy in the eyes of morality. Many of MKULTRA's methods at the time were downright terrifying violations of human rights and many individuals, prisons, universities, pharmacies and institutions involved in carrying out experiments either didn't know who was paying out overhead or what the information was being used for. And, of course, there were those who certainly did and either got out right then or carried it on to even higher levels of violation when told by government to stop. This was a very dark chapter in the history of the U.S. Government, a time of rampant abuse of the mentally ill behind closed doors after the work of reformation in institutions in the earlier part of the century and a time we cannot gloss over or forget because the horrors of that generation led the way to the healing of the current one.

Just like the horrific experiments done on victims of the Holocaust in WWI and WWII led to untold advances in medicine and science after the war, so too the pain of those victims of experimentation in mind control gave their minds so that we today have more and safer options to battle various mental illnesses. I regard of all of these patients and those before them as my common ancestors and I respect what they have given to me as a descendent. Let's look for a moment on the process by which projects MKULTRA and ARTICHOKE used ECT, starting with the work done during WWII in this area of study (LSD, Mind Control, and the Internet: A Chronology, n.d.).

To begin with, experiments with ECT on children as young as three were conducted at Bellevue Hospital, New York by Dr. Laura Bender from 1942-1956 and later at Creedmore State Hospital from 1956-1969 were thought to have tamed the symptoms of unruliness and disarray these children exhibited at home and in the classroom due to Autistic Schizophrenia (an old diagnostic term used). Dr. Bender was greatly influenced by the work of Dr. Harold Abramson, an influential name in the field of LSD research under the American group the Josiah Macy Foundation (John Breeding, 2014).

Abramson also did child studies, conducting LSD trials on children from the ages of five to fourteen. After using both ECT and LSD on the children she treated, Dr. Bender was awarded funding from the Society of Human Ecology to continue her own work. She spearheaded a good deal of arcane methodology in testing of ESP; astrology and the like, all of which were being looked into by the government as serious sources of defense. Absolutely no stone could be left unturned in winning the war. But later studies suggested that the opposite was true; while some children became violent and one hardly seen to derive any benefit at all, others seemed happier and Dr. Bender had reasonable hope for a cure. It's speculated that all the subjects of her studies were orphaned or wards of the state and guardians may not have been aware of the experiments or given consent but there isn't much documentation one way or another. Some of the children who were treated in this manner were also exposed to LSD (being studied more and more at the time) and went on to become self-harming and in one sad instance, attempted suicide at nine years of age. While the benefits may have been up to interpretation, one thing was crystal clear: electroshock *influenced behavior*, making it the golden egg of wartime application (Jr., 2010).

The days of experimentation on an entirely captive audience in the mental institutions of America had begun in earnest, spilling over to prisons and other social institutions. We can thank this practice for several key medical advancements that affect us still today from public water fluoridation first studied on children, VA patients, soldiers, pregnant women, African-Americans, infants, prostitutes and student volunteers. We can thank it for progress in the usage of chemotherapy as studied in 1931 with radium-266 injections at Elgin State Hospital. We may ponder the influence these studies had on flu vaccines developed from spraying influenza into the nasal passageways of patients and our understanding of the effects of cold temperature on the body from keeping mentally disabled patients in 30 degree refrigeration for up to 120 hours at University of Cincinnati Hospital. Even as late as 1987 were the mentally ill used in studies to determine LSD levels in the brain by administering LSD and electrodes on the brain. Though society has always wanted their undesirables to be hidden from view, few have thought twice about refusing the gifts of their suffering for the sake of the "greater good (Marks, 1991)

The techniques of war are terrible and fascinating and the mentally ill have always been a conveniently available and captive population to try such things out on. In their own way, lunatics throughout time have advanced the wars of men unwittingly, using the frailty of their minds to contribute to the war effort where others may be sent to engage in fighting on land, by air and by sea. It would be impossible for the U.S. government to use regular patients to do its research. After all, even the enemy Nazis turned away from terminal experimenting on "normal" subjects, preferring to use the undesirables of Germany such as the mentally ill, criminals, prostitutes, minorities and drug addicts.

To prove the point, Rudolf Hess, Nazi Deputy Fuhrer to Adolf Hitler levied the accusation against shock doctor Dr. Ewan Cameron of doing experiments against his patients without consent. In the early 1950s Dr. Cameron had been experimenting in Canada with a process called "depatterning" brought on by a treatment cycle of electroshock treatments, induced sleep and subliminal messages.

Cameron was born in Scotland and had come eventually to practice at Allen Memorial Institute in Montreal, holding the title of head of the American Psychology Association in 1953. The hospital became a prime site for CIA-funded studies in "brainwashing." (Zetter, 2010) Whether Cameron actually knew his projects were funded by the CIA is speculated on but not proven. What he and the CIA *were* aware of at the time were that shock treatments caused memory loss, behavior changes and confusion. The CIA had invested a good deal of time and money during this time via PROJECT ARTICHOKE to come up with the most effective ways of brainwashing and these methods included the use of ECT, LSD and the old favorite, Metrazole. In the early '50s, Metrazole may have fallen out of favor in public hospitals, but its side effects of violent shaking and contractions made it an excellent interrogation drug used against Communist prisoners of war. This was also a time in history when, under the auspices of building the best war machine, highly-regarded scientists and psychiatrists such as Donald Hebb and John Lilly began intense experiments in sensory deprivation, which would later cross paths directly with ECT (Institute, n.d.).

The CIA found that electroshock effects were kicked up a notch with the addition of Dr. Cameron's depatterning technique and jumped at the chance to have this studied further. In terms of treating mental illness, depatterning a human brain was rooted in the idea that if one could break the mind through wiping it of memory, the brain's *memory* of illness symptoms (namely Schizophrenia, which Cameron was trying to treat) would be *forgotten* as well and allow the patient to start over in a healthy mental state and have a fair shot at healing and working normally. This theory depended on the persistent idea that the mentally ill are born with a broken brain to begin with.

On one hand, it seems common sense that the most complex and mysterious part of the human body can't simply be split apart and put back together but with what science knows today of neuroplasticity, perhaps this is entirely possible in theory. The brain can and does mend itself in many situations throughout the lifespan of a human without our ever knowing it. The CIA came in on the idea that if one could rebuild a broken brain, it stood to reason one could use the same process to break an unbroken one and wash out enemy secrets or reverse the process and send back a re-programmed prisoner of war to sabotage an enemy country. Patients who participated in Cameron's depatterning experiments were mainly women (a statistic which still stands in ECT treatment today in the U.S.) and some who gave consent and much later felt they were coerced into doing so. The anti-feminist notion of women being more prone to hysteria also lent to the usage of ECT in that men whose wives acted out of turn for the social mores of the day could have them treated and in theory made more docile.

The shock treatments were done in a *sleep room* as they were called because of the alternating cycles of induced sleep and shock and these were feared by patients throughout psychiatric hospitals everywhere they were set up in. Patients and staff alike walked on the other side of the corridor where a sleep room might be located and it was not uncommon for patients to attempt escaping the hospital. Staff later interviewed stated they were hard-pressed to find these frightened patients and bring them back to endure more treatments.

Doctors used what today would be considered extremely condescending, bordering on manipulative language to convince patients they needed to submit to this type of treatment method. The character Nurse Ratched sums up the manipulative nature shock treatment could take on at the time in the 1962 novel *One Flew Over the Cuckoo's Nest* when she notes that troublemaker McMurphy will be free from shock treatment *this* time if he confesses his wrong (Kesey, 1962).

In depatterning, success was measured in terms of long term or permanent memory loss. Dr. Cameron claimed the patient to be cured as the offending behaviors (due to his theory of "differential amnesia") were also *lost* (Scotland, 2008). But it was noted in later years that the memories sometimes did return and so also did the features of the illness. However, as Mr. John Marks points out in *The Search for the Manchurian Candidate*, schizophrenic patients who suffered continued memory loss and were later put under testing did in fact still show the illness's hallmark disordered thinking so it's possible it may be that the treatment course attacked the symptoms but not the actual disease.

The procedure of depatterning went was carried out specifically as such: ECT at up to 150 watts two to three times daily based on the Page-Russell method (this was used in Britain at the time at 110 watts administered once daily) fifteen to thirty days sleep therapy in which the patient was put into induced sleep with a combination of 100mg Thorazine, 100 mg Nembictal, 200 mg Seconal, 150 mg Veronal, 10 mg Phenersan, administered three times daily when awakened for meds, fed and then put back to sleep (1964 Allen Memorial Institute Procedure Book). There is debate over whether patients at the time had two or three doses of medication. Staff would testify to three in later inquiry, Dr. Cameron asserted it was two. (Marks, The Search for the Manchurian Candidate: The CIA and Mind Control: The Secret History of the Behavioral Sciences, 1991)

In Mr. Marks' interview with *Lauren G*, who received treatment in 1959 with Dr. Cameron's approach, it was revealed that Dr. Cameron thought he could break up disordered thought patterns in Schizophrenia (essentially non-surgically doing the same as what a leucotomy or lobotomy does). Based on this, he thought the side effect of memory loss and confusion was a sign of the treatment working because it was breaking up these patterns. Agent Morse Allen, part of the CIA's ARTICHOKE project reported the process was like "creating a vegetable," with the entire process of shock and sleep cycles lasting anywhere from fifteen to sixty-five days depending on the patient. When they regained consciousness, some patents tried to escape from Allen Memorial though most didn't get very far as in the case of Lauren G who was caught trying to scale a large hill outside of the hospital. The CIA had funded additional research into Cameron's depatterning treatment to not only create a blank slate of the mind or brainwash, as the term would be used, but to *re*program it (Marks, The Search for the Manchurian Candidate: The CIA and Mind Control: The Secret History of the Behavioral Sciences, 1991).

Because the CIA is not able to carry out operations on U.S. soil, it does such research through a third party outside of U.S. borders. In order to do this, a new approach named *psychic driving* was being developed. During the sleep portions of depatterning following ECT, patients were overwhelmed with audio messages of either positive or negative statements played in the treatment room as they slept. These statements, read onto a recorded tape, were personalized to each patient based on information gleaned during a patient's intake into the hospital. Some statements attacked a person's character and were intentionally emotionally inciteful to make the patient feel inadequate or unloved or hateful. The goal of these was to tear a person down to zero (for example, "*Your mother hit you because you were a bad child.*"). Positive statements followed. These were created as well from intake information and were played to build up confidence a patient may have never experienced in the first place ("*Your mother loved you because you were such a good child.*"). It's not a stretch to see how mastering such a skill could erase the hatred of an enemy soldier and reprogram them against their own people.

To begin psychic driving, negative messages were looped constantly for sixteen hours a day over several weeks with several patients at a time being treated in the same fashion together. As the messages ended, some were also given electric shocks on their legs to reinforce the message in the brain as one might shock a lab rat to teach it to remember the correct way through a maze. After completing the rounds of negative message, positive reports looped with "suggestions" of changes to behavior sprinkled in followed for the next few weeks (Collins, In the Sleep Room). When assessing the validity of claims against Dr. Cameron, one must consider the testimony regarding Canadian patient Val Orlikow, a mother from Ottawa and also an ECT patient who was awarded $750,000 in damages from the CIA in an out of court settlement in 1988 (though the CIA would not accept responsibility officially), the first of a later 250 victims ruled by a Canadian judge to also have the right to pursue compensation by the Canadian government in regards to abuses during this period under the MKULTRA project (The Scotsman, 2006).

Evidence turned up in later years that the devil was in the details: patients did give consent in many instances but for those who maintained they did not, the consent given was a general consent to authorize treatment which was taken as a go-ahead for ECT. These patients deeply felt they had been tricked into signing.

Orlikow was reported to have been fed "truth serum," *sodium amytal* which is a barbiturate substance given slowly via IV and is thought to loosen inhibitions and thus inspire a person to tell their own secrets. The CIA was deeply interested in the so-called truth drug for obvious reasons, though it later was debunked from its reported magical qualities. On top of the drug treatment, Ms. Orlikow was administered high doses of ECT at six times the normal dose and given LSD as well as being treated with the psychic driving method. It's alleged that she was treated while pregnant with one child and after treatment had no memory of any her children or husband (Bimmerle, 1993).

During treatments involving depatterning and psychic driving, patients were confused about who they were, where they were and what time they were in. Dr. Cameron found the amnesia and regression in patients wasn't controllable and memory loss was spotty and could reach back many years. It did not produce a blank slate to fill with new information as was hoped for. Nursing staff at the time and indeed, today still, saw both the ineffective treatments and those that truly worked come and go and took great pride in their work. They took the ups and downs in regard to getting the desired result: a patient free of mental illness that could take their place in society and achieve independence and personal happiness. They felt that they were using treatments other hospitals had given up on and they took care of patients in the sleep room by the physical turning and bathing when needed as any nurse would a patient who could not do these things for themselves in a medical ward.

Even so, staff such as Nurse Peggy Edwards noted there were things not always so transparent when it came to Cameron's methods. Her statement that a lot of what patients had said in their initial interview was later used against them during psychic driving echoes what it still the experience of the mentally ill across the world. In the ER this may be a necessary evil, but how quickly patients realize this and alter their answers to protect themselves from the ills of treating illness. But though he was hated by many patients for his work, Dr. Cameron was also adored by others, *including* Val Orlikow They looked to Dr. Cameron as a sort of god, holding an elusive cure for their illnesses. Some were even proud to be his patients. It's true that Dr. Cameron had some great ideas in the beginning. He felt the hospital should look more like the surroundings of the outside world to be easier for the patient to transition back to life outside after treatment so that healthy behaviors learned during hospitalization would be easier to maintain. Originally Alan Memorial Institute was named Ravenscrag Hospital and a new wing to mirror this theory was built onto it under his guidance. In 1957 Dr. Cameron joined the ranks of scientists in the U.S. for his contributions to the study of sensory deprivation. Like John C. Lilly, who had worked with sensory deprivation in isolation tanks for NIMH in 1953, Cameron also worked with sensory deprivation among his patients in the ever-pressing quest to "break" a human being and restart them in a controlled manner.

But back at NIMH, Dr. Maitland Baldwin had told Morse Allen with the CIA that his experiments with isolation (meaning isolation from all touch, sound, smell, etc.) during a period of forty hours proved that isolation itself could break *any* human and anything beyond this point was a state of no return. With this admission that a human's psyche couldn't be repaired past the point of forty hours in isolation, NIMH declared the technique to be inhumane and experiments were shut down. In the U.S., perhaps, but on foreign soil, under Dr. Cameron's directive, the former horse stables behind Allen Memorial were converted for his own work in sensory deprivation. Again, with an available population of mental patients there was little to stop Dr. Cameron's work. Ever obsessed with pushing the time limit of how long a person could withstand deprivation and still come out coherent, one incredible woman survived isolation for thirty-five *days* straight followed by subsequent with cycles of shock treatment and depatterning and then positive psychic driving for a total of 101 days in treatment of anxiety and hypochondria. Known as Mary C., I'd like to think it was the unique stubbornness of a woman that allowed her to break the unbreakable record. Following her ordeal there is no official record of what happened to Ms. C. and Cameron decided not to pursue any more treatment (Nickson, 1994) (Rejali, 2009).

Dr. Cameron also tested the drug Curare, giving injections of it to sensory deprivation patients. His method of psychic driving was used in conjunction with LSD treatments by the US government (the usage of which is a main plot line in the Stephen King classic, *Firestarter*) with LSD being given specially to induce schizophrenic behavior in order to observe and create a "crazy model" in which to study and develop treatment from. But Dr. Donald Ewan Cameron, despite his many other contributions to the CIA's research, will always primarily be recalled as the CIA's number one "shock doctor."

Cameron went on to retire early in 1964 and then died in 1967. Afterwards Dr. Robert Cleghorn, a colleague of Dr. Cameron through McGill University had independent studies commissioned on ECT treatment. The findings of these studies postulated that 60% of depatterned patients suffered amnesia ranging from six months to ten years before the therapy was given and did not find the intensity of the treatment to be more or less effective than general ECT treatment. He advised against further use of Cameron's methods, and depatterning as a viable treatment ended.

However, it was neither patient abuses or the debunking of success rates that plummeted ECT's numbers. The advent of psychotropic medications was upon the world, and why bother with electroshock if you could simply take a pill?

As Dr. Cameron was still pioneering depatterning in Canada, the first wave of psychotropic drugs was coming into use in the early 1950s. Antipsychotic drugs such as chlorpromazine, tricyclic antidepressants and monoamine oxidase inhibitors (MAOIs) brought relief of symptoms to patients in ways former treatments couldn't hold a candle to; namely, preserving the whole of a patient's self while separating them from their illness. The early 1960s brought another class of drugs usually thought of when talking about the "original" psychiatric medications, those being the barbiturates and benzodiazepines. While seemingly miraculous, these heavy drugs were not without their side effects and unwanted reactions. Their inception knocked ECT for a loop but did not knock it out for the count. Shock therapy endured as an alternative to medication therapy and as a front-line treatment for very serious cases of mental illness. It was in the 1980s that ECT's usage greatly declined.

The '80s were a time of social instability and mental health was no stranger to its effects. In a move to lessen the burden of long-term care of the mentally ill on taxpayers, *again*, long-term facilities were closed in a sweeping move of deinstitutionalization. The movement was characterized by the idea of moving the mentally ill who had lived a great deal of their lives in state hospitals back into the community where they would be followed in the outpatient arena by doctors and therapists in what was termed their "continuity of care." In an ideal world, one's continuity of care would include their family, group support, the medical doctor's office and all related caregivers as well as the therapist and psychiatrist so that there are no gaps in services in the patient's life. Because mental illness never sleeps, so does the patient with mental illness always need care in some form, be it medicinal or therapeutic or supportive (Steven P. Reidbord, 2014-2017).

We do not live in an ideal world and the 1980s, while excessive, did not bode well for those turned out by deinstitutionalization. For the public it made sense to put people back into the world who may be construed as living off the dole in the psychiatric sense. Why pay for people who could probably work? Those who were truly incurable would continue on in a much smaller number of state hospitals, leaving those freed to get jobs and pay taxes like the rest of us. The problem with this was scheme was its supporting players. Mental health workers of all stripes were generally for the independence of their patients, absolutely. But dumping thousands of patients into a society knee-deep in recession without job training to enter the workforce, social skills to make it on the street or families and homes to return to created an explosion in the homeless population, backfiring against any positive outcome it may have started to build and continuing on even today in the disbursement of services we use at present.

What the '80s did directly to ECT was decrease the number of captive patients who may have received it, closed the locations mobile patients may have come to in order to pursue it, and flood the market with a second and much more widely available wave of medications which included the power-drugs of the 1990s: atypical antipsychotics and serotonin reuptake inhibitors (SSRIs).

The 1990s brought the United States into the "decade of the brain," an initiative between the Library of Congress and NIMH to make the public aware of research being undertaken on brain functions. During these years the stigma of talking about mental illness came down a notch with the influence of popular books such as *Listening to Prozac* (Peter D. Kramer), *An Unquiet Mind* (Kay Redfield Jamison) and *Awakenings* (Oliver Sacks). How did ECT then come back to be administered in the numbers it is today? What was the driving factor in this controversial treatment that has ridden so high and ridden so low despite totally conflicting facts?

In a word: time.

It only took a decade for a whole new bevvy of books, movies and testimonials to refute the magic of medication and put us right back where we started at the beginning of the 1950s with an entire population of mentally ill patients with no insurance, no support and no options for treatment outside of the side effects of those medications then in circulation long enough to show their true colors in the public light.

Today one can find data to corroborate or refute their own views just about anywhere with the constant river of information we're plunged in from our televisions to our computers, to our phones and tablets and gaming devices and for us old-fashioned sorts, the public library. What we choose to believe about ECT will stem largely from our own experience and what we seek to find. There is no doubt that ECT has played a sinister role in many people's lives and this should never be forgotten. But in looking backward, we can still derive some benefit even from that role via the CIA's driving need to pick apart the souls of men.

Today's psychiatric drugs and behavior modification therapies, besotted with their own issues of course, came out of such programs such as PROJECTS BLUEBIRD, ARTICHOKE and MKULTRA. Many theories still abound all over the internet that these experiments never really stopped but went even further underground in order to continue. As for the files that chronicle them, those were destroyed by the CIA in 1973 per order of then-Director Richard Helms. The only private citizen to ever acquire these (under the Freedom of Information Act) was John Marks, author of *In Search of the Manchurian Candidate*.

As for the rest of us, it is disrespectful of our collective ancestors to look away from the good that came of their suffering and miss taking advantage of the use of it. It is also just as damning to allow it to go on. Yes, we have to take the sweet with the sour.

# First Impressions are Everything

WE live in a media-saturated world.

At any given time of day or night, we have access to real-time news from every corner of the globe like no other civilization in history. It appears nothing can hold back the flood of information from today's digital media. The problem is not in the quantity of data or even the quality, for sources of every stripe can be had for virtually nothing, but rather the *integrity*. The rule of thumb when I was in school for writing any critical essay was to cite no fewer than three independent sources per point. It would seem that in a world where communications have been dominated by social media and wide distribution there would be a high incidence of verification. After all, what cannot be found at the behest of one's fingertips and a keyboard?

Thus, it's alarming to observe that online habits mirror offline appetites for popular opinion over journalistic fact. News entertainment sites are incredibly popular due to their propensity to circulate viral content and search engine ranking systems reward what's popular over what's necessarily true by making it more easily found. It is up to us to go digging if we wish to find balanced material. In a society where stigma cripples efforts of recovery, nowhere is this more true than in mental health where a reluctance to know overshadows the need to.

It's become cliché to blame the media for just about everything and certainly it's inaccurate to because while we put our trust in the authors and distributors to report fair and balanced reports, we also must accept responsibility for demanding accountability in reporting and sourcing out intelligence for ourselves. It is we, individually, who stop at first impressions and look no further.

That being said, the arts offer us a unique narrative of mental illness and electroconvulsive therapy within the environment of the story which stay with us and incite curiosity. While verifiable facts are not always present to check the validity of, the unique voices of the characters and tone of the situations give us a rare insight into experiences we may have no other window on. And film in particular gives us more of an immersive manner of telling a story about a subject so diffuse with ambiguity and secrecy.

While ECT has been portrayed in many film and television works, one finds that it overwhelmingly takes on a negative light, either as used deliberately as a punishment or means to control another human being. I don't believe in sweetening up true experiences of ECT patients for the screen. As we see in *An Angel at my Table*, the striking scenes of ECT in the first part of the twentieth century come right from book author Janet Frame's personal experience. To soften these scenes would be to negate her very personal fear and thus that of millions like her whose stories died with them. But likewise, there is a great deal of difference in not shielding viewers from true horror and exploiting the same horror to get viewers. Let's look at some of the more modern film depictions of ECT.

## Nonfiction

**An Angel at my Table** is a film based on the three autobiographies *To the Island*, 1982, *An Angel at My Table*, 1984, and *The Envoy from Mirror City*, 1984 by New Zealand author Janet Frame, born 1924. It was directed by Jane Campion and released by Fine Line Films in the U.S. in 1990.

A talented young writer from a poor family in the New Zealand countryside, Janet experiences a depressive episode during college and overdoses on pills while staying with a relative. Janet is visited during a class she is teaching by her superiors and informed they think she needs a bit of a rest in hospital and this news is delivered to her in a patronizing, though well-meaning way in soft voices as though no one wants to "set her off" so to speak. A complete vagueness about this "rest" is maintained which serves only to generate more fear of the unknown for Janet and a promise to "come visit" which materializes as little more than just that. After a stay in hospital Janet is discharged but realizes she has left the routine world of her family unmarked by insanity and as Janet watches the swinging door to the Psychiatric Ward on her release, she expresses that she doesn't want to go home. She is sent to a long-term institution, where the brilliant writer is diagnosed with Schizophrenia; a condition for which there was little hope in the 1940s. Janet is told that there is a new treatment able to cure her Schizophrenia and so off to the Sleep Room she goes, which is depicted by an old-style hospital corridor where the treatments are done en masse.

Female patients are trying to escape with frantic nurses in hot pursuit. An orderly wheels in a tray with patients' sets of dentures in glass jars labeled with their names. A nurse asks young Janet for her teeth which she informs her have just been pulled. The doctor arrives, states he knows "what this is all about" and with no explanation the headphones are put onto Janet's head bilaterally and she is held down and administered a shock. Her head rears back against the pillow and she screams as if in terrible pain. The orderlies, of whom we see no faces, hold her down as her body writhes on the bed. The nurse quickly puts a roll of gauze protectively in her mouth. Janet passes out. In voiceover, Janet tells us that over eight years she received over 200 treatments. She felt each one to be as fear-inducing as the prospect of execution.

During the eight years Janet undergoes ECT, she manages to publish some of her manuscripts and is saved from having a leucotomy when one of her doctors discovers she has won the prestigious Hubert Church Memorial Award for her work. Having had the surgery cancelled, Janet goes home to collect the award but is then returned to the institution for another four years. The film does not depict any side effects she may have had from her treatments aside from the obvious visual effects of living in an overcrowded asylum. It is thought later that Janet Frame was misdiagnosed with Schizophrenia from the start.

**Frances** stars Jessica Lange and was directed by Graeme Clifford. The film was released in 1982 by Universal Pictures. Frances is the biopic of 1930s actress Frances Farmer's harrowing journey through an asylum after a scandal lands her under commitment by her mother. The film graphically depicts what many patients of the time would have suffered- being put away by their families from a society that didn't want to see their illness. A scene between Frances and her psychiatrist illustrates the all-too-common situation of medical personnel taking the word of the family as gospel over the patient (of course in real life psychiatric care would swing wide the other way as well with the family being suspect of bringing on mental illness before settling into the uneasy armistice we have today). It would seem in the film that Frances is given a round of drug-induced seizures during her first commitment but then as she is dragged back down the hall by orderlies, screaming in a straight-jacket, we see shock treatment is next in the cards. She is shown struggling mightily against the arms of unseen orderlies, the electrodes placed on her head and the only words spoken are from one professional to another, conferring the wattage to be used.

Her body writhes and in the next shot we see men wheeling in what appears to be a dead woman who may or may not be Frances. She is transferred to a bed and restrained, the camera panning down to the floor where a disheveled Frances sits lost in her memories. Later we see her restrained in her sleep in a crowded room of crying patients, being woken up to face the commitment board of review. As she relates her story in lifeless tones, we see flashbacks of her treatment in classic horror-film style: girls tied to beds, pacing in the padded room in a straight-jacket, hydrotherapy. Frances too must go home and pretend the illness never happened.

No ill effects are shown from the ECT save the line Frances later says to her lover, "*That place nearly killed me.*"

**Shine** is the Australian biographical film starring Geoffrey Rush. Directed by Scott Hicks, the film was released in the U.S. in 1996 by Fine Line Features. Australian child piano prodigy David Helfgott's life under an emotionally distant and abusive father is chronicled in the acclaimed *Shine*. Helfgott's father teaches him to play piano and after winning the state championship and being offered a chance to study in the United States, David is crushed when his father forbids him to leave the family. A local novelist takes interest in the boy and when he competes again he is offered a scholarship to study in London. With his friend's encouragement, Helfgott leaves but is disowned by his father.

While abroad David elects to enter another competition playing Rachmaninov's Third Concerto, a piece he played as a child that his father was especially proud of. But amidst studying and grueling practices Helfgott has his first break of Manic Depression (Bipolar Disorder) and is taken to psychiatric hospital and administered shock therapy.

The depiction of this is so understated it might be missed if not paying attention. We see a composite of images; the camera breaks from the concert hall where Helfgott is playing Rachmaninov, we have just seen a glimpse of his father back in Australia listening on the radio after his wife has died (another subtle vignette), and the camera pans across David's prone form, cleaned and gowned, his mouth fitted with a plastic mouth guard.

Only a glimpse of the machinery is shown, the initial pass of electric and then only his bare feet twitching as the seizure begins. It appears he is already unconscious when the treatment starts, which is consistent with methods of ECT in the late 1960s when a sedative would have been issued before the actual shock. No ill effects are shown from the ECT, in fact we see little of David's early treatment at all as the movie uses another popular methodology of showing the patient as emerged fresh and new with none of the actual work of recovery acknowledged at all.

## Fiction

**Passions,** *American daytime television drama.* In season five, ECT portrayed is portrayed as a form of mind control. Daughter of millionaire Alistair Crane, Sheridan Crane is seen wrestled onto the table laden with heavy, old-style restraints by a doctor, all the while shouting *"This is where you took me before; this is where you hurt me!"* and *"You can't do this to me again!"* The scene rises dramatically with Sheridan screaming for help and the apologetic but obviously ill-intentioned doctor wrangling her down single-handedly and strapping her to the table.

He plunges her with a needle of some unknown substance and the doctor comments to an off-camera voice that the patient is out of her mind after what they did to her "last time" and fearful for her life. The off-camera voice replies that she should be. The doctor now assures Sheridan she won't feel anything. The voice, who identifies as Alistair Crane states they know that's not true and seems to be intent on wiping Sheridan's memory out with the procedure.

The conversation which ensues between the two men enlightens us to the fact that electroshock is used for certain types of illnesses such as clinical Depression but the machinery is so old it should be outlawed and the doctor could lose his license for using it. What ensues suggests a horrifically painful procedure with a fair share of screaming and writhing around by a completely conscious patient. Alistair calls for the voltage to be increased over and over until the doctor protests that he can't hurt another human being.

We learn that this is all over trying to erase Sheridan's feelings of love over a lover. The voltage is increased again and we have the doctor begging her to lie to her father as the shock isn't working to wipe her memory. But after an extremely long scene of increasing the voltage to levels no human could withstand, it would seem nothing can erase the memory of true love in daytime drama at least.

**American Horror Story: Asylum** depicts electroshock as the consequences of being where one ought not to be. In one example, a journalist is held prisoner by sadistic Sister Jude. The journalist informs Sister Jude that her editor knows where she is because she came in originally to write a story on the asylum and now she'll have plenty to report back about from what she's seen, remarking she has "an excellent memory." Retorts Sister Jude, *"We'll see about that."*

In what turns out to be one of the screwiest conversations about mental health treatment on television, Sister Jude makes her case to the psychiatrist that the journalist's memories are impeding her and asks would he suggest ECT to treat? He points out this is a surprise as when he suggested it *last*, Sister Jude accused him of being a sadistic barbarian.

However, she's been praying about it and now thinks it's one of G-d's "tools." On the table, the journalist screams she's been kidnapped and the psychiatrist remarks she's a noisy one as Sister Jude watches impassively. The psychiatrist suggests Sister Jude assist as it was her idea after all and asks if she's squeamish. The patient in this case remains conscious, strapped down to the table and given a mouth guard.

Sister Jude applies the electroshock with an over-the-top sized headset and the current is assumed to be strong enough to be making the lights overhead flicker. The scene ends and cuts to another part of the story.

**Shock Treatment** is the obscure follow up to cult classic *The Rocky Horror Picture Show*, directed by Jim Sharman. It was released in 1981 by Twentieth Century Fox. Set after the events of *Rocky Horror*, mousy Brad Majors is stuck in Denton, a small town where the citizens are brainwashed into complacency inside a life-sized game show. His wife Janet unwittingly gets him committed to

Dentonvale, the local institution operating within a televised soap opera to be "treated" for being a lousy husband.

As Janet is simultaneously trapped in the game and forced into competing for ratings on-air, Brad is subjected to shock treatments. At his intake, Brad tries to reason with the overly passive and cloyingly sympathetic psychiatrists while an orderly sneaks up behind him and jabs his neck with a syringe of sedative. Aware of the proceedings, wife Janet is not sure about this but cannot manage to protest against the word of the doctors.

A sexy, less-than-brilliant nurse comes to wheel him down a white, padded hall to the Terminal Ward where his existence in a man-sized canary cage will be broadcast as part of the Dentonvale show. This is certainly a movie that hits all the social stereotypes equally on race to homosexuality to gender to immigration and puts tongue in cheek in nearly every scene. Being a follow up to *Rocky Horror*, *Shock Treatment* is a campy musical and not meant to be taken all that seriously.

But it does lend to the pervasive perception that ECT is always against the will and always as a punishment which is sold to the patient and their family as a "treatment" to cover up what really goes on in the sleep room. *"I've never found the time to have a nervous breakdown,"* says Janet's father in regard to Brad, whom he calls him a weirdo. The odd turn of phrase "faith factory" is the euphemism used for the mental ward, the psychiatrists are cruel and untrustworthy, and the public is totally in the dark until someone sees Brad in his cage and protests there are regulations against these things.

The staff protests they've used drugs to keep him quiet and nothing has worked. This is for his own good; he needs *"a bit of shock treatment"* to make him *"jump like a real live wire."* In the end a little bit of TV and egomania brainwashes Janet far worse than anything Brad goes through sitting in his cage. The only shot of anything suggesting actual ECT is an aerial shot of a policeman being strapped down in the middle of the TV set once the townspeople get what's going on but goes no farther than this during the dance number. We are left to imagine through the whole film what the "treatment" involves. And art imitates life.

**Shock Corridor** is a 1963 film directed by Samuel Fuller and released by Allied Artists Pictures. Journalist Johnny Barrett signs himself into a mental hospital to masquerade as a patient so he can investigate a suspected murderer, hoping to win the Pulitzer prize for his article. The film excellently portrays a pervasive social belief that a person without mental illness can "catch" mental illness by exposure to it, which lends to the stigma of treatments such as ECT to the point that even speaking about them may somehow taint the minds of those who have not experienced insanity.

Barrett is administered ECT as a routine treatment for Schizophrenia and inappropriate feelings and dreams about his sister Cathy (his girlfriend who is in fact only posing as his sister to help get him into the hospital). We are privy to his thoughts throughout the film about a colorful cast of characters range from his obese roommate who wakes him up to chew gum to the black student who steals pillow cases and believes he is a KKK member, and the young man who believes he is five months pregnant. The inmates show the usual humor of those who are more aware of their stigma than their captors give them credit for.

Cathy gives permission to give electric shock treatments because she thinks Barrett can't recognize her for who she is and tells her never to kiss him again "that way" after spending a time with another inmate in restraint. Barrett's boss asks Cathy if she's "lost her marbles?" stating that "*Johnny can't take that kind of punishment. He'll crack! They'll find out he's a fake!*" This is Cathy's intent, to break him so he will be found to be sane in order to save him. The scene of shock therapy itself is interesting in that we can see overlays of different back-drops throughout the movie of patients experiencing the Hollywood version of madness en masse, Barrett's shaking body being held down by orderlies (his mouth stuffed with a rolled-up towel) and the fantasy of Cathy cutting in and out so that screaming, speaking and singing become a true cacophony of sight and sound meant to depict madness.

The electric pulse stops and the scene stops, ending abruptly in the body of Barrett falling back to the table in silence. The next scene finds Barrett sitting calmly on his bed, none worse to the wear for all we can tell but we still hear his thoughts asking himself why he cannot speak? He attempts to and says he is fine to the doctor. The doctor asks if he needs another treatment and he responds that only if the doctor is going to throw the switch the whole way because he's "learned his lesson." The doctor laughs and affirms there will be no more race riots in the corridor instigated by Barrett. He later lies back and thinks he's beaten the system. Barrett hasn't given up his identity to the hospital but is still worried about losing his voice and subsequently his memory of facts he's just learned about the murder case he's investigating.

As predicted, Barrett loses his mind by the end of the movie. As the film ends we see the doctor telling Cathy that a man can't tamper with his mind and subject himself to tests and expect to come out sane; Barrett is a catatonic schizophrenic now. The screen bears a quote from Euripides in 425 B.C.: *Whom G-d wishes to destroy, He first makes mad.*

**One Flew Over the Cuckoo's Nest** released in 1975 by United Artists. Probably the most enduring portrayal of ECT comes from the 1962 novel by Ken Kesey and subsequent film that showcases a tableau of unmodified ECT and the culture of mental health treatment in the mid part of the twentieth century.

Randle McMurphy is facing a long-term sentence with hard labor for the raping of a fifteen year-old but sees a ticket out of his situation by claiming mental illness in order to be committed for the rest of his time to an institution. He is surrounded by a standout cast of characters including mute Native American

"Chief" Bromden, who is the narrator in the book version. McMurphy defies authority at every turn, rousing the ire of the ward nurse, Nurse Ratched. As he inspires the other patients to come out of their shells and wreaks havoc on the ward, his short term stay to recuperate from his "illness" turns into a long-term sentence and pits him against Nurse Ratched in earnest.

McMurphy plots to escape the institution with the help of the Chief but ends up in a tousle with other patients and staff and is sent to have ECT by the enraged nurse. The Sleep Room here is referred to as the "shock shop" and while waiting to go in they discover the Chief can speak and like McMurphy, is keeping up the appearance as he waits out his time.

Feigning brain damage on return from the shock shop, McMurphy reveals he's back and better than ever, plotting a Christmas party for the ward after staff have gone home to have a last fling before his escape. After a night of revelry no one is awake when Nurse Ratched comes in the next morning to catch them red-handed. In an act of defiance, timid wardmate Billy stands up to her but is quickly cut down by her sadistic threat to tell his mother of his antics at the party and he locks himself in a doctor's office and kills himself.

McMurphy attempts to avenge Billy by choking Nurse Ratched but is knocked out and taken away. Later the inmates decide he must have successfully escaped in the aftermath but instead we see him incapacitated in his bed discovered by Chief. McMurphy has had a lobotomy. Chief smothers him to death with a pillow as an act of mercy and escapes using the plan he and McMurphy concocted. The end credits play over Chief running off into the dawn as is heard one of the most sincere musical tributes ever made to the world of the mentally ill.

# Resources

HERE are some of the tools I found helpful with recovering and staying healthy that I hope you'll check out as well. I find that hearing the personal stories of others helps motivate me more than anything else because sometimes all you need to get going is to hear someone else say *"Hey kid, I was there once too."*

## Books

*An Unquiet Mind: A Memoir of Moods and Madness* by Kay Redfield Jamison

*Night Falls Fast: Understanding Suicide* by Kay Redfield Jamison

*A Brilliant Madness: Living with Manic-Depressive Illness* by Patty Duke and Gloria Hochman

*Awakenings* by Oliver Sacks

*One Flew Over the Cuckoo's Nest* by Ken Kesey

*The Brain that Changes Itself: Stories of Personal Triumph from the Frontiers of Brain Science* by Norman Doidge

*The Brain's Way of Healing: Remarkable Discoveries and Recoveries from the Frontiers of Neuroplasticity* by Norman Doidge

*Depression Fallout: The Impact of Depression on Couples and What You Can Do to Preserve the Bond* by Anne Sheffield

*Somebody Else's Kids* by Torey Hayden

*I'll Carry the Fork! Recovering a Life After Brain Injury* By Kara L. Swanson

*Brain Injury Survival Kit: 365 Tips, Tricks and Tools to Deal with Cognitive Function Loss* by Dr. Cheryl Sullivan MD

*Coping with Concussion and Mild Traumatic Brain Injury* by Diane Roberts Stoler, Ed.D. and Barbara Albers Hill

*New Order: A Decluttering Handbook for Creative Folks (and everyone else)* by Fay Wolf

*Buddha's Book of Sleep: Sleep Better in Seven Weeks with Mindfulness Meditation* by Joseph Emet and Thich Nhat Hanh

*Making Sense of Your Senses: A Workbook for Children with Sensory Processing Disorder* by Christopher R. Auer

*Fervent: A Woman's Battle Plan to Serious, Specific and Strategic Prayer* by Priscilla Evans Shirer

*An Angel at My Table: An Autobiography* by Janet Frame

*The Power of Habit* by Charles Duhigg

*Nothing Left Over: A Plain and Simple Life* by Toinette Lippe

*Making Space: Creating a Home Meditation Practice* by Thich Nhat Hanh

The *"Little House"* books by Laura Ingalls Wilder

*The Joy Luck Club* by Amy Tan

## Therapeutic Helps

Psychotherapies: www.nimh.nih.gov/health/topics/psychotherapies/index. shtml

Lovingkindness Meditation: *Awakening Loving-Kindness* by Pema Chödrön

Radically Open Dialectical Behavioral Therapy (RO-DBT): www.radically-open.net

*The Science of Mindfulness: a Research-based Path to Well-Being* by Ronald Siegel (DVD, 2014)

The Nightmare Protocol: www.aasmnet.org/Resources/bestpracticeguides/ NightmareDisorder.pdf

# Works Cited

*1964 Allen Memorial Institute Procedure Book.* (n.d.).

American Cancer Society. (2016, March 23). *Lifetime Risk of Developing or Dying From Cancer.* Retrieved from www.cancer.org: www.cancer.org/cancer/cancer-basics/lifetime-probability-of-developing-or-dying-from-cancer.html

American Heart Association. (2017). *Answers by Heart.* Retrieved from www. heart.org: www.heart.org/idc/groups/heart-public/@wcm/@hcm/documents/down-loadable/ucm_300340.pdf

American Heart Association. (2017). *What Is an Automated External Defibrillator?* Retrieved from www.heart.org: www.heart.org/idc/groups/heart-public/@wcm/@hcm/documents/down-loadable/ucm_300340.pdf

Andrew C. Papanicolaou, R. B.-M. (2005). *The Amnesias: A Clinical Textbook of Memory Disorders.* Oxford University Press.

Aruta, A. (2011, July). *Shocking Waves at the Museum: The Bini–Cerletti Electroshock Apparatus.* Retrieved from US National Library of Medicine : www.ncbi.nlm.nih.gov/pmc/articles/PMC3143851/

Association for Natural Psychology. (n.d.). *Famous Persons who have Undergone Electroshock Therapy.* Retrieved from Association for Natural Psychology: aycnp.org/ect_treatment_famous_people.php

Bimmerle, G. (1993, September 22). *"Truth" Drugs in Interrogation*. Retrieved from Central Intelligence Agency: www.cia.gov/library/center-for-the-study-of-intelligence/kent-csi/vol5no2 /html/vo5i2a09p_0001.htm

Biography.com Editors. (2017, May 14). *Benjamin Rush Biography.com*. Retrieved from Biography.com: www.biography.com/people/benjamin-rush-9467074#the-revolution-and-beyond

Bittar, E. (1999). Biological Psychiatry 14 (Principles of Medical Biology). In E. E. Bittar, *Biological Psychiatry* (p. 614). Elsevier Science.

Black, E. (2003, September). *The Horrifying American Roots of Nazi Eugenics*. Retrieved from Columbian College of Arts & Sciences : historynewsnetwork.org/article/1796

Black, E. (2003, September). *The Horrifying American Roots of Nazi Eugenics*. Retrieved from Columbian College of Arts and Sciences: historynewsnetwork.org/article/1796#sthash.QDUNJhYN.dpuf

Black, E. (2017). *The Horrifying American Roots of Nazi Eugenics*. Retrieved from Columbian College of Arts and Sciences: historynewsnetwork.org/article/1796

Boodman, S. G. (2016, June 23). *Shock Therapy...It's Back*. Retrieved from www.healthyplace.com: www.healthyplace.com/depression/articles/shock-therapyits-back/is-shock-therapy-suicide-preventive

Boyles, S. (2003, June 19). *Memory Loss Common Complaint With ECT*. Retrieved from www.webmd.com: www.webmd.com/depression/news/20030619/memory-loss-common-complaint-with-ect#1

Breeding, J. P. (2014, February 11). *Electroshocking Children: Why it Should be Stopped*. Retrieved from Madinamerica.com: www.madinamerica.com/2014/02/electroshocking-children-stopped/

Carter, R. (2010). *Mapping the Mind.* University of California Press.

Cooke, J. (2017). *Bedlam 1946.* Retrieved from Jerry Cooke Archives, Inc.: www.jerrycookearchives.com/photo-essays/bedlam-1946/

Daily Mail. (2004, November 15). *Health.* Retrieved from Daily Mail: www.dailymail.co.uk/health/article-326201/Why-broken-escalator-make-dizzy.html

Day, E. (2008, January 13). *He was Bad, so They Put an Ice Pick in his Brain.* Retrieved from Theguardian.com : www.theguardian.com/science/2008/jan/13/neuroscience.medicalscience

Day, E. (2008, January 13). *Neuroscience the Observer.* Retrieved from Theguardian.com: www.theguardian.com/science/2008/jan/13/neuroscience.medicalscience

DeAngelis, T. (2002, February). *New data on lesbian, gay and bisexual mental health.* Retrieved from www.apa.org: www.apa.org/monitor/feb02/newdata.aspx

deathpenaltyinfo.org. (1998, January). *The Shocking Truth About Death in the Electric Chair.* Retrieved from deathpenaltyinfo.org: web.archive.org/web/20080202095956/capitaldefenseweekly.com/chair.htm

Dept of Psychiatry of University of Michigan Health Department . (2016). *Electroconvulsive Therapy Program.* Retrieved from psychmed.umich.edu: www.psych.med.umich.edu/ect/common-side-effects.asp

Derek S. Beal, M. L. (n.d.). *fMRI of Overt Speech& Stimulated Stuttering.* Retrieved from Department of Speech-Language Pathology University of Toronto: www.asha.org

Devanand DP, D. A. (1994, July). *Does ECT alter brain structure?* Retrieved from US National Library of Medicine National Institutes of Health: www.ncbi.nlm.nih.gov/pubmed/8010381

Diane Roberts Stoler, E. a. (2013). *Coping with Mild Concussion and Mild Traumatic Brain Injury.* Avery .

Dienstmann, G. (n.d.). *Scientific Benefits of Meditation- 76 Things You Might be Missing out on.* Retrieved from Live and Dare: liveanddare.com/benefits-of-meditation-2/

Donald B. Tower, D. M. (1948). Cholinesterase Patterns and Acetylcholine in the Cerebrospinal Fluids of Patients with Craniocerebral Trauma. *Canadian Journal of Research, 27,* 105.

Dr. Andrew Weil. (n.d.). *Three Breathing Exercises.* Retrieved from www.drweil.com:

www.drweil.com/health-wellness/body-mind-spirit/stress-anxiety/breathing-three-exercises/

Dukakis, K. a. (2007). *Shock: The Healing Power of Electroconvulsive Therapy .* Avery.

ect.org. (n.d.). *ECT Machines.* Retrieved from www.ect.org: www.ect.org/resources/machines.html

Ed. David J. Thurman, J. F. (1995). *Standards of Surveillance of Neurotrauma .* World Health Organization.

Editors of Encyclopedia Britannica. (2017). *Sir Francis Galton British Scientist.* Retrieved from Encyclopedia Britannica:

www.britannica.com/biography/Francis-Galton

Elizabeth J Kramer, K. K. (2002, September). *Cultural factors influencing the mental health of Asian Americans.* Retrieved from Western Journal of Medicine:

www.ncbi.nlm.nih.gov/pmc/articles/PMC1071736/

Elizabeth J. Kramer, P. G. (2009). *No Soy Loco/ I'm Not Crazy: Understanding the Stigma of Mental Illness in Latinos.* Retrieved from ethnomed.org: ethnomed.org/clinical/mental-health/Facilitators%20Guide%20123108%20final%20_2_.pdf

Emet, J. (2012). *Buddha's Book of Sleep: Sleep Better in Seven Weeks with Mindfulness Meditation .* TarcherPerigee.

Fink, M. (2014, February 12). *What was learned: studies by the consortium for research in ECT (CORE) 1997–2011.* Retrieved from Wiley Online Library: onlinelibrary.wiley.com/doi/10.1111/acps.12251/full

Fish, S. T. (2016, January 14). *Mental Health in Lesbian, Gay, Bisexual, and Transgender (LGBT) Youth.* Retrieved from US National Library of Medicine Naitonal Institutes of Health: www.ncbi.nlm.nih.gov/pmc/articles/PMC4887282/

Frame, J. (1984). An Angel at My Table . In J. Frame, *An Angel at My Table* (pp. 68, 72, 75, 112, 114, 131-141). New York: G. Braziller.

Gaddis, J. (2010, November 19). *The Shamanic View of Mental Illness.* Retrieved from JaysonGaddis.com: www.jaysongaddis.com/the-shamanic-view-of-mental-illness/

Gale Group, Inc. (2003). *Electroconvulsive Therapy.* Retrieved from www. encyclopedia.com: www.encyclopedia.com/medicine/psychology/psychology-and-psychiatry /electroconvulsive-therapy

Gale Group, Inc. (2003). *Gale Encyclopedia of Mental Disorders Electroconvulsive Therapy.* Retrieved from www.encyclopedia.com: www.encyclopedia.com/medicine/psychology/psychology-and-psychiatry /electroconvulsive-therapy

Gleissner, U. (2004, October 14). *Epilepsy Study Shows Memory Loss After Brain Surgery.* Retrieved from Science Daily : www.sciencedaily.com/releases/2004/10/041014081055.htm

Grandin, T. (2015). *Electric Stunning of Pigs and Sheep.* Retrieved from Grandin .com: www.grandin.com/humane/elec.stun.html

Grant, J. E. (2006, August). *ECT Wipes Out 30 Years of Memories.* Retrieved from Current Psychology: www.mdedge.com/currentpsychiatry/article/62301/ect-wipes-out-30-years-memories

*Hamilton Depression Rating Scale (HDRS)*. (n.d.). Retrieved from dcf.psychiatry.ufl.edu:

dcf.psychiatry.ufl.edu/files/2011/05/HAMILTON-DEPRESSION.pdf

Hartelius, H. (1952). *Cerebral Changes Following Electrically Induced Convulsions: An Experimental Study on Cats.*

Health, C. o. (20002). Retrieved from New York State Assembly Committee on Mental Health 2002 Report on Electroconvulsive Therapy: nyassembly.gov/comm/Mental/20020416/#SAFETY

Health, N. I. (2008). *Use of Mental Health Services and Treatment Among Adults.* Retrieved from www.nimh.nih.gov:

www.nimh.nih.gov/health/statistics/prevalence/use-of-mental-health-services-and-treatment-among-adults.shtml

Herculano, H. S. (2009, November 9). *The Human Brain in Numbers: A Linearly Scaled-Up Primate Brain.* Retrieved from www.ncbi.nlm.nih.gov: www.ncbi.nlm.nih.gov/pmc/articles/PMC2776484/

Hersh, J. (2016). *Julie Hersh on ECT.* Retrieved from Psych Central: psychcentral.com/lib/julie-hersh-on-ect/

Hersh, J. K. (2013, June 27). *TMS or ECT? A Mental Health Consumer Weighs the Options.* Retrieved from www.psychologytoday.com:

www.psychologytoday.com/blog/struck-living/201306/tms-or-ect-mental-health-consumer-weighs-the-options

Hersh, J. K. (2015, April 24). *The Shocking Truth about ECT.* Retrieved from Struck by Living:

www.psychologytoday.com/blog/struck-living/201504/the-shocking-truth-about-ect

History.com staff. (2009). *Dorothea Lynde Dix.* Retrieved from History.com: www.history.com/topics/womens-history/dorothea-lynde-dix

Holland, A. C. (2010, January 11). *Emotion and Autobiographical Memory.* Retrieved from www.ncbi.nlm.nih.gov:

www.ncbi.nlm.nih.gov/pmc/articles/PMC2852439/

Institute, J. C. (n.d.). *The Story*. Retrieved from John C. Lilly Homepage: www.johnclilly.com/thestory.html

International, C. C. (2017). *Potential Conflicts of Interest between ECT researchers, ECT device manufacturers, FDA/ NIMH*. Retrieved from Citizens Commission on Human Rights: www.cchrint.org/pdfs/conflicts-of-interest-ect-researchers-apa-task-force .pdf

Jamison, K. R. (2000). *Night Falls Fast: Understanding Suicide*. Vintage.

John Breeding, P. (2014, February 11). *Electroshocking Children: Why it Should be Stopped*. Retrieved from Madinamerica.com: www.madinamerica.com/2014/02/electroshocking-children-stopped/

Johnson, G. (2010). *Traumatic Brain Injury Survival Guide*. Retrieved from www.tbiguide.com: www.tbiguide.com/memory.html

Jones, R. (2012, December 14). *Brain Battery*. Retrieved from www.knowingneurons.com: knowingneurons.com/2012/12/14/brain-battery/

Jones, R. (2012, December 14). *Knowing Neurons*. Retrieved from knowingneurons.com: knowingneurons.com/2012/12/14/brain-battery/

Jr., D. J. (2010, August 11). *The Hidden Tragedy of the CIA's Experiments on Children*. Retrieved from truthout.org: truth-out.org/archive/component/k2/item/91211:the-hidden-tragedy-of-the-cias-experiments-on-children

Kandel, E. R. (2007). *In Search of Memory: The Emergence of a New Science of Mind*. W.W. Norton & Company.

Kesey, K. (1962). *One Flew Over the Cuckoo's Nest*. Signet.

*Kirkbride Buildings History*. (2017). Retrieved from www.kirkbridebuildings. com: www.kirkbridebuildings.com/

K. Rose Quayle

L R Squire, P. C. (1983, January). *Electroconvulsive therapy and complaints of memory dysfunction: a prospective three-year follow-up study.* Retrieved from BJPsych:

bjp.rcpsych.org/content/142/1/1

Larry R. Squire, P., Slater, P. C., & Miller, P. L. (1981, January). *Retrograde Amnesia and Bilateral Electroconvulsive Therapy: Long-Term Follow-Up.* Retrieved from The JAMA Network:

jamanetwork.com/journals/jamapsychiatry/article-abstract/492469

Law, H. R. (2009, September 22). *Mental Illness, Human Rights, and US Prisons.* Retrieved from Human Rights Watch:

www.hrw.org/news/2009/09/22/mental-illness-human-rights-and-us-prisons

Leighton P. Mark, R. W.-B. (2001, November). *Pictorial Review of Glutamate Excitotoxicity: Fundamental Concepts for Neuroimaging.* Retrieved from American Journal of Neuroradiology:

www.ajnr.org/content/22/10/1813#sec-2

Leiknas, K. A.-v. (2012, May). *Brain and Behavior.* Retrieved from www.ncbi.nlm.nih.gov:

www.ncbi.nlm.nih.gov/pmc/articles/PMC3381633/

Levinson, H. (2011, November 8). *The strange and curious history of lobotomy.* Retrieved from:

www.bbc.com/news/magazine-15629160

Loo, C. K. (2012, March). *A review of ultrabrief pulse width electroconvulsive therapy.* Retrieved from www.ncbi.nlm.nih.gov:

www.ncbi.nlm.nih.gov/pmc/articles/PMC3513900/

*LSD, Mind Control, and the Internet: A Chronology.* (n.d.). Retrieved from University of Virginia:

www.people.virginia.edu/~jmu2m/SLS.htm

Marks, J. (1991). *The Search for the Manchurian Candidate: The CIA and Mind Control: The Secret History of the Behavioral Sciences.* W. W. Norton & Company.

Mastin, L. (2010). *Declaritive (Explicit) and Procedural (Implicit) Memory.* Retrieved from The Human Memory:

www.human-memory.net/types_declarative.html

Matsin, L. (2010). *Episodic and Semantic Memory.* Retrieved from The Human Memory:

www.human-memory.net/types_episodic.html

Mayo Clinic. (1998-2017). *Tests and Procedures: Electroconvulsive Therapy (ECT).* Retrieved from www.mayoclinic.org:

www.mayoclinic.org/tests-procedures/electroconvulsive-therapy/basics/risks/prc-20014161

Mayo Clinic. (2015, October 13). *Diseases and Conditions Mental Illness.* Retrieved from www.mayoclinc.org:

www.mayoclinic.org/diseases-conditions/mental-illness/basics/risk-factors/con-20033813

Merriam-Webster. (2017). *Propoganda.* Retrieved from Merriam-Webster.com:

www.merriam-webster.com/dictionary/propaganda

Ming Lu, M. S. (2011). *Qi Gong in Chinese Medicine.* Peopole's Medical Publishing House.

Mrs. Sushma. C, D. M. (2016). *Moral Treatment: Philippe Pinel.* Retrieved from International Journal of Indian Psychology:

oaji.net/articles/2016/1170-1457809587.pdf

MS., P. (2006, April). *Dorothea Dix (1802–1887).* Retrieved from American Journal of Public Health:

www.ncbi.nlm.nih.gov/pmc/articles/PMC1470530/

Mukerjee, S. (2016). *The Gene: In Intimate History* . Scribner.

NAMI. (2017). *Mental Health by the Numbers*. Retrieved from www.nami.org: www.nami.org/Learn-More/Mental-Health-By-the-Numbers

Nancy A. Payne, L. M. (2009, September). *Electroconvulsive Therapy Part I: A Perspective on the Evolution and Current Practice of ECT.* Retrieved from U .S. National Library of Medicine, National Institutes of Health: www.ncbi.nlm.nih.gov/pmc/articles/PMC3042260/

National Institutes of Health. (2017). *National Institute of Mental Health (NIMH)*. Retrieved from The NIH Almanac: www.nih.gov/about-nih/what-we-do/nih-almanac/national-institute-mental-health-nimh

National Security Archive. (1975, January 31). *Memorandum for the Record: Project Artichoke*. Retrieved from National Security Archive: nsarchive.gwu.edu/NSAEBB/NSAEBB54/st02.pdf

Neuroskeptic. (2015, January 11). *The Tragic History of Surgery for Schizophrenia*. Retrieved from Discover Magazine: blogs.discovermagazine.com/neuroskeptic/2015/01/11/tragic-surgery-for-schizophrenia/#.WQaJp_nyuUk

Newitz, A. (2013, December 11). *A disturbing "care pamphlet" given to families of lobotomized soldiers*. Retrieved from io9.gizmodo.com: io9.gizmodo.com/a-disturbing-care-pamphlet-given-to-families-of-lobot-1481219125

Nickson, E. (1994). *Mind Control: My Mother, the CIA and LSD*. Retrieved from arizona.edu: dgibbs.faculty.arizona.edu/sites/dgibbs.faculty.arizona.edu/files/MindControl.pdf

NIMH. (2008). *Use of Mental Health Services and Treatment Among Adults*. Retrieved from www.NIMH.nih.gov: www.nimh.nih.gov/health/statistics/prevalence/use-of-mental-health-services-and-treatment-among-adults.shtml

NIMH. (2015, April 23). *A New Look at Racial/Ethnic Differences in Mental Health Service Use Among Adults*. Retrieved from National Institute of Mental Health:
www.nimh.nih.gov/news/science-news/2015/a-new-look-at-racial-ethnic-differences-in-mental-health-service-use-among-adults.shtml

Norman Doidge, M. (2016). The Brain's Way of Healing : Remarkable Discoveries and Recoveries from the Frontiers of Neuroplasticity. In M. Norman Doidge, *The Brain's Way of Healing : Remarkable Discoveries and Recoveries from the Frontiers of Neuroplasticity* (p. 211). Penguin Books.

Norman Doidge, M. (2016). The Brain's Way of Healing: Remarkable Discoveries and Recoveries from the Frontiers of Neuroplasticity. In M. Norman Doidge, *The Brain's Way of Healing: Remarkable Discoveries and Recoveries from the Frontiers of Neuroplasticity*. Penguin Books.

Okura, L. (2014, August 14). *Krickitt and Kim Carpenter, Couple Who Inspired "The Vow" Talk About Love that Endures*. Retrieved from Huffington Post:
www.huffingtonpost.com/2014/08/14/krickitt-and-kim-carpenter-the-vow_n_5676474.html

Penn Medicine. (2017). *DR. THOMAS STORY KIRKBRIDE*. Retrieved from www.uphs.penn.edu:
www.uphs.upenn.edu/paharc/timeline/1801/tline14.html

Peter R. Breggin, M. (1997). *Brain Disabling Treatments in Psychiatry : Drugs, Electroshock and the Role of the FDA*. Springer Publishing Company.

Phillips, M. M. (n.d.). *The Lobotomy Files: Forgotten Soldiers*. Retrieved from Wall Street Journal:
projects.wsj.com/lobotomyfiles/

Productions, R. P. (Director). (2016). *Quakers, that of God in Everyone: Utold Stries from the Society of Friends* [Motion Picture].

*Project MKULTRA, the CIA's Program of Research in Behavioral Modification.* (1977, August 3). Retrieved from wikimedia.org:

upload.wikimedia.org/wikipedia/commons/0/01/ProjectMKULTRA_-Senate_Report.pdf

Rejali, D. (2009). *Torture and Democracy* . Princeton University Press .

Resuscitation Central. (n.d.). *Understanding Defibrillation Waveforms.* Retrieved from resuscitationcentral.com: www.mayoclinic.org/diseases-conditions/mental-illness/basics/risk-factors/con-20033813

Resuscitation Central. (n.d.). *UNDERSTANDING DEFIBRILLATION WAVEFORMS.* Retrieved from www.resuscitationcentral.com: www.resuscitationcentral.com/defibrillation/biphasic-waveform/

Romeo Vitelli, P. (2015, November 11). *Ending the Nightmares.* Retrieved from Psychology Today: www.psychologytoday.com/blog/media-spotlight/201511/ending-the-nightmares

SAMHSA. (2016, February 18). *Racial and Ethnic Minority Populations.* Retrieved from Substance Abuse and Mental Health Services Administration: www.samhsa.gov/specific-populations/racial-ethnic-minority

Sarah H. Lisanby, M., Jill J. Maddox, B., Joan Prudic, M., & al, e. (2000, June). *The Effects of Electroconvulsive Therapy on Memory of Autobiographical and Public Events.* Retrieved from The JAMA Network: jamanetwork.com/journals/jamapsychiatry/fullarticle/481613

Saul Levin M.D., M. R. (2016, January 29). *Time is Now to Support the ECT Reclassification Effort.* Retrieved from American Psychiatric Association: www.psychiatry.org/news-room/apa-blogs/apa-blog/2016/01/time-is-now-to-support-the-ect-reclassification-effort

Scotland, F. (Director). (2008). *The Memory Thief: The Story of Dr. Ewen Cameron* [Motion Picture].

Scull, A. (2015, April 22). *Madness and MEaning.* Retrieved from The Paris Review: www.theparisreview.org/blog/2015/04/22/madness-and-meaning/

Segen's Medical Dictionary. (2012). *Madhouses Act of 1774.* Retrieved from Segen's Medical Dictionary: medical-dictionary.thefreedictionary.com/Madhouses+Act+1774

Shafer, P. O. (2013, November). *Suicide Risk.* Retrieved from www.epilepsy.com: www.epilepsy.com/learn/impact/mortality/suicide-risk

Shashina, E. B. (1985). The Structure of Psychiatry in The Soviet Union. In *The Structure of Psychiatry in The Soviet Union* (pp. 86-87).

Somatics, L. (1983-2015). *Somatics, LLC Makers of Thymatron.* Retrieved from www.thymatron.com: www.thymatron.com/main_faq.asp#Health

Somatics, LLC. (1983-2015). *Somatics, LLC Makers of the Thymatron.* Retrieved from www.thymatron.com: www.thymatron.com/main_home.asp

Squire LR, S. P. (1983, January). *Electroconvulsive therapy and complaints of memory dysfunction: a prospective three-year follow-up study.* Retrieved from US National Library of Medicine National Institutes of Health: www.ncbi.nlm.nih.gov/pubmed/6831121

Starr, M. (2014, August 17). *Violinist has Brain Surgery, Fiddles Throughout.* Retrieved from cnet.com: www.cnet.com/news/violinist-has-brain-surgery-fiddles-throughout/

Steven P. Reidbord, M. (2014-2017). *A brief history of psychiatry.* Retrieved from stevenreidbordmd.com: www.stevenreidbordmd.com/history-of-psychiatry/

Sugarman, R. (2014, August 07). *Electroconvulsive Therapy Saved My Life & Helped Me Be Myself Again.* Retrieved from kveller.com: www.kveller.com/electroconvulsive-therapy-saved-my-life-helped-me-be-myself-again/

Susan Dillon, G. (2012, June 15). *Maintaining Mobility The Feldenkrais Method and Multiple Sclerosis.* Retrieved from The Feldenkrais Method of Somatic

Education:

www.feldenkrais.com/article_content.asp?article=44

Task Force on Electroconvulsive Therapy. (n.d.). *The Practice of Electroconvulsive Therapy: Recommendations for Treatment, Training and Privileging Second Edition (Completely Revised).* Retrieved from ECT.org: www.ect.org/resources/apa/5.html

The Scotsman. (2006, January 02). *Stunning tale of brainwashing, the CIA and an unsuspecting Scots researcher.* Retrieved from scotsman.com: www.scotsman.com/lifestyle/stunning-tale-of-brainwashing-the-cia-and-an-unsuspecting-scots-researcher-1-466144

Trafton, A. (2015, September 23). *How the brain encodes time and place.* Retrieved from MIT News: news.mit.edu/2015/brain-circuit-encodes-episodic-memories-0923

U.S. Department of Health and Human Services. (2016, January 19). *Electroconvulsive Therapy (ECT) Devices for Class II Intended Uses Draft Guidance for Industry, Clinicians and Food and Drug Administration Staff.* Retrieved from www.FDA.gov: www.fda.gov/downloads/MedicalDevices/.../UCM478942.pdf

U.S. Department of Health and Human Services. (2016, January 19). *Electroconvulsive Therapy (ECT) Devices for Class II Intended Uses Draft Guidance for Industry, Clinicians and Food and Drug Administration Staff.* Retrieved from www.fda.gov: www.fda.gov/downloads/MedicalDevices/.../UCM478942.pdf

UC Davis Health System. (2009, March). *Building Partnerships: Conversations with Native Americans about Mental Health Needs and Community Strengths.* Retrieved from dhcs.ca.gov: www.dhcs.ca.gov/services/MH/Documents/BP_Native_American.pdf

UC San Diego School of Medicine. (2017). *What is fMRI?* . Retrieved from Center for Functional MRI in the Department of Radiology: fmri.ucsd.edu/Research/whatisfmri.html

United States Holocaust Memorial Museum. (n.d.). *Forced Sterilization*. Retrieved from United States Holocaust Memorial Museum: www.ushmm.org/learn/students/learning-materials-and-resources/mentally-and-physically-handicapped-victims-of-the-nazi-era/forced-sterilization

University of California Press. (n.d.). *The Romance of American Psychology*. Retrieved from UC Press E-Books Collection: publishing.cdlib.org/ucpressebooks/view?docId=ft696nb3n8&chunk.id=doe5267&toc.id=doe5184&brand=ucpress

University of Michigan Department of Psychiatry. (2016). *Electroconvulsive Therapy Program*. Retrieved from www.psych.med.umich.edu: www.psych.med.umich.edu/ect/common-side-effects.asp

US DEPARTMENT OF HEALTH AND HUMAN SERVICES. (n.d.). *MENTAL HEALTH: CULTURE, RACE, AND ETHNICITY A Supplement to Mental Health: A Report of the Surgeon General.* Retrieved from Connecticut's Official State Website: www.ct.gov/dmhas/lib/dmhas/publications/mhethnicity.pdf

US Department of Health and Human Services National Institutes of Health. (1985, June 10-12). *Electroconvulsive Therapy*. Retrieved from National Institutes of Health Consensus Development Conference Statement: consensus.nih.gov/1985/1985electroconvulsivetherapy051html.htm

Valenstein, E. S. (2010). *Great and Desperate Cures : The Rise and Decline of Psychosurgery and Other Radical Treatments for Mental Illness.* Createspace.

Weiner, R. D. (2010, February 01). *Does electroconvulsive therapy cause brain damage?* Retrieved from Behavioral and Brain Sciences: www.cambridge.org/core/journals/behavioral-and-brain-sciences/article/does-electroconvulsive-therapy-cause-brain-damage/330201DC63275BF1E683ABCD7F3DFAE9

Whitaker, R. (2010). *Mad in America: Bad Science, Bad Medicine, and the Enduring Mistreatment of the Mentally Ill* . Basic Books .

White Swan Foundation. (2016). *How far can ayurveda go in treating mental health issues?* Retrieved from White Swan Foundation: www.whiteswanfoundation.org/article/how-far-can-ayurveda-go-in-treating-mental-health-issues/

Wong, E. (2013, January 11). *A Shameful History: Eugenics in Virginia.* Retrieved from American Civil Liberties Union of Virginia: acluva.org/10898/a-shameful-history-eugenics-in-virginia/

World Health Organization. (2014, September 4). *First WHO report on suicide prevention.* Retrieved from World Health Organization: www.who.int/mediacentre/news/releases/2014/suicide-prevention-report/en/

World Health Organization. (2017). *Gender and women's mental health.* Retrieved from World Health Organization: www.who.int/mental_health/prevention/genderwomen/en/

Worsley, L. (2013, April 15). *What was the truth about the madness of George III?* Retrieved from BBC.com: www.bbc.com/news/magazine-22122407

WW2History.com. (n.d.). *Hitler Authorizes Killing of Disabled.* Retrieved from WW2history.com: ww2history.com/key_moments/Holocaust/Hitler_authorizes_killing_of_-disabled

Zetter, K. (2010, April 13). *April 13, 1953: CIA OKs MK-ULTRA Mind-Control Tests.* Retrieved from Wired.com: www.wired.com/2010/04/0413mk-ultra-authorized/

Zoech, I. (2003, October 12). *Named: the Baby Boy who was Nazis First Euthanasia Victim.* Retrieved from Telegraph.co.uk: www.telegraph.co.uk/news/worldnews/europe/germany/1443967/Named-the-baby-boy-who-was-Nazis-first-euthanasia-victim.html

# About the Author

K Rose Quayle is a wife, Salvationist, amateur zoo keeper, photographer, and strong believer in mental health rights. You can connect with her at www.lookleftwalkright.com

Tell her the chickens sent you.

www.ingramcontent.com/pod-product-compliance
Lightning Source LLC
Chambersburg PA
CBHW032102280326
41933CB00009B/731